CORPORAL PUNISHMENT
AND
LOW-INCOME MOTHERS

CORPORAL PUNISHMENT AND LOW-INCOME MOTHERS

The Role of Family Structure, Race,
and Class in America

Lorelei Mitchell

CAMBRIA PRESS

PRESS

AMHERST, NEW YORK

Requests for permission should be directed to:
permissions@cambriapress.com, or mailed to:
Cambria Press
20 Northpointe Parkway, Suite 188
Amherst, NY 14228.

Library of Congress Cataloging-in-Publication Data

Mitchell, Lorelei.
    Corporal punishment and low-income mothers : the role of family structure,
race, and class in America / Lorelei Mitchell.
        p. cm.
    Includes bibliographical references and index.
    ISBN 978-1-60497-531-4 (alk. paper)
    1. Corporal punishment of children—United States. 2. Discipline of
children—United States. 3. Low-income mothers—United States. 4. Child
rearing—United States. I. Title.

    HQ770.4.M58 2008
    649'.64086240973—dc22

2008014628

For Andy, Lydia, and Silas

TABLE OF CONTENTS

List of Figure and Tables   ix

Foreword   xiii

Acknowledgments   xix

Introduction   1

Chapter 1: The Evolving American Family   15
    Trends in Family Formation and Configuration   16
    Effects of Family Structure on Children   24
    Conclusion   36

Chapter 2: Corporal Punishment in the United States   39
    Definitions of Corporal Punishment   40
    Rate, Severity, and Effects of Corporal Punishment   42
    Punishment as a Packaged Variable   45
    Factors Associated With Corporal Punishment   57
    Conclusion   64

Chapter 3: Family Structure and Corporal Punishment   65
    Conceptual Frameworks   65
    Review of the Literature   68
    Study Approach   72
    Study Hypotheses   73

Chapter 4: Study Methodology   79
    Study Design   79
    Study Participants   81
    Measures   82
    Dependent Variables   87

Independent Variables   89
Control Variables   93
Procedures   101
Approach to Data Analysis   103

Chapter 5: Results   **111**
Sample Description   111
Bivariate Associations With Discipline Practices   129
Constructing the Multivariate Models   135
Multivariate Analyses: Spanking and High Spanking   136
Spanking   137
High Spanking   142
The Role of Race in Spanking   146
Multivariate Analyses: Minor Assault
     and High Minor Assault   148
Minor Assault   148
High Minor Assault   152
The Role of Race in Minor Assault   156

Chapter 6: Discussion   **161**
Primary Study Findings   162
Measures of Family Composition   171
Control Variables   172
Implications for Policy and Practice   178
Implications for Future Research   193
Limitations of the Study   198

Conclusion   **203**

References   **207**

Index   **241**

LIST OF FIGURE AND TABLES

Figure 1. Family structure and corporal punishment:
Hypothesized relationships between
study variables.   74

Table 1.   Study variables according to domain.   83

Table 2.   Maternal demographics according to study site.   113

Table 3.   Child characteristics according to study site.   114

Table 4.   Maternal demographics according to race.   116

Table 5.   Relationship history and quality according
to race.   117

Table 6.   Maternal mental health and history
of victimization according to race.   118

Table 7.   Parenting attitudes according to race.   119

Table 8.   Discipline practices.   121

Table 9.   Discipline practices according to study site.   122

Table 10. Discipline practices according to race.   123

Table 11. Differences according to family structure.   124

Table 12. Differences according to marital status.   127

Table 13. Variables associated with spanking.   130

Table 14. Variables associated with high spanking.   132

Table 15. Variables associated with minor assault.   133

Table 16. Variables associated with high minor assault.   134

Table 17. Logistic regression analysis: Family structure
           and likelihood of spanking.   138

Table 18. Family structure and likelihood of spanking:
           Separate regressions according to race.   141

Table 19. Logistic regression analysis: Family structure
           and likelihood of high spanking.   143

Table 20. Logistic regression analysis: Marital status
           and high spanking—Separate regressions
           according to race.   146

Table 21. Summary of findings: Spanking
           and high spanking.   147

Table 22. Logistic regression analysis: Family structure
           and likelihood of minor assault.   149

Table 23. Logistic regression analysis: Family structure
           and likelihood of high minor assault.   153

Table 24. Logistic regression analysis: Family structure
and likelihood of high minor
assault—Separate regressions by race.   154

Table 25. Logistic regression analysis: Marital status
and high minor assault—Separate
regressions by race.   156

Table 26. Summary of findings: Minor assault
and high minor assault.   157

FOREWORD

Parenting in the American context is no easy task. The pace of American life, the social dangers our children experience in their neighborhoods and schools, the rampant materialism that exerts its unrelenting pressure—these, and many other social difficulties, all challenge parents under the best of circumstances. For many, the best circumstances hardly exist. Twenty percent of American children are being raised in poverty (Fass & Cauthen, 2006), 32% of American children are raised by single parents (U.S. Census Bureau, 2006), and 11% of American children lack health insurance (U.S. Census Bureau). The challenges facing children of color in this country are compounded, with rates of poverty, single parenthood, and other similar factors often doubling the national average (Fass & Cauthen; Lyter, Sills, & Oh, 2002).

Parenting has always had its challenges. Reviewing historical texts from centuries ago, we find that social commentators have long worried about the state of the American family, and parents' capacities to raise their children well (Fass, 2008). Today's parenting concerns somehow seem different, with the potential for lethal consequences if children are found in the wrong place at the wrong time.

Therefore, parents do their best, many using a firm hand to control their children, to establish parental authority, and to teach children right from wrong. According to recent evidence, 90% or more of American parents use physical discipline as one strategy to manage their children's safety, gain their compliance, and teach them appropriate behavior (Straus & Stewart, 1999). Parenting strategies in other counties appear to be somewhat different. In several European countries, for example, national law restrains the use of corporal punishment (Durrant, 2000). In the United States however, physical punishment is normative. Although it may not be parents' *only* strategy for managing their children's behavior, it is certainly a principal tool.

The use of corporal punishment varies according to social class, ethnicity, and—as we see in this volume—other important factors. Nonetheless, overall, corporal punishment is widely used. If this disciplinary technique is pervasive, what's the problem? When behavioral patterns are found across states and localities, is it appropriate to consider child rearing any differently? Also, if corporal punishment is an effective means to raise children, why the fuss?

Of course, taken to an extreme, corporal punishment can be seriously hazardous for children. Parents' use of corporal punishment can go awry; sometimes parents physically abuse their children, and sometimes children are harmed (Garbarino, 1977; Gil, 1973; Vasta, 1982). The most recent National Incidence Study of Child Abuse and Neglect, the NIS-3, showed that maltreatment in the United States had increased from 1986 to 1996 (Sedlak & Broadhurst, 1996). What is more worrisome is that the number of children who were seriously injured as a result of maltreatment almost quadrupled. Furthermore, in the United States, over 1,000 children die each year as a result of child maltreatment (Lindsey, 2003).

Corporal punishment is not the same as physical abuse, but there are those who suggest a link (Strauss, 2001). Some, viewing the issue from a human rights perspective, also question the moral undertones of state-sanctioned assault (Gershoff & Bitensky, in press; U.N. Committee on the Rights of the Child, 1994). Regardless of these ethical considerations, questions regarding the effectiveness of corporal punishment abound (see, e.g., Gershoff, 2002). If more effective methods of child management exist, these methods should be employed regularly in parenting.

While many parenting books and magazines exist, little research has been conducted to examine *who* uses corporal punishment, under *what* circumstances they use it, and *why* they do so. Lorelei Mitchell tackles these challenging subjects in *Family Structure and Use of Corporal Punishment by Low-Income Mothers*. Using a large-scale sample of vulnerable families, Mitchell provides a close-up view of corporal punishment from the vantage point of family structure and race/ethnicity. Importantly, she also examines parents' motivations for its use. Rather than universally condemning or sanctioning corporal punishment, Mitchell's contextual understanding of disciplinary strategies for individual families provides a balanced, reasoned approach which can help to move us forward. No political platforms are proclaimed, nor are large-scale social service interventions suggested. Mitchell takes the reader on a journey which allows one to better understand the diversity of America's families, and the wide-ranging circumstances that ultimately promote physical disciplinary tactics. Her voice is one of optimism, sensitivity, and reflective consideration for American parents and their potential to raise their children well.

Professor Jill Duerr Berrick
University of California, Berkeley

REFERENCES

Durrant, J. (2000). Trends in youth crime and well-being since the abolition of corporal punishment in Sweden. *Youth & Society, 31*(4), 437–455.

Fass, P. (2008). The past is not a foreign country: The historical education of policy. In J. Berrick & N. Gilbert (Eds.), *Raising children: Emerging needs, modern risks, and social responses* (pp. 9–26). New York: Oxford University Press.

Fass, S., & Cauthen, N. (2006). *Who are America's poor children? The official story.* New York: National Center for Children in Poverty.

Finkelhor, D., & Jones, L. (2006). Why have child maltreatment and child victimization declined? *Journal of Social Issues, 62*(4), 685–716.

Garbarino, J. (1977). The human ecology of child maltreatment: A conceptual model for research. *Journal of Marriage and the Family, 39*(4), 721–735.

Gershoff, E. T. (2002). Corporal punishment by parents and associated child behaviors and experiences: A meta-analytic and theoretical review. *Psychological Bulletin, 128*(4), 539–579.

Gershoff, E. T., & Bitensky, S. H. (in press). The case against corporal punishment of children: Converging evidence from social science research and international human rights law and implications for U.S. public policy. *Psychology, Public Policy, and Law.*

Gil, D. G. (1973). *Violence against children: Physical abuse in the United States.* Cambridge, MA: Harvard University Press.

Lindsey, D. (2003). *The welfare of children* (2nd ed.). New York: Oxford University Press.

Lyter, D., Sills, M., & Oh, G. T. (2002). *Children in single parent families living in poverty have fewer supports after welfare reform.* Washington, DC: Institute for Women's Policy Research.

Sedlak, A., & Broadhurst, D. (1996). *The national incidence study of child abuse and neglect.* Washington, DC: U.S. Department of Health and Human Services, Administration for Children and Families.

Straus, M. (2001). *Beating the devil out of them: Corporal punishment in American families and its effects on children* (2nd ed.). New Brunswick, NJ: Transaction Publishers.

Straus, M., & Stewart, J. (1999). Corporal punishment by American parents: National data on prevalence, chronicity, severity and duration, in relations to child and family characteristics. *Clinical Child and Family Psychology Review, 2*(2), 55–70.

U.S. Census Bureau (2006). *America's families and living arrangements.* Washington, DC: U.S. Census Bureau.

Vasta, R. (1982). Physical child abuse: A dual-component analysis. *Developmental Review, 2*, 125–149.

ENDNOTE

1. Although David Finkelhor and associates claim that maltreatment may be on the decline, their evidence rests upon various data sources using mixed methods and disparate samples. See Finkelhor and Jones (2006).

ACKNOWLEDGMENTS

The data used in this publication were made available by the National Data Archive on Child Abuse and Neglect, Cornell University, Ithaca, NY, and have been used with permission. Data from the Longitudinal Studies of Child Abuse and Neglect (LONGSCAN), Assessments 0–4, Project were originally collected by the LONGSCAN Consortium. Funding for the project was provided by the Office on Child Abuse and Neglect, Children's Bureau, U.S. Department of Health and Human Services. The collectors of the original data, the funder, the Archive, Cornell University, their agents and employees bear no responsibility for the analyses or interpretations presented here. Financial support for this secondary analysis was provided by the Normative Time Fellowship granted by the University of California, Berkeley, Office of the Dean.

It is a pleasure to acknowledge and thank the members of my dissertation committee at the University of California, Berkeley, for all of their support and guidance. Jill Duerr Berrick was a wonderful chair and advisor: challenging, yet always positive and enthusiastic. Over the years, I have come to know her as a tremendously intelligent, compassionate person with a lovely sense of humor. Jane Mauldon offered much appreciated pragmatism, while pushing me to really examine the theoretical basis for my work. Neil Gilbert brought a keen eye for methodological issues, and was never hesitant to raise difficult questions about policy implications. I truly enjoyed and benefited from working with each and every one of them.

I am especially grateful for the warmth and encouragement offered by my committee with regard to my other primary responsibility during the course of my doctoral studies: that of new motherhood. I would also like to thank my former advisor, former dean of the Graduate Division, Mary Ann Mason, for her unfailing efforts on behalf of student parents. Without such support, I would have been tempted many times to throw in the towel. Likewise, Toni Tan at Cambria Press has been an enthusiastic cheerleader and always there to help.

I also owe a great big thank-you to my dear friends, Jamie Kautz and JoAnna Caywood, who have done so much to bolster my confidence and spirit during this process. I am very lucky to have them in my life, and their work with and on behalf of children is a great inspiration to me.

Finally, I want to thank my husband Andy for his staunch support and neverending belief in me. To him, I offer my love and deep gratitude for taking this journey with me. Most of all, I am grateful beyond words for my children, Lydia and Silas, a constant source of joy, amazement, and consternation. They are the ones who made it all relevant, and I dedicate this work to them.

Corporal Punishment
and
Low-Income Mothers

INTRODUCTION

The 20th century saw profound changes in American families, generating considerable anxiety about children's well-being and the future of society. For many years, the problem was cast primarily as single motherhood among poor African Americans. In the 1980s, however, the issue centered on divorce, and the focus shifted perceptibly to the (white) middle class (Stacey, 1998). By the 1990s, a new buzzword—"father absence"—had appeared, and with it, a movement to restore men to their proper place in the rapidly disappearing traditional American family. As such trends have continued into the 21st century, many observers fear that the family itself is "breaking down," and social science seems to suggest the effects could well be disastrous. Many of today's social problems, including poverty, teen pregnancy, high school dropouts, delinquency, drug abuse, and family violence, have been attributed, at least in part, to the absence of biological fathers from increasing numbers of families (although the evidence for such claims is not uncontested).

Of course, this notion of the "American" family has always been essentially Eurocentric, as has been most of the research regarding the causes and consequences of family formation and functioning. In retrospect, it seems ironic that early changes in African American family formation predicted subsequent trends in other ethnic groups. Historically pathologized as deviant and dysfunctional, "African American domestic organization has become the prototypical postmodern family" (Tucker & James, 2005, p. 90). According to stereotype, the hallmark of the African American family, and the primary reason for its so-called downfall, is its model of family organization, supposedly based upon a strong/harsh matriarch and weak/absent father. Today, many fathers' rights groups argue that feminism has brought about the same power imbalance in white, middle-class families, and propose solutions based, in large part, on rolling back hard-won rights such as no-fault divorce. When welfare reform was reauthorized in 2006, $150 million per year was included to promote "healthy marriage" and "responsible fatherhood."

What this highlights is the essentially political nature of public discourse regarding family life in America. Although there is good reason to consider seriously the potential effects of changing family structures and roles, it is also apparent that the topic is deeply embedded in complex issues of power and control, both within families, and in the larger society. Implicit in the single motherhood debate are disagreements about the appropriate balance of power between men and women; between parents and children; between whites and nonwhites; and between the state and the family. The movement to ban corporal punishment of children by parents provides a compelling example of how such realignments in power relations intersect in discussions of parenting. As Fass and Mason (2000) point out, anxiety regarding social change has long been manifested in changing notions of childhood and appropriate child rearing. Disagreements about how children should be disciplined, and who has the power or right to exercise such authority speak directly to the burning question: Who, exactly, is in control of families today?

For the most part, corporal punishment is considered by social scientists and helping professionals to be an undesirable disciplinary tactic and indicative of "harsh parenting" (Whipple & Richey, 1997). Rather than being viewed as a deliberate parenting strategy, corporal punishment is seen most often as being reactive and impulsive, as coming from a place of anger and loss of control. One often hears the argument that many incidents of physical abuse begin with an act of corporal punishment (which is true). Parents who use corporal punishment are portrayed as being over stressed, uneducated, or otherwise compromised by substance abuse, relationship problems, a history of abuse in their own childhood, and so forth. For these same reasons, it is widely assumed that single mothers are more likely than married mothers to engage in harsh parenting—and by extension, to abuse their children. Harsh parenting, in turn, is assumed to be a significant contributor to the myriad social problems linked to single motherhood.

Surprisingly, however, the relationship between family structure and the use of corporal punishment has remained largely unstudied. Likewise, considerable research indicates that corporal punishment is almost universal in American families, suggesting that it may be normative parenting practice for many families rather than an indication of dysfunction. Corporal punishment is especially prevalent among low-income and/or some ethnic minority groups, resulting in what some claim to be the denigration of legitimate cultural differences in parenting (Larzelere, 2000). Others go so far as to argue that the child welfare system discriminates wholesale against African Americans, routinely misconstruing customary and appropriate child discipline as child abuse. Such claims, however, must be considered first and foremost in light of the research regarding the effects of corporal punishment on children. If corporal punishment is universally harmful to children, the notion of respecting cultural differences in parenting is not sufficient justification for continuing to use corporal punishment.

The literature regarding the effects of corporal punishment on children is quite mixed and difficult to interpret, due, in large part, to serious methodological challenges involved in studying complex parent-child interactions. There is increasing evidence to suggest, however, that the effects of corporal punishment vary significantly according to race and income, with negative effects found primarily among white, middle-class samples, and neutral or even beneficial effects found among low-income and African American samples (Deater-Deckard & Dodge,

1997a; Gunnoe & Mariner, 1997; McLeod, Kruttschnitt, & Dornfeld, 1994; Straus, Sugarman, & Giles-Sims, 1997). The degree of parental warmth toward the child, and the child's own perception of the parent as accepting or rejecting seem to be particularly important in mediating the effects of corporal punishment. Indeed, some argue that physical discipline may not be harmful for African American children precisely because it is used (for the most part) nonimpulsively, as a conscious discipline strategy, and in the context of a warm and accepting parent-child relationship (Deater-Deckard & Dodge, 1997a; Parke, 2002).

Family structure is closely tied to both race and class, making it difficult to disentangle the role of each of these factors in predicting the use of corporal punishment. In fact, one explanation for why corporal punishment is more common among low-income and African American families than other families is that low-income and African American families are more likely to be headed by single mothers. Of course, this model pathologizes corporal punishment, seeing it as being an indicator of maternal dysfunction, rather than a culturally distinct parenting practice. Furthermore, much of the research that indicates a possible relationship between single motherhood and harsh discipline has relied on predominantly white, middle-class samples with a high proportion of divorced mothers—low-income and African American single mothers are much more likely never to marry. It is possible that corporal punishment represents compromised parenting for such mothers, yet normative discipline for others. In that case, if corporal punishment represents functional parenting for low-income families, low-income single mothers under stress might actually be expected to engage in corporal punishment *less* frequently, rather than more frequently.

Parke (2002) maintained that the inconsistency of findings regarding the effects of both corporal punishment and other disciplinary tactics can be attributed to a fundamental failure to ask the right question:

> The problem with asking about the effects of punishment per se is that punishment is not a single variable but in reality is situated in the context of other practices...Punishment is a *packaged*

variable [italics original] that requires 'unwrapping' to isolate the components that account for its effectiveness. (p. 597)

The effects of corporal punishment on any given child are likely to vary according to particular characteristics of the child, the characteristics of the punishment, the quality of the parent-child relationship, and the cultural context within which parenting takes place. Historically, we have relied on excessively simple conceptual and statistical models to study relationships that are in fact multiply determined phenomena. Researchers increasingly recognize the need to move away from a main effects model toward an ecological model that locates the child within multiple, nested systems, from the micro level of the family to the macro level of the culture, and allows the identification of indirect and transactional effects (Belsky, 1993; Bronfenbrenner, 1979).

This study is unique in that it offers and tests a conceptual model for predicting maternal use of corporal punishment according to family structure using a large sample of low-income, predominantly African American families, and advanced analytical methodology. Most research on child discipline has relied heavily on (typically small) white, middle-class samples, and only a handful of studies have attempted to examine the relationship between family structure and corporal punishment, often with mixed and contradictory findings. Likewise, few studies have explored the diversity of discipline styles and strategies within poor and/or ethnic minority populations. Just as a range of parenting styles have been identified among white, middle-class parents, parenting by African Americans is unlikely to fit a single mold. Using a uniformly low-income sample reduces the likelihood that large differences in corporal punishment according to race and income will mask the influence of other, subtler influences on corporal punishment. Most importantly, perhaps, special attention is paid in this study to the interaction of variables in predicting maternal use of corporal punishment, especially the interaction of race with family structure.

The results indicate that motivations for using corporal punishment among low-income mothers are indeed mixed. Indicators of maternal *warmth,* as well as of maternal stress, were associated with corporal punishment, suggesting that corporal punishment may be a normative parenting practice for some mothers, but a sign of dysfunction for others. Likewise, the relationship between family structure and corporal punishment proved to be quite complex, varying according to race, relationship status, and the relative severity of punishment. Contrary to popular belief, this study found that mothers were significantly more likely to spank when living with the *biological father* or in a multigenerational family than when living alone or with a surrogate father figure. Mothers living with surrogate father figures were more likely to engage in higher, potentially problematic levels of corporal punishment, a finding consistent with prior research showing an elevated risk of child maltreatment in surrogate-father families. An important difference emerged by race, however: white mothers were just as likely to report high minor assault whether they were living with the biological fathers of their children or with surrogate fathers.

These findings suggest that slightly different dynamics may be at work in low-income white and African American families. For African American mothers in this sample, the two-biological-parent family structure and the multigenerational family structure seem to provide the most consistent discipline with the lowest risk of abuse. Mothers living with surrogate father figures appear less likely to discipline, yet more likely to use severe physical punishment. Single motherhood without cohabitation seems to offer children some protection from higher levels of physical punishment, but may also be associated with reduced structure or maternal involvement which can be equally or more detrimental to a child's well-being (Baumrind, 1997).

For low-income white mothers, having a biological father in the home does not seem to serve as a protective factor against potential abuse by mothers. This discrepancy might be explained by a difference in relationship quality. As Edin and Kefalas (2005) pointed out, there is a preponderance in low-income communities of men "of fairly uniformly low quality" who arguably do not make good husband material, for example, they may be unemployed, unfaithful, abusive, involved in drugs, crime, and so forth (p. 209). In some cases, low-income fathers or father figures may actually cause stress rather than provide assistance, undermining effective parenting. Nonetheless, low-income white mothers are far more likely than African American mothers to cohabit and/or marry. Therefore, for African American mothers, living with the biological fathers of their children may be an indication of a particularly strong relationship. African American mothers may "have a higher standard for marriage than whites" (Edin & Kefalas, 2005, p. 213).

What is clear is that the relationship between family structure and use of corporal punishment is far from straightforward and cannot be considered independently of the cultural context. Since the completion of this study, additional research has been reported that supports the notion of punishment as a packaged variable, with culture playing a key role in mediating the effects of corporal punishment on children. Using a large sample of African American mothers, McLoyd, Kaplan, Hardaway, and Wood (2007) found that maternal endorsement of corporal punishment moderated the links between maternal distress and use of corporal punishment, and between corporal punishment and child depressive symptoms. Mothers who did *not* endorse corporal punishment were more likely to report using corporal punishment when distressed; likewise, the relationship between corporal punishment and child depressive symptoms was only significant for children of nonendorsing mothers. McLoyd et al. (2007) pointed out that these results mirror those reported by other studies comparing the effects of corporal punishment according to race: when corporal punishment is perceived as undesirable, the effects seem to be negative, but when corporal punishment is perceived as normative, negative effects are minimized—whether one is making between-race or within-race comparisons.

Another study compared the moderating effect of cultural normativeness of physical discipline on the relationship between corporal punishment and child adjustment in six different countries: China, India, Italy, Kenya, the Philippines, and Thailand (Lansford et al., 2005). As expected, perceived normativeness (especially perceived normativeness on the part of the child) did reduce the negative effects of corporal punishment, yet in all cases, more frequent corporal punishment was still associated with adverse outcomes. Likewise, four studies reported in a Special Issue of *Cross-Cultural Research* (2006) dedicated to corporal punishment each found evidence that child perception of corporal punishment had a moderating effect on child adjustment: When punishment was perceived to be rejecting, corporal punishment was more likely to affect child adjustment negatively. Corporal punishment by itself did not significantly affect child adjustment unless it was more frequent or severe. Samples were drawn from Turkey, Jamaica, U.S. Virgin Islands, and a southern rural population in the United States. As Rohner (2006) argued,

> Results of studies contained in this Special Issue converge on one major and overarching conclusion: much of the research done so far on the issue of corporal punishment draws misleading conclusions about the direct relations between punishment and negative psychological and behavioral outcomes. (p. 217)

Other new ethnographic research provides more in-depth information regarding the motivations among low-income African American mothers for using corporal punishment. In their interviews with 9 Head Start mothers over 5 years, Ispa and Halgunseth (2004) found in the majority of cases that use of corporal punishment was decidedly not parent-centered, as is commonly assumed. Mothers clearly believed corporal punishment to be in the best interests of their children and repeatedly expressed concern about lax discipline leading to a lifetime of trouble. As the authors point out, the mothers' attributions regarding normal toddler behavior may not have been developmentally "correct," but the decision to use corporal punishment was largely conscious, rational, and made with the children's interests foremost in mind. Whether one agrees with this strategy, it does appear to be a bona fide parenting approach, rather than simply a sign of stress or loss of control.

At the same time, it is apparent that some proportion of corporal punishment in both affluent and low-income families is driven by dysfunction rather than positive values or deliberate parenting strategies

(Pinderhughes, Dodge, Bates, Pettit, & Zelli, 2000). A substantial minority of mothers who use corporal punishment do so impulsively and out of anger, and it is understood that many instances of child abuse begin as disciplinary interactions (Straus, 2000; Straus & Mouradian, 1998). The cross-cultural evidence regarding the significant negative effects of frequent and/or severe corporal punishment on children is uncontested. Furthermore, some studies have found negative effects of corporal punishment for African American children as well as white children (McCabe, Clark, & Barnett, 1999; McLoyd & Smith, 2002). In this study, African American mothers were found to be significantly more likely than white mothers to report using high, potentially problematic levels of corporal punishment, and even low levels of corporal punishment were linked to maternal alcohol use and psychological disturbance. Therefore, even if corporal punishment is normative in some communities, it cannot be viewed as universally harmless.

To the best knowledge of the author, no new research regarding the relationship between family structure and corporal punishment has appeared since the completion of this study. However, one new study did report some interesting findings regarding parenting efficacy, child conduct problems, and family structure among African Americans (Simons, Chen, Simons, Brody, & Cutrona, 2006). It found that mothers in single-parent families, two-biological-parent families, multigenerational families, and stepfamilies all provided basically equivalent levels of parenting (including with regard to a dimension labeled consistent discipline). Children, however, fared the best in two-biological-parent and multigenerational families, leading the authors to conclude that two parents are simply better than one; even if single African American mothers are effective and appropriate parents, there just isn't as much parenting to go around. The exception to this was the stepfamily, where the study found higher levels of conduct problems among children.

Findings from the study presented in this book suggest that family structure does indeed influence the likelihood of maternal use of corporal punishment in a low-income, high-risk sample, but also that the relationship is multiply determined. To further complicate matters, it is not clear what the impact of corporal punishment (or a lack thereof) might be from one family to the next. Judging from the literature on the subject, the effects of corporal punishment depend in large part on the specific context. Given these complex scenarios, it seems clear that simple marriage promotion, funding for which is now provided under Temporary Assistance For Needy Families (TANF), is unlikely to be the best approach to encouraging safe, effective child discipline in low-income families. Indeed, it might even prove to be counterproductive.

For example, marriage to a child's biological father may in fact support more appropriate child discipline for low-income African American mothers, but put white children at risk of higher levels of physical discipline, and perhaps even maltreatment. Likewise, for both African American and white children, it appears that the presence of a surrogate father puts them at higher risk for potentially abusive punishment. This suggests that if anything, an anticohabitation message might be of greater benefit to children than a promarriage message. Even recommending marriage for low-income African Americans—the group most likely to benefit, according to this study—might not be a good idea, if African American women are already self-selecting out of dysfunctional relationships. Scott, Edin, London, and Mazelis (2001) found that many welfare-reliant African American women worried that marriage, or even involvement in a relationship, would not be in their children's best interests, given the pool of apparently unacceptable mates, and their prior negative experiences with men.

Other studies indicate that early ("shotgun") marriages are more likely to fail, resulting in increased family conflict and instability (Ludtke, 1997). This may help to explain the discrepancy in risk for high minor assault found in this study between African American and white mothers living with their children's biological fathers. Because whites are more likely than African Americans to marry, there may be a higher proportion of unstable or conflictual marriages among poor white mothers than poor African American ones. Likewise, a much higher percentage of unplanned or nonmarital pregnancies result in marriage for whites than for African Americans (Mauldon, 1998). "Consequently, we walk a thin line when we attempt to promote matrimony as a public good if many or most marriages turn out to be unstable or conflict-ridden" (Frank Furstenburg, quoted in Ludtke, 1997, p. 424). In some cases, stable, single motherhood, or perhaps single parenting within a multigenerational family setting, may be better options for protecting children from overly harsh punishment or abuse.

At the same time, it is also understood that a lack of child discipline may be a matter of equal or even greater concern than the possible excessive use of corporal punishment. In fact, emotional neglect has been found to be a better predictor of externalizing behaviors than harsh punishment, remaining significant even after controlling for harsh punishment has been carried out (Baumrind, 1997). As Straus (2001) noted, this finding may also explain, in part, why corporal punishment looks relatively benign, or even beneficial, for minority children: "Corporal punishment may not be good for children but failure to properly supervise and control is even worse" (p. 199). How, then, do we better support single-mother families if marriage promotion is not the answer? Although no longer a popular idea, the best strategy would seem to be provision of more supports for poor single mothers and their children. Greater economic stability and access to much needed services would likely enhance parenting by single mothers, while decreasing the pressure to cohabit or enter to into dysfunctional marriages.

A recent comparative study of 14 European countries found that the gap in educational achievement associated with single parenthood was greatly reduced in countries where comprehensive supports were provided to single parents, whether through state-funded programs or private charities and the informal sector (Hampden-Thompson & Pong, 2005). Significantly, larger gaps in achievement were found in so-called liberal welfare regimes (similar to the United States), where family well-being is largely left up to market forces, and a more individualistic culture does not encourage the kind of family and charitable support seen in the conservative welfare states. Interestingly, the gap in achievement was not the lowest in the social democratic states, for example, the Scandinavian countries, despite the generous provision of social supports. According to the authors, this finding may be explained by the emphasis in social democratic states on maternal employment outside the home. Although childcare is provided by the state, it likely does not replace reduced parental involvement in children's education. In any case, Hampden-Thompson and Pong's (2005) study clearly demonstrated the potential feasibility of better supporting single-parent families, were the political will to exist.

Finally, it would be advisable to do some public education around corporal punishment that goes beyond automatically equating corporal punishment with child abuse. Encouraging parents to try alternative disciplinary approaches and perhaps decrease their use of corporal punishment is likely to be more successful when preexisting beliefs about corporal punishment are treated with respect and empathy (Davis, 1999). Larzelere (2000) recommended using the metaphor of a parenting toolbox. According to this metaphor, spanking is one possible tool among many other, potentially useful tools for child discipline. For all parents, regardless of whether they use corporal punishment, discipline is most likely to be effective when it is delivered early in an interaction, consistently, calmly, and with an explanation. The actual choice of disciplinary strategy (for example, time-out, spanking, verbal reprimand, response cost, and so forth) should be flexible and responsive, customized to the particular circumstances and unique characteristics of any given child. Excessive reliance on any one approach is likely to be less effective and potentially more harmful than using a variety of tactics appropriate to the particular situation. It could be added that spanking is not necessary because other techniques work just as well; given the potential for harm, the most prudent path might be to avoid spanking. However, for parents who do choose to use corporal punishment, guidelines could be offered to maximize effectiveness and minimize potential harm.

This would seem to both to be a more respectful approach to parenting differences in society, as well as a more pragmatic strategy for protecting children, given that the vast majority of young children are likely to experience corporal punishment at some point. This study, as well as others, suggests that corporal punishment may be a legitimate discipline strategy, depending upon how, and with whom, it is used. Indeed, it would appear that most Americans, especially African Americans and low-income Americans, agree with this perspective, although expert opinion largely disagrees. Because the evidence does not support a simple condemnation of corporal punishment, the issue, at least for now, seems to boil down to a question of personal values, choices, and judgment.

It does seem likely, however, that public support for corporal punishment will decline on its own without the more drastic step of a government ban. Although the proportion of parents who report using corporal punishment remains high, public support for corporal punishment has fallen dramatically in past several decades. The percentage of Americans who agreed with the statement, "A good hard spanking is sometimes necessary" dropped 20 percentage points in just 10 years (Straus, 2001, p. 206). Parent-child relations have become increasingly egalitarian as motivations for child bearing have shifted away from an economic model of family and notions of universal rights for children have expanded (Fass & Mason, 2000). Here in the United States, the so-called "violent socialization" of children may well come to be seen as inherently inhumane and unethical, as it has in a growing number of other countries.

CHAPTER 1

THE EVOLVING AMERICAN FAMILY

The past century has seen a number of significant changes, such as the decline in fertility, rise in divorce, rise in nonmarital childbirth, increase in single parenthood, widespread entry of women into the paid workforce, and growth in income inequality. Such changes have generated considerable anxiety about the state of the traditional American family and the future of society. The so-called breakdown of the family has been linked to a variety of social ills including poverty, family violence, juvenile delinquency, and teen pregnancy (Blankenhorn, 1995; Popenoe, 1996), although the evidence for such effects is hotly debated (Stacey, 1998). This chapter provides a context for understanding these claims by presenting an overview of major demographic changes in the family and a brief review of the relevant social science evidence regarding the effects of single parenthood and father absence on children.

TRENDS IN FAMILY FORMATION AND CONFIGURATION

Fertility

The rate of childbirth, both inside and outside of marriage, has obvious consequences for women's employment, family structure and dynamics, and children. The fertility rate in the United States, as well as other indus- trialized nations, has decreased significantly and steadily since about 1870, with the brief exception of the Baby Boom period (Jones, Tepper- man, & Wilson, 1995). In the late 1990s, the birth rate again rose slightly in the United States, due mostly to rising fertility among Hispanics and African Americans. Today, the total fertility rate, or total number of expected lifetime births per woman, is 2.05, just below the replacement rate of 2.1 (Hamilton, Martin, & Ventura, 2006). In general, caring for fewer children has allowed women greater freedom to obtain education and pursue work outside the home, which has, in turn, generated more economic independence for women.

The same period of time has seen a dramatic increase in the rate of nonmarital births, a phenomenon that has garnered widespread media coverage, especially with regard to teen pregnancy. Although the rate of increase recently leveled off or even decreased slightly, only 4% of all births were to unmarried women in 1950. As of 2004, this figure reached 35.8% (43% for first births) (Martin, Hamilton, Sutton, Ventura, Menacker, & Kirmeyer, 2006). Again, there are significant racial and ethnic differences in the total nonmarital birth rate: 24.5% of all births to non-Hispanic whites are to unmarried women, versus 69.3% of all births to African American women, and 46.4% of births to Hispanic women. However, whites still account for the greatest proportion of total nonmar- ital births (Martin et al., 2006). For whites, but not for African Americans, the increase in nonmarital births is largely due to births within cohabit- ing relationships (Wu & Wolfe, 2001). The majority of nonmarital births (76%) are to women over the age of 20, contradicting the stereotype that unwed mothers are all teenagers (Martin et al., 2006).

Similarly, despite the media controversy surrounding teenage pregnancy, rates of adolescent childbearing have actually declined dramatically (by 43%) since the early 1990s (Martin et al., 2006). In 2004, births to teenagers accounted for only 10.3% of all births, reflecting a consistent decline in the teen birth rate since 1991 (Martin et al., 2006). The sharpest decline in teen-childbearing rates has been observed for African American teenagers (more than a 50% decline since 1991), but the rate of teen births for African Americans is still close to twice the rate for whites (Martin et al., 2006). However, white, unwed teen mothers account for the greatest proportion of all nonmarital adolescent childbearing, constituting 38% of the total (Martin et al., 2006). The vast majority, or 82.4 percent of teen births, are to unmarried teens, although white teen mothers are much more likely to be married (22%) than African American teen mothers (3.4%). Finally, the rates of childbirth for teens under the age of 15 are negligible; the majority of teen births are to women aged 18–19, arguably falling into the category of young adults rather than "teenagers" (Mauldon, 1998).

Marriage, Cohabitation, and Divorce
Rates of marriage have changed relatively little over the last century, with the majority of men and women marrying at some point in their lifetimes, although the overall marriage rate is slightly lower than it was during the Baby Boom years. What has changed more significantly is the length of time people spend being married. Today, people typically spend a smaller proportion of their lifetimes married than they previously did, due to later age of marriage, longer life expectancy, and a much higher divorce rate (Executive Office of the President, 2000). Again, racial differences exist in the rate of marriage, with African Americans being much less likely to marry than whites, more likely to delay marriage, more likely to divorce, and less likely to remarry (Bramlett & Mosher, 2002). As of 1995, the most recent year for which data is available, only about one quarter of African American women (aged 15–44) were married and residing with their spouse, as compared to more than half of all whites (Bramlett & Mosher, 2002).

Another trend with potential consequences for family structure and child well-being is cohabitation. The rate of "cohabitation," or unmarried coresidential relationships, has dramatically increased over the past several decades: "Only 3 percent of women born between 1940 and 1944 had lived in a nonmarital cohabitation by age 25, whereas for women born 20 years later, 37 percent had cohabited by that same age" (Executive Office of the President, 2000, p. 7). Today, about half of all young adults cohabit prior to marriage and almost half of all births to unmarried mothers take place within the context of cohabitation (Bumpass & Lu, 2000). Indeed, for many couples, both poor and middle-class, cohabitation seems to function as a kind of "trial marriage" phase, although African Americans are less likely than whites or Hispanics to cohabit (Edin & Kefalas, 2005). Same-sex partnerships also fall, by default, into the category of cohabitation, since lesbians and gays are legally barred from marriage. Such households numbered 1.7 million in 1998, representing 1.6% of all households (Executive Office of the President, 2000). In general (at least for heterosexual couples), cohabiting relationships are considered less stable than marriages, and cohabitation prior to marriage may be a predictor of divorce (Jones et al., 1995). For example, close to half of the cohabiting couples in Cherlin and Fomby's (2002) study had ended their relationship after less than a year and a half, but more than 80% of children of the married couples in the study experienced no such disruption during that time period. Interestingly, cohabiting parents in Europe typically remain together for many years, so the instability of cohabitation appears to be a particularly American phenomenon (Edin & Kefalas, 2005).

It is the rapid jump in the divorce rate that probably has generated the most anxiety regarding the future of the family. Although the divorce rate actually began to rise early in the 20th century (being interrupted by the Baby Boom era), it was not until the 1970s that the divorce rate seemingly doubled overnight. Today, it is estimated that approximately half of all marriages will result in divorce, a rate that seems to have stabilized or even decreased slightly since the early 1980s (Kreider & Fields, 2002). Of all divorces, about 60% involve children; a total of 1.5 million children experience divorce each year (Arbuthnot & Gordon, 1996). White children are more likely than African American children to experience divorce, for the simple reason that African American children are more likely to have always lived in single parent families than their white counterparts are.

A significant proportion of divorced Americans go on to remarry, with the result that about 25% of children become part of a stepfamily before they reach age 18 (Furstenberg & Cherlin, 1991). Many more probably experience a stepfamily-like arrangement through cohabitation. The vast majority of stepfamilies (86%) are composed of a custodial mother, her children, and a stepfather (Mason, 1998). African Americans are much less likely to remarry or cohabit than whites are. Children who maintain relationships with nonresidential or noncustodial parents may gain additional stepparents and siblings. The risk for divorce is even more elevated for second and subsequent marriages than for first marriages, and as many as a quarter of all second marriages end within 5 years (Bramlett & Mosher, 2002). Almost half the children whose parents remarry experience a second divorce by late adolescence (Furstenberg & Cherlin, 1991). Taken together, all of these changes suggest, for better or for worse, that many children are experiencing increasingly complex family arrangements.

Family Structure
For many years, the predominant model—at least the white, middle-class model—of the family in the United States has been that of the single-earner (male) married couple. Today, less than a third of families fit that model, as compared to about two-thirds in 1952 (Fields, 2003). About half of all families with children are dual-earner married couples, while the proportion of single-parent families has grown from 13% in 1949 to 28% in 2006 (Fields, 2003; U.S. Census Bureau, 2006). Contrary to popular stereotypes of unwed single motherhood, the majority of single mothers were once married, although the proportion of never-married single mothers is now almost equal to the proportion of divorced single mothers (Bianchi, 1995; Sorensen & Halpern, 1999). A little less than one-quarter of all white families are headed by single parents, as compared to only a little over half of African American families (U.S. Census Bureau, 2006). Despite the disproportionate representation of

African American single mothers, white single mothers comprise the largest proportion of all single mothers. Interestingly, 17% of all single-parent families are now headed by fathers rather than mothers, a three-fold increase since 1970 (Executive Office of the President, 2000; U.S. Census Bureau, 2006).

Of particular relevance to the topic of father absence, the rising proportion of single-parent families means that more than a third of children now live separately from their biological fathers, and more than half of all children are expected to live apart from their biological fathers for a substantial period of time before turning 18. Forty percent of children in single-parent families have not had contact with their fathers in at least 1 year (Executive Office of the President, 2000). In other words, the definition of and effects of "father absence" may be contested, but the trend toward children living apart from their biological fathers is certainly real. Relatively few children, however, spend their entire childhoods without some type of father figure, whether through delayed parental marriage, cohabitation, or remarriage following divorce. The average spell as a single parent lasts 6.9 years; if one considers cohabitation as akin to remarriage, that time is reduced to 3.7 years (Bianchi, 1995). Indeed, recent studies suggest that the rate of single motherhood has fallen slightly since the late 1990s, especially among low-income populations, primarily due to growing numbers of single mothers cohabiting with men who are unrelated to their children (Cherlin & Fomby, 2002).

Of all American children, African American children are most likely to be born into, and grow up in, a single-parent family. Indeed, only a little more than a third of all African American children live with both parents, versus almost three-quarters of white children (U.S. Census Bureau, 2006). Likewise, single parenthood may be less of a transitory event for some African American children. However, if one takes into account the relative instability of cohabitation and/or shared living arrangements with extended families, African American children may experience more frequent family transitions than their white counterparts. A significant proportion of African American children will spend time living with their mother and another relative (often a grandmother), either prior to the disruption of a marital or cohabiting relationship, or following it. Whether or not these multigenerational family structures, often found in the African American community, are equivalent to the two-parent model has long been a matter of debate (Gadsden, 1999).

A number of authors have raised the issue of whether today's family instability, including marriage dissolution, remarriage, and the high proportion of single-parent families, truly represents a unique development, or is rather simply a new twist on an old theme (Coontz, 1992; Stacey, 1998). For example, the risk of parental death used to be much higher than it is today. It is estimated that about a quarter of all children in 1900 lost a parent by age 15, with one-third living in single-parent families for some portion of their childhood (Furstenberg & Cherlin, 1991). Similarly, remarriage, and the formation of stepfamilies following parental death, were extremely common. The same authors point out that African American families have always experienced—and coped with—more family "instability" than white families. The comparatively stable family of the 1950s, therefore, is often regarded more as a nostalgic myth than as the "traditional" family form. At the same time, however, Coontz (2005) pointed out that the *reasons* for such fluctuations in family structure have fundamentally changed because the meaning of marriage has fundamentally changed. In the past, marriage functioned primarily as an economic and political institution, but the contemporary Western view of marriage is based on notions of love and free choice. This transformation of marriage into something "optional" has made marriage less likely and rendered it inherently unstable, a state that is unlikely to be reversed in the future (Coontz, 2005).

Women's Labor Force Participation
Accompanying the above changes in family formation and structure, and perhaps in part driving such changes, women's labor force participation has also increased significantly during the 20th century. Not only are more women working for pay than previously, a substantially greater proportion of women with children are working for pay. In 2006, 71% of

women with children under the age of 18 worked in paid employment, while 56% of mothers of children under the age of 1 participated in the workforce (U.S. Department of Labor, 2007). The percentage of mothers with infants in the paid workforce has increased dramatically over the past few decades (in 1976, only 31% of mothers of infants worked outside the home), yet has decreased from a high of 59% in 1998 (U.S. Census Bureau, 2001b). It is important to note, however, that this decrease has been observed primarily in white, married women over 30; the labor-force participation of young, African American and Hispanic mothers has not decreased. Seventy-seven percent of single mothers in America worked outside the home in 2006, and single mothers are more likely than married mothers to work full time (Executive Office of the President, 2000; U.S. Census Bureau, 2006). Young, never-married women, by contrast, are the least likely to work, and the most likely to require public assistance (Executive Office of the President, 2000).

Many commentators have discussed the impact of women's growing economic independence on the high divorce rates and supposed marginalization of the father. At the same time, it is important to keep in mind that women's wages still lag behind men's wages, and single mothers' wages lag behind married women's wages, largely due to differences in education. Today, married women's wages only account for 30% of a couple's total income, and single mothers, on average, only earn about a third as much as dual-earner married couples do, and half as much as single-earner married couples (Executive Office of the President, 2000). Therefore, it is premature to conclude that women have achieved true economic independence. Indeed, poverty is a significant problem for single mothers and their children, as shall be discussed later in this study.

Income Inequality
Economic changes in the second half of the 20th century may also be seen as relevant to gender relations, the future of the family and the well-being of children. As many have noted, the disappearance of "family wage," low-income jobs and the widening income gap between the poorest Americans and the wealthiest Americans has been greatly

disruptive to the male breadwinner model, especially among the less educated segments of society. Some argue that the so-called "breakdown" of the African American family in particular can be traced to the lack of economic opportunities (and accompanying high rate of incarceration) for African American men, as manufacturing jobs have disappeared from the inner cities (Wilson, 1996). Similarly, many low-income (or unemployed) fathers—often villainized as "deadbeat dads"—simply cannot afford to pay child support, perhaps discouraging ongoing contact with the mother and/or children in a society that associates fatherhood with paying bills (Roberts, 1998). Thus, in part, the problem of father absence may be an economic one, rather than simply a "moral" or cultural shift. Indeed, it long has been acknowledged that marriage rates increase (and divorce rates decrease) as one moves up the income ladder. Empirical studies looking at the relationship between the declining earning potential of African American men and rates of marriage among African Americans have provided modest support for this theory (Edin & Kefalas, 2005). It is estimated that about 25% of the decline in marriage among African Americans can be attributed to worsening economic conditions for African American men (Wilson, 1996).

The growing number of single-parent families, combined with the income disparity between married mothers and single mothers, means that many children must make do with fewer resources, despite the fact that the majority of single mothers are working, and are working full time. Although mothers' earnings have increased average family income, the gains have disproportionately favored middle-class and already affluent families. It is the well-educated women, most often married to well-educated, high-income men, who have the highest rate of work participation among women with children today (Executive Office of the President, 2000). Moreover, a little less than half of all single mothers receive any child support, and only a little more than a third of poor single mothers receive child support (Sorensen, 2003). As a result, more than a quarter of all single-mother families (28%) live in poverty, as compared to only 5.4% of married-couple families; around two-fifths of both African American and Hispanic single-mother families live in poverty (U.S. Census Bureau, 2004). Even women who are not poor experience roughly 50% reduction in household income following divorce, which may not put such households below the poverty line, but certainly has important ramifications in terms of parental stress and quality of life for children (Wallerstein, 1998).

EFFECTS OF FAMILY STRUCTURE ON CHILDREN

After reviewing these major demographic shifts, it is apparent that father-lessness, at least as defined as the physical absence of the biological father from the child's custodial home, is a real phenomenon. Expert and public opinion has vacillated between viewing changes in family struc-ture as being completely disastrous or relatively benign (Cherlin, 1999). Increasingly, social science has weighed in on the debate. A growing body of research suggests that single parenthood may, in fact, carry some neg-ative consequences for children (Amato & Keith, 1991; McLanahan & Sandefur, 1994). There may also be reason to believe that fathers in par-ticular contribute something unique and important to child well-being (Marsiglio, Amato, Day, & Lamb, 2000). However, such findings are far from conclusive and, "No consensus, but lively debate, characterizes the contemporary social scientific discourse on the sources and/or effects of [all the] routes to 'fatherlessness'" (Stacey, 1998, p. 66). In many ways, the literature on the subject probably provides more clues as to what is *not* known than to what is.

One of the first difficulties encountered in examining the literature regarding the effects of single motherhood and/or "father absence" is the poorly defined nature of such terms. Not only might one expect the effects of single motherhood to differ according to the precipitating conditions, but conditions themselves may represent diverse categories of motherhood. For example, single motherhood may be voluntary or involuntary; single mothers may be very young or mature professional women; single mothers may be divorced, never married, or even remar-ried. Much of the existing literature on the subject fails to make such distinctions and typically conflates research regarding several disparate family forms: single-parent (mother) families formed through divorce, single parent families formed through nonmarital (often teenage) pregnancy, and intentional families formed with little to no involvement of the father aside from the biological contribution (e.g., single parent adoption or insemination and sometimes lesbian parenthood).

Furthermore, it is not clear what is meant by the separate terms "father" and "absence." Does "father" refer only to biological fathers, or does it include stepfathers, boyfriends, and other potential father figures? Could the term "father" conceivably refer to a second parent of any gender? How does one understand "absence": Does it refer to physical absence and/or emotional absence? If a father lives in the same house as his children, but works 80 hours a week, is he absent? If a father lives separately from his children, but maintains a high level of involvement, is he present? Fatherlessness itself does not appear to be a static condition, further complicating the matter. The reality is that a contemporary child is likely to spend his/her childhood in various household configurations, rather than growing up within one basic structure. Many children, for better or for worse, are experiencing increasingly complex family arrangements that cannot be captured using a simple single-parent/two-parent categorization.

However, most of the research regarding family structure uses just such a categorization, making interpretation of the findings somewhat challenging. The good news is that researchers today increasingly recognize the importance of looking beyond this dichotomy in understanding children's experiences (Carlson & Corcoran, 2001). In the meantime, it is important to glean what one can from the existing literature. Because relatively little research has been conducted regarding family structure and corporal punishment specifically, it is helpful to begin with a brief review of the broader literature. Conceptually, there is reason to think that if single motherhood poses a risk to children's development in one area, it might pose risks in other areas.

By and large, research regarding the effects of family structure on children seems to indicate that the great majority of children raised in single-mother families develop normally (Amato & Keith, 1991). Single motherhood simply is not an unmitigated disaster for children, as it is often portrayed in the media. Similarly, the differences observed between children of single mothers and intact families, even when statistically significant, are relatively small in magnitude. For example, Amato and Keith's (1991) meta-analysis of 92 studies on the effects of divorce found that the average increase in risk associated with divorced single parenthood was only 0.14 of a standard deviation. In other words, the variation within single-parent families and within intact families is often greater than any differences between the two family structures, implying that variables other than family structure are primarily responsible for child outcomes (Demo & Acock, 1996).

However, this does not mean that the observed differences between children in intact families and so-called "disrupted" families should be treated as meaningless. A sizeable minority of children raised in such households do experience more severe and long-lasting problems (Simons & Chao, 1996). Thus, although little research exists to support the claim that family structure is a primary determinant of various contemporary social problems, it may be a contributor, especially as the numbers of children experiencing divorce and remarriage continue to accumulate (Amato, 1999).

The more robust findings regarding the effects of family structure on children seem to be found in the research on divorce, and to a lesser extent, on stepfamilies and cohabiting families. It appears that divorce and/or remarriage may pose some threats to children's healthy development, as compared to growing up in a "traditional" two-parent family. On average, children of divorced parents and children living in reconstituted families seem to be at approximately twice the risk of behavioral problems, academic difficulties, compromised psychological adjustment, teen delinquency, and early sexual behavior and childbearing, as well as longer-term effects such as lowered socioeconomic attainment, decreased marital quality, and diminished well-being in adulthood (Amato & Keith, 1991).

Rather than family structure per se, however, it appears to be processes within the family that are largely to blame for the difficulties experienced by children in reconstituted families (Amato & Keith, 1991; Furstenberg &

Cherlin, 1991). In many studies, for example, adjusting for predivorce conflict, as well as predivorce child behavioral problems, eliminated or significantly reduced the magnitude of effects initially attributed to family disruption (Furstenberg & Cherlin, 1991; Kelly, 2000). Vandewater and Lansford (1998) found that family structure was not significantly associated with child internalizing or externalizing behavior, but that the level of family conflict was associated with both. As Kelly (2000) argued, "Marital conflict is a more important predictor of child adjustment than is divorce itself," and divorce may actually serve to reduce tension between parents and result in behavior improvements for children (p. 2).

Hetherington (1999), however, found that even after controlling for predivorce conflict, there was a significant increase in the risk of behavioral problems among children. It appears that in some situations, postdivorce conflict may exacerbate preexisting behaviors, while in others, separation may ease tension in the home and benefit children (Hetherington, 1999). Others have suggested that child problem behaviors actually put intact marriages at risk, increasing the likelihood of disruption, in which case the causal direction would be reversed (Furstenberg & Cherlin, 1991). As many as half of the behavioral problems observed among children of divorce were actually present years prior to the divorce, and similar levels of behavioral problems are found among children raised in intact high-conflict marriages and children of divorce (Kelly, 2000).

It also appears that children in reconstituted families may face more emotional difficulties than children in single-parent families, due to adjustment difficulties and friction among nonbiological family members (Hetherington, 1999; Jeynes, 2000). Demo and Acock (1996) found that child problems were strongly associated with family process variables such as mother-child disagreement, parent-child interaction, and parental supervision. Divorced-single-parent families and stepfamilies reported the highest levels of mother-child conflict and the lowest levels of parent-child interaction and parental supervision. Much of the conflict between parents in second or subsequent marriages seems to revolve around issues of stepparenting and child behavior, and may predict failure of the marriage (Hetherington & Stanley-Hagan, 1999).

Interestingly, one study that compared child externalizing behavior among four family structures—intact families, stepfamilies, single-parent families, and cohabiting families—found that children from cohabiting families had significantly higher externalizing scores than children from any of the other family forms (Ackerman, D'Eramo, Umylny, Schultz, & Izard, 2001). The authors suggest that the presence of an ambiguous father figure may be even more deleterious to children than a legally defined stepfather. Conversely, the higher externalizing scores were also explained, in part, by the mother's relationship history. A history of serial relationships was associated with higher child externalizing behaviors, and when controlled for, decreased the magnitude of the family structure effect. Thus, it may be family instability, as much as cohabitation, which exerts a negative influence on child behavior outcomes (Ackerman et al., 2001). Carlson and Corcoran (2001), however, after controlling for maternal characteristics such as education and age at first birth, did not find that children from families with multiple transitions exhibited higher levels of behavioral problems.

The loss of income that commonly accompanies divorce also appears to play a very significant role. McLanahan and Sandefur (1994) estimated that income accounts for about 50% of the observed differences—with the notable exception of children living in stepfamilies (in such cases, the increased family conflict seems to outweigh any increases in income resulting from remarriage). Single mothers, on average, have significantly lower incomes than married mothers, and divorced mothers often experience a substantial decrease in family income following divorce (Wallerstein, 1998). An alarming percentage of single mothers, and thus their children, spends at least some time living in poverty. Poverty itself is strongly linked to developmental problems in children:

> One reason may be that low-income families are not able to afford adequate food, shelter and other material goods that foster healthy cognitive and social development of children...Family income also affects the type of neighborhood in which families can afford to live, and children in higher income communities are more likely to receive positive peer influences that encourage achievement

> and prosocial behavior...In addition, poverty and economic
> stress may lead to less effective parenting which, in turn, has
> adverse consequences for children's development and adjustment.
> (Carlson & Corcoran, 2001, p. 780)

Numerous studies have found that differences between children in intact
families and children in other family structures are reduced or eliminated
when family income is taken into account (Carlson & Corcoran, 2001;
Jeynes, 2000; McLanahan & Sandefur, 1994; Pong & Ju, 2000).

Much less research exists regarding the effects of growing up in a
never-married-single-mother family, and the findings of what research
does exist appear less consistent. Many studies show an apparent effect
that disappears or is significantly reduced once income is included
in the equation (Carlson & Corcoran, 2001; Demo & Acock, 1996;
Jeynes, 2000; Pong & Ju, 2000). This tendency is consistent with the
argument that never-married mothers represent a distinct population of
disproportionately young, poor women whose children are already at
risk regardless of family structure. Interestingly, several studies have
found less variation in child outcomes according to family structure
for African Americans and Hispanics (Amato, 1999; McLanahan &
Sandefur, 1994; Pong & Ju, 2000). This makes sense, if—as is often
argued—marriage offers fewer economic benefits for women from
disadvantaged populations than it does their more affluent counterparts (Carlson & Corcoran, 2001). In effect, if African American and
Hispanic men have high rates of unemployment, or are only able to
obtain low-income jobs, one might expect children to fare as equally
well in single-parent families as in two-parent families. It is not clear,
however, that poverty is the only factor, or even the most salient one.
Since always-single mothers, on average, start out with lower incomes
than divorced white mothers, "controlling for income in more heterogeneous samples tends to reduce effects for poverty co-factors and
obscures the diversity of disadvantaged families" (Ackerman et al.,
2001, p. 290). In other words, there may be undetected disadvantages
to growing up in an always-single-mother family, above and beyond
the effects of income level.

There is some evidence to suggest there may be emotional advantages to being raised in a never-married-single-mother family, compared with a disrupted family. A number of studies find that children of single, non-cohabiting mothers are indistinguishable from children of intact families, or at least appear to fare better than children of divorced or reconstituted families (Demo & Acock, 1996; Jeynes, 2000). Some authors argue that in the African American community, single parent status does not carry the same stigma as in the white community (Thomas, Farrell, & Barnes, 1996). More generally, never-married motherhood may not be associated with the residential mobility and loss of community resources often linked to divorce and remarriage (Bray, 1999). Similarly, there may be less exposure to interparental conflict (Kelly, 2000). In some cases, low-income fathers or father figures may cause stress rather than provide assistance: "If the male figure is not providing economic or social support to an already deprived household, then he could be an additional burden on the already stressed mother" (Radhakrishna, Bou-Saada, Hunter, Catellier, & Kotch, 2001, p. 287). Indeed, Edin and Kefalas (2005) found that low-income women, especially low-income African American women, choose not to marry precisely because the men in their communities are "of fairly uniformly low quality" and would not make good husband material (p. 209). Even more important than the lack of financial support may be the widespread drug and alcohol abuse among young men, domestic violence, participation in crime, and unfaithfulness to mates (Edin & Kefalas, 2005).

Interestingly, socioeconomic status seems to have a greater influence on cognitive and educational outcomes than on socioemotional adjustment (McLanahan, 1999), so adjusting for income may well eliminate any apparent differences between children of never-married mothers and children of two-parent families. Family conflict—which most often accompanies divorce and remarriage, rather than always-single parenthood—seems to be more salient to issues of socioemotional adjustment. Indeed, "In two epidemiologic samples...[the investigators]... discovered that stable single parent status was not associated with child externalizing behavior after controlling for chronic poverty, however, divorce remained a significant predictor of externalizing behavior" (Shaw, 1999, p. 744).

Children raised in less common family structures, such as same-sex families or single-mother families formed through sperm donation, do not seem to suffer any appreciable negative effects—and in fact, may even be at an advantage in some regards (Golombok, 1999, 2000; Golombok, Tasker & Murray, 1997; Patterson & Chan, 1997, 1999; Stacey, 1998). Research regarding gay and lesbian families, as well as families formed through assisted reproduction, indicates that such couples, whose parenthood is necessarily intentional, are likely to demonstrate greater warmth and less stress than their mainstream counterparts. As Golombok (1999) argued, "The findings suggest that genetic ties are less important for family functioning than a strong desire for parenthood" (p. 432). However, research in these areas is new and extremely sparse, sample sizes are small, many of the children themselves are still young, and little time has elapsed in which to study longer term outcomes.

The Role of Fathers
Father advocates argue that it is not just the interparental conflict or low-income status often associated with single-parent families, but the specific absence of a biologically related father that causes problems for children raised in such homes (Blankenhorn, 1995; Popenoe, 1996). Across a number of social science disciplines, including anthropology, sociology, and psychology, it is commonly assumed that a two-parent biological family conveys more child benefits than any other family structure. Particularly influential perspectives include the Freudian argument that the heterosexual married unit is critical for healthy gender identification and sexual development, and Parson's structural-functional theory that emphasizes the importance of sex role differentiation within traditional nuclear families (Demo & Acock, 1996).

In actuality, relatively little empirical evidence exits to support the father absence perspective: "Research on father 'presence' or 'absence' has frequently found that presence alone does not significantly influence child outcomes" (Dubowitz, Black, Cox, et al., 2001, p. 300). Even in two-parent families, fathers spend relatively little time with, or available to, their children—only about a fifth to a quarter of the time that mothers spend—and they "assume essentially no responsibility (as defined by participation in key decisions, availability at short notice, involvement in the care of sick children, management and selection of alternative childcare, etc.) for their children's care or rearing" (Lamb, 1997, p. 4). Unsurprisingly, therefore, few studies have been able to identify direct paternal influences on child development (Lamb, 1997).

Similarly, most studies have found no positive effects of contact with noncustodial fathers (Lamb, 1997; Simons & Chao, 1996). There may be some benefit to children when the noncustodial parent-child relationship most closely approximates an everyday parent-child relationship, for example, one that includes mundane activities and responsibilities rather than only recreational weekend activities, but relatively few noncustodial parent-child relationships fit this description (Kelly, 2000). In fact, a number of studies have found contact with the noncustodial parent to be deleterious to child adjustment, perhaps, in part, because conflict with the mother is ongoing, but also because fathers' hands-on parenting skills may be relatively undeveloped prior to divorce (DeMaris & Greif, 1997). The effects of noncustodial father involvement for African Americans are also unclear, with some evidence to suggest that low-income African American boys with less noncustodial father involvement may be better adjusted, perhaps due to reduced exposure to the drug culture and criminal activity (Thomas et al., 1996). Other studies, however, indicate that contact with fathers and father figures can improve self-esteem, lower rates of anxiety and depression, and perhaps decrease delinquency among poor African American teenage boys (Coley, 1998; Zimmerman, Salem, & Maton, 1995).

Furthermore, there is evidence to indicate that remarriage and/or cohabitation—with the introduction of a surrogate father figure—does not automatically mitigate the effects of single parenthood. If anything, it appears that reconstituted families may be the most deleterious family structure for children (Bray, 1999, Hetherington & Stanley-Hagan, 1999). The vast majority of research in this area, however, has been conducted with middle-class white families. Newer studies examining father surrogates in low-income and minority populations find that father surrogates may play positive roles in children's lives if they function as highly involved parents (Dubowitz, Black, Cox, et al., 2001; Dubowitz, Black, Kerr, Starr, & Harrington, 2000). Other research suggests that boys, and especially African American boys, may benefit more from their parents' (generally mothers') remarriage than girls, and that younger children may adjust more readily than older children to life in a stepfamily (Hetherington & Stanley-Hagan, 1999). Interestingly, many studies find no differences according to the biological status of the father (Furstenberg & Harris, 1993; Black, Dubowitz, & Starr, 1999; Dubowitz et al., 2000; Dubowitz, Black, Cox, et al., 2001).

In general, child development research supports the notion that parental sex identification is relatively unimportant in determining child adjustment. It is not so-called "masculinity" that seems to affect child adjustment, but rather the degree of warmth and involvement in the father-child relationship (Lamb, 1997). The same has been found for mothers' influence on child outcomes, suggesting that fathers and mothers actually influence children via similar mechanisms. Likewise, some studies do find significant benefits of father "presence" when the father in question is highly involved in the direct care of the child. For example, Pleck (1997) found that children of such fathers demonstrated greater cognitive skills, more empathy, a stronger internal locus of control, and fewer sex-stereotyped beliefs. However, highly involved fathers remain an extremely small minority among two-parent families, and it is unclear whether findings regarding this small, unusual population of fathers realistically can be applied to father involvement more generally.

Newer models of father involvement suggest that fathers play multiple, mutually reinforcing roles in family systems, including economic, social, and emotional roles (Lamb, 1997). Accordingly, the father's individual relationship with a given child may be less important than the father's role in the overall family system: "Fathers have beneficial effects on their children when they have supportive and nurturant relationships with them…when they are competent and fulfilled breadwinners, when they are successful and supportive partners, and so on"

(Lamb, p. 13). Father absence may prove detrimental to some children in some circumstances, not because of the absence of a male role model per se, but because one or more aspects of the father's (or second parent's) roles must be assumed by the single parent—or simply go unfilled, potentially compromising the primary mother-child relationship (Belsky & Vondra, 1989). If paternal influence is more indirect than direct, this might explain, in part, why so few studies have been able to document any significant effects of father absence; traditional main effects models of family structure would not capture the more subtle interactions at work (Marshall, English, & Stewart, 2001).

Ultimately, one must keep in mind that such roles are culturally bound, so appropriate and beneficial father involvement may look different from family to family, in various cultural groups, and throughout history (Lamb, 1997). A number of authors have pointed out that father involvement, as typically defined in the single parenthood literature, is a very white, middle-class notion, based primarily on economic contribution (Shaw, 1999; Thomas et al., 1996). Due to fewer economic opportunities and high rates of unemployment, African American fathers may not be able to meet this definition of father involvement, but still may play other important roles in their children's lives that usually go unexamined (and unappreciated by the public at large). Chase-Lansdale, Gordon, Coley, Wakschlag, and Brooks-Gunn (1999) found that over half of the African American fathers they studied were substantially involved in their children's lives, as measured by financial contributions, number of visits, participation in childcare, level of involvement in decision making regarding the children, and overall closeness of relationship with the child. However, the level of father involvement was not significantly associated with any of the child outcomes. Of course, it is important to keep in mind that the children in this study were only 3 years old at the time; effects might yet be seen in later years.

Multigenerational Families
A number of researchers have highlighted the important role played by grandparents in providing assistance to single mothers and in easing the

transition following divorce (e.g., by providing a temporary home, child-care, and monetary support) (Furstenberg & Cherlin, 1991). Extended families, however, are often assumed to play a larger and more lasting role in African American single-parent families. Dating back to Moynihan's (1965) infamous study of the Black family, a number of authors have described the strengths of the African American family, highlighting the importance of multigenerational relationships, most especially between mothers, grandmothers, and children (Chase-Lansdale et al., 1999). A recent study by the National Institute for Child Health and Development found that among the poorest African American families, half of all single mothers lived in multigenerational households and relied heavily on extended family to help them with childcare, financial support, and emotional support (Gadsden, 1999). This family structure has been discussed as a pragmatic response to poverty, a mechanism for "mentoring" very young mothers, and/or a remnant of traditional African family practices (Chase-Landsdale et al., 1999).

The multigenerational family, however, has remained outside mainstream research on family structure and father absence. In fact, it was not until the Personal Responsibility and Work Opportunity Act of 1996, otherwise known as "welfare reform," that the U.S. Census Bureau was mandated to begin collecting data on multigenerational households (Chase-Lansdale et al., 1999). As Shaw (1999) argued, the African American extended family structure may be an important mediating variable in determining child outcomes in fatherless families, and may explain why the research regarding child outcomes in African American single-parent families appears less consistent than research regarding white single-parent families, with some studies even showing *lower* rates of externalizing behaviors among African American children raised in single-mother families than among white children raised in single-mother families. Similarly, Demo and Acock (1996) noted that, "These relationships and the support they provide may explain why adolescents in continuously single parent families fare better than generally expected" (p. 484).

However compelling such arguments may be, the limited research available does not provide consistent support for the notion that multigenerational households buffer the impact of single motherhood, or that African American nonresidential fathers exert an unrecognized, positive influence on their children. Aquilino (1996), using data from the National Survey of Families and Households, found that coresidence with a grandparent householder resulted in increased educational attainment and delayed assumption of adult roles (e.g., childbearing and independent living). Interestingly, Aquilino (1996) also found little difference in the rate of coresidence between African Americans and whites.

Conversely, McLanahan and Sandefur (1994) found that living with a grandmother actually increased the risk of dropping out of school (twofold), and had no statistically significant effect on the risk for early childbearing. Chase-Lansdale et al. (1999) found that in some situations, especially in cases of prolonged coresidence, the multigenerational family structure was associated with reduced parenting skills on the part of both mothers and grandmothers. In effect, mothers and grandmothers in multigenerational families seemed to engage in a kind of "coparenting" that often is characterized by conflict and competition that benefits neither themselves nor the child(ren). Grandmothers who lived nearby, but not in the same residence, however, seemed to have a far more beneficial influence, suggesting that it may not be multigenerational families per se, but rather coresidence, that is problematic for children.

CONCLUSION

The research reviewed here suggests that the relationship between family structure and child well-being is a very complex one, mediated by the interplay of multiple factors. Indeed, one explanation for the often weak, or apparently nonexistent, effects of family structure on child outcomes is the historical excessive simplicity of the conceptual models utilized by most authors (Marshall et al., 2001). Researchers increasingly recognize the need to move away from a main effects model toward an ecological model that locates the child within multiple, nested systems, from the micro level of the family, to the macro level of the culture (Belsky, 1993; Bronfenbrenner, 1979). It is also apparent that the simple dichotomy between married, two-parent, heterosexual families, and divorced, single (white) mothers is a fallacy. The phenomenon of fatherlessness, whether framed as a problem of single motherhood, nonmarital birth, divorce, stepfamilies, cohabitation, same-sex parenthood, or even assisted reproduction, is deeply embedded in issues of gender, race, and class.

Chapter 2

Corporal Punishment in the United States

Corporal punishment is a normative parenting practice in the United States. Surveys of parenting behavior report slightly different figures, but all find that the great majority of parents (e.g., 90% or more report using corporal punishment with their children at some point in time (Flynn, 1996; Straus & Stewart, 1999). A similar proportion of adults report having experienced corporal punishment as a child (Graziano & Namaste, 1990; Hemenway, Solnick, & Carter, 1994). Even as the states moved to pass child abuse legislation in the 1960s, lawmakers were careful to exclude corporal punishment from the definition of child abuse, reinforcing the normative view of corporal punishment (Straus, 2000). Similarly, corporal punishment by schools is still permitted in almost half the states in the United States (Whipple & Richey, 1997). Nonetheless, attitudes toward corporal punishment may be changing, with support for corporal punishment having fallen significantly over the past few decades. For example, the percentage of parents who agreed with the statement, "A good hard spanking is sometimes necessary" dropped 20 percentage points in just 10 years (75% agreed in 1988, as compared to 55% in 1998). Changes in practice, however, have seemingly lagged behind changes in attitude.

DEFINITIONS OF CORPORAL PUNISHMENT

Some debate exists regarding the definition of corporal punishment, as well as the appropriateness of the term itself. In particular, the debate revolves around the distinction between child abuse and corporal punishment, and the distinction between "punishment" and "discipline." In general, discipline is thought to include a teaching/internalization component, while punishment is seen as being more punitive and concerned primarily with behavior suppression. Both of these terms are highly value-laden and few parenting responses to misbehavior are likely to fall neatly into one category or another. This study, therefore, simply uses the most commonly accepted terminology and definition, as offered by Straus (2001). Straus (2001) defined corporal punishment as, "The use of physical force with the intention of causing a child to experience pain but not injury for the purposes of correction or control of the child's behavior" (p. 4). The most widely used instrument for measuring the use of physical force against children is the Conflict Tactics Scale (CTS) developed by Straus and colleagues (Straus, Hamby, Finkelhor, Moore, & Runyan, 1998). Under the rubric of corporal punishment, the CTS includes a range of so-called "minor assaults," such as spanking on the bottom with a bare hand, belt, stick, hairbrush, and so forth; slapping on the hand, arm, leg, face, head or ears; pinching; and shaking (children over 2 years old).

Baumrind, Larzelere, and Cowan (2002) have argued that this definition is too broad and likely to include acts that are excessively harsh or abusive. Instead, they advocated using a definition that reflects "the more moderate application of normative spanking within the context of a generally supportive parent-child relationship" (p. 580). According to Baumrind et al. (2002), the majority of corporal punishment involves a mild to moderate spank to the buttocks with an open hand that causes minimal pain, and is most often used as a "backup" to other strategies such as reasoning or time-outs. This kind of spanking is referred to as "physical discipline" and is considered a potentially positive parenting behavior that is qualitatively different from child abuse.

As Gershoff (2002b) pointed out, however, the types of behaviors included in the Minor Assault subscale of the CTS are more common than Baumrind et al. (2002) maintained. For example, Straus and Stewart (1999) found that somewhere between a quarter and a third of the parents of 2- to 4-year-olds and 5- to 8-year-olds reported spanking with an object, and corporal punishment in schools usually takes the form of "paddling." Similarly, the language used by parents to describe customary corporal punishment is often harsh, with the term "beat" used widely throughout the United States. Gershoff argued that it is important to study corporal punishment as it is defined and practiced in reality, rather than how one thinks it should, or could be practiced. She and others maintain that corporal punishment is part of a continuum of violence against children, rather than a qualitatively different parenting practice, and as such, should be subject to close scrutiny.

Indeed, many scholars in this area argue that the distinction between abuse and corporal punishment represents contemporary social norms rather than a real dichotomy between harmless and harmful behaviors (Straus & Gelles, 1990). Some evidence in support of this perspective is provided by the apparent association between corporal punishment and physical abuse. Parents who abuse their children are more likely than parents who do not abuse their children to use corporal punishment (Whipple & Richey, 1997). Furthermore, a sizable proportion of physical abuse incidents appear to be cases of corporal punishment that escalated into injurious behavior (Straus, 2001). Straus goes so far as to describe corporal punishment as "one of the most prevalent and best documented risk factors for physical abuse" (p. 1109).

Baumrind et al. (2002) on the other hand, pointed out that the vast majority of parents who use corporal punishment do not abuse their children and argue that correlation in this case does not imply causation. Parents who are likely to escalate, they argue, have distinct characteristics that predispose them to abuse, rather than corporal punishment being the factor that incites them to violence. Such parents are likely to use corporal punishment impulsively and explosively, as a mechanism for venting their own frustration, not as a rational strategy for shaping child behavior. According to Baumrind et al. (2002), this distinction has been obscured in research regarding corporal punishment precisely because excessively severe definitions of corporal punishment have been utilized: "If both corporal punishment and physical abuse are measured with overlapping levels of severity, the conclusion that they are closely linked is tautologous" (p. 584).

RATE, SEVERITY, AND EFFECTS OF CORPORAL PUNISHMENT

Methodological problems certainly have plagued the research on corporal punishment, making it very difficult to evaluate the "true" rate, severity, and effects of corporal punishment. Numerous studies have simply asked respondents to endorse corporal punishment behaviors without defining those behaviors, asking about frequency, or asking about severity. In other words, a question might be worded as, "Have you spanked your child in the past year?" The term "spanking" may carry different meanings for different respondents, ranging from a light swat on the bottom to a full-fledged "whipping" with a belt. Likewise, it is unknown how findings might be affected by respondent willingness to report parenting behaviors that potentially fall into the realm of child abuse, although some authors argue that Americans have been surprisingly forthcoming in acknowledging violence against their children (Straus & Gelles, 1990).

Furthermore, one might expect that occasional spanking could have different effects than frequent, chronic corporal punishment which perhaps spills over into physical abuse. When questions about frequency have been asked, the time frame utilized has not been conducive to accurate recall. For example, using the time frame of one week, Giles-Sims, Straus, and Sugarman (1995) found that corporal punishment was used approximately 3 times a week with 2- and 3-year-old children. Most studies of corporal punishment, however, have asked about use over the past *year*. When corporal punishment is used that frequently, it is not likely that respondents will accurately report the total number of incidents in a year. Thus, most estimates of frequency are "almost certain to drastically underestimate the use of corporal punishment" (Straus et al., 1998, p. 253). In fact, when Whipple and Richey (1997) averaged data from three studies that reported corporal punishment during a 24-hour time frame, they found that parents spanked an average of 2.47 times a day, with a "normal range" of spanking frequency of 0–5.73 times a day. Efforts such as parental diaries, nightly phone calls, or extended observation in the laboratory are currently underway to explore alternate methodologies for capturing the true rate of corporal punishment (Parke, 2002).

The greatest controversy exists surrounding the question of corporal punishment's effects on children. General agreement seems to exist that corporal punishment is effective in the short term, at least with regard to suppressing unwanted behavior, and especially when it is well-timed (early in the interaction), consistent, accompanied by a verbal rationale, and practiced in the context of a nurturing relationship (Parke, 2002). It also appears that when all of the above criteria are met, a lower intensity of punishment is necessary to achieve behavior suppression. Much disagreement exists, however, regarding the long-term effects of corporal punishment. Short-term suppression, it is argued, is not sufficient to produce long-term internalization, and "In the long run the degrading aspects of corporal punishment may be more likely to cause resentment and a desire to defy the parent and others" (Whipple & Richey, 1997, p. 434).

Hundreds of studies have attempted to address this question over the past several decades, yet the evidence is far from conclusive. Some studies have found negative effects of corporal punishment, most notably subsequent antisocial or aggressive child behavior, whereas other studies have found positive or neutral benefits. Gershoff's (2002a) meta-analysis of 88 studies represents the most up-to-date attempt to synthesize the literature in this area. Her analysis found that corporal punishment did indeed result in immediate compliance by children, yet decreased moral internalization, increased aggression, and negatively affected mental health in the long run. Effect sizes were consistently in the moderate range. Gershoff (2002b) concluded that public policy should discourage the use of corporal punishment: "Why should we risk harming our children when there are a range of alternative methods of punishment and discipline?" (p. 609).

Baumrind et al. (2002), however, have criticized Gershoff's methodology on many fronts, arguing that her analysis confounded corporal punishment with physical abuse by including studies that used excessively severe definitions of corporal punishment; that her analysis relied for the most part on cross-sectional studies; that her analysis failed to delineate effects according to race/ethnicity; and that a majority of the studies included suffered from a variety of major methodological problems such as shared method variance (the same respondents reports both the punishment behavior and the effects on the child), retrospective recall, and failure to define the behaviors in question.

Reanalyzing Gershoff's data by severity of corporal punishment, research design, and independence of informants, Baumrind et al. (2002) found that effect sizes were significantly larger for cross-sectional studies, for studies that included excessively severe measures of corporal punishment, and for studies with shared method variance. Larzelere's (2000) qualitative review likewise found that the effects of corporal punishment differed according to study methodology. In fact, the randomized clinical trials included in his review (four in total) found primarily positive outcomes of corporal punishment (increased compliance, decreased fighting, increased parental warmth). About half of the uncontrolled studies found primarily negative outcomes for children (antisocial behavior, mental health problems, and reduced competencies), while the other half found neutral outcomes. Findings indicating beneficial child outcomes were more likely when data were observational or based on daily maternal reports, and when measured within 6 months of punishment. Findings indicating negative outcomes were more likely when only one reporter was utilized, when global measures of behavior were used, and when outcomes were measured more than 6 months after punishment. Effect sizes were smallest when study methodology was strongest. Effects were much larger for studies with samples drawn from clinically referred children and/or parents.

Given these contradictory findings, Baumrind et al. (2002) concluded that "a blanket injunction against disciplinary spanking is not warranted by the data" (p. 828). Indeed, when compared to nonviolent disciplinary tactics, there is little in the literature on the subject to suggest that corporal punishment is more harmful. For example, several analyses using data from the National Longitudinal Study of Youth have found similar associations between aggressive behavior and other discipline techniques such as withdrawal of privileges, suspension of allowance, grounding, and sending the child to the his or her room (Larzelere & Smith, 2000; McLeod et al., 1994). When the child's initial level of aggressive behavior was controlled for, however, these associations all became nonsignificant, suggesting that the aggressive behavior itself may in part trigger increased punishment, as well as predict later aggression (Gershoff, 2002b; Larzelere, 2000). Several of the studies included in Gershoff's (2002a) meta-analysis actually found larger negative effects for alternative disciplinary tactics than for corporal punishment, especially when used with younger children (Sears, 1961; Straus & Mouradin, 1998; Yarrow, Campbell, & Burton, 1968). Similarly, one recent study linked child mental health problems to high levels of *nonphysical* punishment (Vostanis et al., 2006). Other studies have found primarily beneficial (or sometimes neutral) effects of spanking, most notably with young children, children with behavior problems, African American children, and children of conservative Protestants (Deater-Deckard & Dodge, 1997a; Ellison, Musick, & Holden, 1999; Larzelere, 2000; McLeod et al., 1994; Straus et al., 1997).

PUNISHMENT AS A PACKAGED VARIABLE

Parke (2002) maintained that the inconsistency of findings regarding the effects of both corporal punishment and other disciplinary tactics can be attributed to a fundamental failure to ask the right question:

> The problem with asking about the effects of punishment per se is that punishment is not a single variable but in reality is situated in

the context of other practices.... Punishment is a *packaged variable* [italics original] that requires 'unwrapping' to isolate the components that account for its effectiveness. (p. 597)

The effects of corporal punishment on any given child are likely to vary according to characteristics of the child, characteristics of the punishment, the quality of the parent-child relationship, and the cultural context within which parenting takes place. What is needed, therefore, is the development and testing of transactional models of parental discipline that incorporate all of these elements. To date, very little research has attained this high standard, but careful interpretation of the literature yields a number of clues as to the contexts in which corporal punishment may be more or less effective and/or harmful.

Child Age

There is a general consensus that corporal punishment is clearly detrimental when used with teenagers, but may convey positive benefits (or at least result in neutral outcomes) when used with preschoolers (Gershoff, 2002a; Larzelere, 2000). Perhaps not coincidentally, corporal punishment is most likely to occur during the preschool years. One study found that 94% of the parents of 3- to 4-year-olds used corporal punishment (Straus & Stewart, 1999). Smaller, yet still significant percentages of parents report using corporal punishment with infants (35%) and teenagers (50%) (Graziano & Namaste, 1990; Straus & Stewart, 1999). Drawing on these findings, Larzelere (2000) recommended that if corporal punishment is used, it should not be used until a child is at least 18 months old, and should then be phased out after age 6.

Severity of Punishment

There is also widespread agreement that very frequent or severe corporal punishment results in negative outcomes for children (Gershoff, 2002a). This mirrors the literature on child physical abuse, the negative effects of which are rarely debated. However, a number of studies have found that when respondents reporting frequent/severe corporal punishment are dropped from the analysis, beneficial or neutral outcomes emerge

(Baumrind & Owens, 2001). The debate continues, of course, about where to draw the line between excessively frequent/excessively severe corporal punishment and customary (presumably harmless) corporal punishment. Support seems to be growing for Deater-Deckard and Dodge's (1997a) suggestion that the relationship between corporal punishment and aggressive behavior is nonlinear: "that is, the degree of association may vary, depending on the severity or frequency or intensity of the physical discipline" (p. 164).

Parenting Style

Numerous researchers have emphasized the importance of parenting style and the quality of the parent-child relationship in determining children's responses to corporal punishment. A number of parenting typologies have been offered, beginning with Baumrind's (1967) classic conceptualization of parenting style as the interaction of parental warmth or responsiveness with parental control or "demandingness." Three distinct parenting styles are described: "authoritarian" (low on warmth, high on control), "authoritative" (high on warmth, high on control), and "permissive" (high on warmth, low on control). Other scholars have identified additional parenting dimensions such as child-centered versus parent-centered (Pulkkinen, 1982) or involvement versus indifference (Martin, 1981). Maccoby and Martin (1983) expanded Baumrind's (1967) typology to include a fourth parenting style: "neglecting" (low on warmth, low on control).

The literature on parenting style and child outcomes is too vast to review here, but suffice it to say that the authoritarian and permissive styles have consistently been shown to be associated with the worst outcomes, and the authoritative style with the best outcomes, with regard to multiple dimensions: prosocial behavior, impulse control, moral development, independence, and self-concept (Maccoby & Martin, 1983). The authoritative style is described as follows:

1. Expectation for mature behavior from child and clear standard setting
2. Firm enforcement of rules and standards, using commands and sanctions when necessary

3. Encouragement of the child's independence and individuality
4. Open communication between parents and children, with parents listening to children's point of view, as well as expressing their own; encouragement of verbal give-and-take
5. Recognition of rights of both parents and children (Baumrind, 1967, summarized in Maccoby & Martin, 1983, p. 46)

Not surprisingly, then, the authoritative style reflects much of what is known about the elements of effective discipline (e.g., clear limits, consistency in enforcement, provision of a rationale, and delivery in the context of a nurturing relationship).

Initially, it was presumed that corporal punishment, as a power-assertive tactic, would be associated primarily with the authoritarian parenting style, but today, parenting style and parenting behaviors are understood to be distinct phenomena, with parenting style seen as more salient to child development (Darling & Steinberg, 1993; Gottman, Katz, & Hooven, 1997). Ahn (1990) found that endorsement of corporal punishment was not equated with frequent use of corporal punishment. In her study, a far lower percentage of respondents who approved of corporal punishment actually reported using it as their usual disciplinary practice. Studies looking at the intersection of parenting style with the use of corporal punishment find that a majority of parents combine physical discipline with nonphysical discipline in the context of a nurturing relationship (high levels of hugging, reading books, playing together, etc.) (Thompson et al., 1999; Wissow, 2001). Wissow (2001) described this group as the "average" spanker. Thus, support for or the use of corporal punishment does not necessarily indicate a harsh or punitive parenting style.

In many ways, this question is at the crux of the debate around corporal punishment: If administered with warmth, and in order to provide a child with appropriate structure and guidance, can corporal punishment represent a positive parenting behavior? The literature on the subject suggests that most parents choose to use corporal punishment because they think it is the right thing to do, rather than administering it in a capricious or vindictive manner (Holden, Miller, & Harris, 1999; Socolar & Stein, 1995), although a sizeable minority does report spanking impulsively and emotionally (approximately a third of all parents who report spanking). Likewise, Straus and Mouradian (1998) found that when mothers reported spanking because they were so angry that they "lost it," there was an association between spanking frequency and externalizing behavior, but for mothers who remained calm while they spanked, the correlation was close to zero. Interestingly, Baumrind (1972) reported that it was actually permissive parents who were most likely to use corporal punishment explosively, presumably as a result of pent up frustration with the power imbalance in the parent-child relationship.

Deater-Deckard and Dodge (1997a) found that acts of parental warmth, such as speaking affectionately about the child, affectionate physical contact with the child, welcoming response to the child's approach, and so forth, mitigated the influence of corporal punishment on subsequent aggressive behavior. A number of other studies have found that the apparent relationships between corporal punishment and undesirable child outcomes became nonsignificant once measures of parental warmth were taken into account (e.g., by controlling for parental rejection or parental involvement) (McCord, 1997; McLoyd & Smith, 2002; Simons, Johnson, & Conger, 1994; Smith & Brooks-Gunn, 1997). Using a sample of poor children in the deep South, Rohner, Bourque, and Elordi (1996) found that corporal punishment was only associated with negative outcomes when the child perceived the punishment as a sign of rejection by the caregiver. Most studies, of course, have not taken such factors into account when investigating the effects of corporal punishment, so the evidence is more limited in this regard. However, it seems reasonable to postulate that corporal punishment associated with either authoritarian or permissive parenting might be more harmful to children than corporal punishment associated with authoritative parenting.

Child Temperament/Disruptive Behavior
A dynamic model of corporal punishment also recognizes the potential role played by the child in eliciting parental behaviors (Parke, 2002).

It has long been recognized in the literature on the subject that children with aggressive or antisocial behavior are more likely to be physically disciplined, confounding the apparent association between corporal punishment and externalizing behavior (Maccoby & Martin, 1983). This is a classic "chicken and egg problem," especially considering the preponderance of cross-sectional studies (Gershoff, 2002b). Although some studies have controlled for initial levels of disruptive behavior, it is difficult to know how or why that behavior developed in the first place (Holden, 2002). Gershoff maintains that externalizing behavior can likely be traced to a history of compromised parenting, while Deater-Deckard and Dodge (1997a) highlighted the research concerning the genetic component of aggressive behavior. Indeed, they noted that the greater frequency of corporal punishment with disruptive children may be due in part to a genetic similarity between child and parent, for example, having an irritable temperament, low tolerance for frustration, impulsivity, and so forth. Aggressive behavior is quite consistent over time and aggressive behavior in childhood is the best predictor of aggressive behavior in adulthood (Gershoff, 2002b). Most scholars, however, including Deater-Deckard and Dodge (1997a), do acknowledge an environmental component as well, especially "poor-quality parenting, specifically capricious, harsh and punitive discipline" (p. 162). Moreover, as Gershoff pointed out, if the very purpose of child discipline or punishment is to affect child behavior, it might be reasonable to assume a primarily parent-to-child direction of effect.

A number of studies have attempted to tease out the dynamics operating in families with aggressive children. On the most basic level, children with externalizing behavior problems seem to cause higher levels of frustration in parents, which may compromise parenting and increase the likelihood of lashing out. Even when parents are trying to stay calm, they are likely to resort to higher intensity attempts to control the child's behavior as milder techniques meet with little success. Patterson's (1982) notion of "coercion training" in families of aggressive boys is widely referenced in understanding how parent-child conflict escalates in such cases. According to Patterson (1982), parents in families of aggressive boys are likely to engage in "nattering," a kind of nagging or scolding with little or inconsistent enforcement of limits. The typical scenario might unfold as follows: Parent attempts to get child to do something (whether to start or stop); the child resists using a variety of noxious tactics such as shouting, whining, and so forth. If the parent backs off, the child's behavior is reinforced. Likewise, when the child ceases his or her noxious behavior, the parent is reinforced for having backed off. As time goes by, the parent is likely to make increasingly harsh attempts to gain compliance, with the child responding in turn.

This dynamic might explain why mild to moderate spanking seems to decrease antisocial behavior for children with behavior problems (Larzelere, 2000). A number of studies have found that parent training to increase child compliance using spanking as a "backup" for time-out significantly reduced child behavior problems (Hamilton & MacQuiddy, 1984; McNeil, Eyberg, Eisenstadt, Newcomb, & Funderburk, 1991; Olson & Roberts, 1987). These improvements also appear to be lasting, with improvements maintained up to 4.5 years later (Baum & Forehand, 1981). One study found that mothers of 2- or 3-year-olds who did *not* back up reasoning with some kind of negative consequence actually saw a progressive increase in unwanted behavior (Larzelere, Sather, Schneider, Larson, & Pike, 1998). It should be noted, however, that most studies using nonclinical samples have found that a brief time-out works equally as well as a mild spank.

Baumrind et al. (2002) argued that for children with behavior problems, improvements in behavior are predicated on achieving a basic, minimum level of compliance—which, for defiant children, may require firmer tactics such as spanking. It is believed that the level of child arousal is a key factor in determining the effectiveness of a given disciplinary tactic. In general, an intermediate level of arousal (not too much distress, but enough to get the child's attention) is thought to be optimal (Gershoff, 2002a). Accordingly, Maccoby and Martin (1983) suggested that aggressive children may constitutionally need a higher level of stimulus in order to attend to the parent's message. Once a minimal level of compliance is obtained, however, the child is more likely to respond to milder disciplinary tactics. Furthermore, Larzelere (2000) noted in his review that several studies have found an increase in parental warmth following spanking, especially regarding children with behavior problems. As Simons, Lorenz, Wu, and Conger (1993) noted, "Parents who report little enjoyment from the parent-child relationship are expected to manifest low levels of supportive parenting and high levels of harsh discipline" (p. 92). In effect, when the nattering dynamic is interrupted and compliance is obtained, parental hostility is reduced, paving the way for more positive interactions.

Children with more sensitive temperaments, on the other hand, may be hyper-aroused by corporal punishment: "Punishment, in particular physical punishment, is not only functionally superfluous for shy, fearful children...but may be traumatic" (Baumrind et al., 2002, p. 585). Indeed, even time-outs or a harsh tone of voice may be overwhelming for some children, and the excessive use of any disciplinary tactic seems to be associated with negative child outcomes (Parke, 2002). As Gershoff (2002a) explained, too much negative emotion on the part of the child may contribute to a feeling of resentment and foster resistance to hearing the disciplinary message. If corporal punishment is linked with later aggressive behavior, this may be the mechanism by which it develops. Similarly, if the corporal punishment is too painful, children may avoid or withdraw from the parent, with the gradual erosion of the child-parent bond that supports effective discipline.

Larzelere (2000) concluded, "It seems to be counterproductive and simplistic to continue viewing some disciplinary tactics as invariably good and others as invariably bad, as long as those tactics are nonabusive" (p. 218). Instead, Larzelere recommended that spanking be thought of as another tool in the parenting toolkit, to be used on a flexible basis and in a responsive fashion, depending on the child's characteristics and the dynamics of a given interaction—but most usually as a last resort, when other, less forceful tactics are not working. Beginning a disciplinary incident with spanking, Larzelere suggested, may increase the likelihood of excessively frequent or excessively severe corporal punishment because if the child resists parental attempts at control, it is difficult to back down and switch to reasoning or time-out. He argued that a ban on corporal punishment, as advocated by some, for example, Straus (2000), or even public policy that actively discouraged all spanking, would deprive parents of a potentially useful tool in the ever challenging business of child rearing.

Cultural Context

A major limitation of the literature on corporal punishment and indeed, on parenting more generally, has been its heavy reliance on white, middle-class samples. As Kelley, Power, and Wimbush (1992) noted, this tendency has resulted in the development of parenting models that are specific to one cultural group, yet defined as the norm. When these standards are applied to nonwhite families, such families may appear dysfunctional or inadequate, especially when race and social class are confounded (e.g., when poor African American families are compared to middle-class white families). African American mothers in particular have often been portrayed as harsh and punitive toward their children, and are generally believed to use a higher level of corporal punishment than white parents (Coolahan, McWayne, Fantuzzo, & Grim, 2002; Kelley et al., 1992). Lareau (2002) argued that lower income parents, both African American and white, may feel the need to teach their children to value external authority, as they will likely enter highly routinized work environments that involve little choice or opportunities for initiative. Likewise, in the midst of a hostile larger culture and potentially dangerous neighborhoods, African Americans in particular may also feel the need to exercise more control over their children's behavior in order to assure their safety (Kelley et al.). This parenting orientation may not be conducive to child success in a society that values self-initiative and independence above all else. However, when parents have little hope of their children "moving up," they may well view obedience to authority as a necessary skill (Lareau).

There is emerging evidence to suggest that the cultural context of corporal punishment heavily influences both the practice and effects of corporal punishment. Kelley et al. (1992) found that low-income African

American mothers who used a child-centered approach to discipline were equally likely as mothers who used a parent-centered approach to use power-assertive tactics such as corporal punishment. "Thus in contrast to middle-class populations, the use of physical punishment may not simply indicate authoritarian parenting but instead may be a behavioral practice under the influence of other factors" (p. 578). A number of well-designed studies have found beneficial or neutral outcomes of corporal punishment for African American children while documenting negative effects for Caucasian children (Deater-Deckard & Dodge, 1997a; Gunnoe & Mariner, 1997; McLeod et al., 1994; Simons et al., 2006; Straus et al., 1997). Likewise, Ellison et al. (1999) found that children of conservative Protestants who were spanked between the ages of 2 and 4 (but not between the ages of 9 and 11) had fewer behavior problems than comparison children who were not spanked.

Other studies using more general measures of parental control have produced similar findings. One study looked at parental "demandingness" (strictness, parental control, high standards for child performance) and school success (Steinberg, Lamborn, Dornbusch, & Darling, 1992). Steinberg et al. (1992) found school success for African American children was associated with a high level of parental demandingness, but the same relationship did not hold for children of other ethnicities. Baldwin, Baldwin, and Cole (1990) similarly found that parental restrictiveness was associated with higher IQ scores for high-risk (low-income) youths but not for low-risk youths. McCabe et al. (1999) found that parental demandingness improved child adjustment (with regard to acting out, anxiety, and social skills) only in families experiencing high stress. Jones (2000) found that in more dangerous neighborhoods (defined as those with a high rate of homicide), a "controlling" parenting style was associated with greater child safety, while in less dangerous neighborhoods, the same parenting style was associated with increased exposure to violence. Coley (1998) reported that high control and discipline by fathers predicted fewer behavior problems at school for African American children, but more behavior problems at school for white children.

If corporal punishment is normative in low-income and/or minority communities, then the practice of corporal punishment, both as a reflection of parenting, and as experienced by children, may well be positive. As Deater-Deckard and Dodge (1997a) explained, corporal punishment may be a sign of something being wrong—being "out of control"—when it represents a rejection of, or inability to accommodate to, social norms. Accordingly, the child is more likely to be harmed, both because the behavior is dysfunctional, and because the child is aware by a certain age that such tactics are not accepted by the community. In the context of a community supportive of corporal punishment, however, it may be that using corporal punishment is a sign of appropriate parenting, and will largely be experienced as an indication of caring and involvement on the parent's part.

Similarly, different social norms may exist regarding alternative disciplinary tactics. According to Jackson (1997), African American parents do not necessarily consider physical punishment to be the harshest disciplinary approach. In fact, alternative tactics such as yelling and time-outs may be viewed within the African American community as more punitive than spanking (Jackson, 1997; Mosby, Rawls, Meehan, Mays, & Pettinari, 1999). Ahn (1990) found that African Americans were indeed much less likely than whites to report yelling or scolding (13.7% compared with 26.8%) or using time-outs (11.6% compared with 58.9%). Mosby et al. (1999) found that African American elders viewed spanking as a strategy to *prevent* child abuse: without spanking, it was argued, child behavior and parent frustration were more likely to escalate until the parent lost control, both verbally and physically.

Conversely, many other studies have found negative effects of corporal punishment for African American children as well as white children (McCabe et al., 1999; McLoyd & Smith, 2002). Straus (2005) estimated that about half of studies have found neutral or beneficial outcomes of corporal punishment for African American children while the other half have found detrimental outcomes (mirroring the broader corporal punishment literature). Of course, part of the uncertainty concerns the definition of corporal punishment from study to study (in particular whether or not items that might be considered abuse were included in the corporal punishment construct). As discussed previously, there is little disagreement that child abuse negatively affects all children, regardless of race or socioeconomic status.

Other authors have suggested that there may be distinct, poorly understood processes operating in African American families. For example, McCabe et al. (1999) found that for African Americans, parental demandingness (which improved child adjustment) was significantly associated with corporal punishment, yet corporal punishment itself was found to decrease child adjustment. Likewise, there was no association between parental warmth and parental demandingness in predicting child adjustment, as has often been found for white children. "It may be that each of these factors contributes to child adjustment separately and not in an interactive fashion among African American families" (McCabe et al., 1999, p. 147). Pinderhughes et al. (2000) found parallel inconsistencies in the prediction of corporal punishment by low-income parents. Life stress, as well as beliefs about the appropriateness of spanking, increased the likelihood of corporal punishment, suggesting that both emotional reactivity and rational deliberation may play a role: "What remains unclear is whether the two paths from these characteristics are mutually distinct or co-occur within individuals" (Pinderhughes et al., 2000, p. 393). Using longitudinal data, McLeod et al. (1994) found that for African American mothers, corporal punishment was a response to child aggression, while for white mothers, corporal punishment was *both* a response to, and a contributor to child aggression.

At the same time, very few studies have looked at within-group variation in parenting styles or parenting behaviors among low-income and/or minority parents. Kelley et al. (1992) found wide variation in attitudes toward corporal punishment as well as in discipline practices among a sample of low-income African American women, highlighting the danger of making overgeneralizations about parenting in this population. Another study of working- and middle-class African American mothers found that corporal punishment was used rarely, with alternative disciplinary tactics such as reasoning used the most often (Bluestone & Tamis-LeMonda, 1999). Just as a range of parenting styles have been identified among white, middle-class parents, parenting by African Americans is unlikely to fit a single mold. Whaley (2000) argued that the key issue is not race per se, but rather whether corporal punishment is parent oriented or child oriented: "A child-oriented view assumes that children need to learn obedience to become self-respecting and responsible adults, whereas a parent-oriented perspective considers obedience to parental authority an end in itself" (p. 6). Both perspectives are likely to be represented to varying degrees within a given ethnic group.

FACTORS ASSOCIATED WITH CORPORAL PUNISHMENT

Clearly, although most children experience corporal punishment at some point, their experiences of corporal punishment are quite varied. The previous section reviewed the literature regarding the possible effects of corporal punishment on children depending on a number of contextual variables. The focus of this study, however, is on predicting maternal use of corporal punishment. Various child, maternal, family, and sociocultural characteristics seem to be associated with an increased likelihood of corporal punishment. Some of these factors have been mentioned already in passing. A more systematic review of relevant child, maternal, and sociocultural characteristics is presented in what follows. A separate chapter is dedicated to the review of research specifically focusing on the role of family characteristics.

Determining the precursors of corporal punishment appears to be as challenging as determining the effects, probably for many of the same reasons (e.g., complexity of the phenomenon under study, competing definitions of corporal punishment, and fundamental measurement challenges). Consequently, the evidence for many of the identified risk factors is often mixed, or even contradictory. It should also be noted that most of the findings described below are, in large part, based on information collected from white, middle-class samples. There is a real possibility that other factors may be more salient to the dynamics underlying corporal punishment in African American or other minority families, and/or that the direction of association may be different.

Child Characteristics

As discussed previously, preschoolers are the age group most likely to experience corporal punishment. Rates of corporal punishment seem to gradually decline with child age, often dropping off considerably by ages 8–10, although 50% of children aged 13 and 14 are still spanked (Day, Peterson & McCracken, 1998; Straus & Donnelly, 1993). Interestingly, Ahn (1990) found ethnicity-related differences in views regarding the effectiveness of corporal punishment according to age: African Americans expressed the belief that corporal punishment was effective with children up until age 10, while whites placed the cutoff at age 7.

There is inconsistent evidence regarding the role of gender in corporal punishment. Many studies show boys to be at higher risk, but other studies find no or very little gender difference (Day et al., 1998; Graziano & Namaste, 1990; Straus & Gelles, 1990). As mentioned previously, many studies have found a positive association between problem behavior and corporal punishment. Other studies looking at child temperament, prematurity, and child disability have similarly concluded that "difficult" children may in part elicit greater parental violence, although the evidence is more mixed (Ammerman, 1990; Belsky & Vondra, 1989; Fox, Platz, and Bentley, 1995). Day et al. pointed out this may be one reason why corporal punishment is used so frequently with toddlers: "The temperament of a 'terrible' 2-year-old can be taxing for even the most skilled parent" (p. 81). Of course, it is also true that alternative tactics such as reasoning are simply less effective with young children. Others similarly argue that more disruptive behavior on the part of boys predisposes them to higher rates of corporal punishment.

Maternal Characteristics

Although both mothers and fathers use corporal punishment, the vast majority of the research has focused on mothers. Thus, references in the literature to "parental" behavior are most often referring to maternal behavior. Relatively little is known about paternal characteristics associated with discipline practices. Mothers and fathers appear equally likely to use corporal punishment, although fathers may spank less frequently simply because they are less involved in day-to-day discipline than mothers are (Feldman & Wentzel, 1990; Flynn, 1996; Straus, 2001). Although it is often assumed in popular culture that fathers are the disciplinarians of the family, one study found that many fathers could be characterized as "low-interacters": "Men who show affection toward and play with their children but who do not engage in much other activity with them" (Wissow, 2001, p. 125). Men who fell into this group tended to be roughly middle income and diverse in terms of race. Only about a fifth of the men in this study could be characterized primarily as disciplinarians, displaying high levels of participation in spanking, but low levels in nurturing activities. Interestingly, these fathers were most likely to be white and affluent (Wissow).

A number of demographic variables have been linked to parental discipline practices. For example, young maternal age has consistently been associated with corporal punishment (Giles-Sims et al., 1995; Straus & Stewart, 1999; Xu, Tung, & Dunaway, 2000). This is usually attributed to a lack of experience and greater overall immaturity on the part of the mother. Maternal education has likewise been linked to parenting practices, with less educated mothers being more likely to use corporal punishment (Arias & Pape, 1999), although some studies find no such relationship (Giles-Sims et al.). Wissow (2001) found a nonlinear relationship between education and corporal punishment, with parents with a high school education reporting more spanking than parents without a high school education or parents with more than a high school education. Other studies have found that family size is linked to corporal punishment, with greater use of corporal punishment observed in larger families (Pinderhughes et al., 2000; Xu et al., 2000).

Some studies have found that parents' own temperaments may be linked to the likelihood of corporal punishment; parents who exhibit aggressive or antisocial tendencies in other areas seem more likely to use corporal punishment with their children than other parents do (Bank,

Forgatch, Patterson, & Fetrow, 1993). As noted previously, a number of scholars postulate that the aggressive behavior exhibited by some children subsequent to corporal punishment may, in fact, be due, in part, to a third variable—an inherited trait—that explains both the parent's use of corporal punishment and the child's aggressive tendencies (Reiss, 1995). Others postulate that parents abused as children are more likely to use corporal punishment with their children, although several studies have found no relationship between history of abuse and attitudes toward corporal punishment among samples of adults who reported injuries as a result of being disciplined in childhood (Bower & Knutson, 1996; Deater-Deckard, Lansford, Dodge, Pettit, & Bates, 2003).

Various measures of psychological functioning, including depression, anxiety, and substance abuse, have also been associated with increased corporal punishment (McLoyd et al., 1994; Paquette, Bolte, Tucotte, Dubeau, & Bouchard, 2000; Smith & Brooks-Gunn, 1997; Youssef, Attia, & Kamel, 1998). Psychological distress and/or impairment, it is argued, tends to compromise parenting by making parents more parent-centered, more emotionally reactive, and more likely to make negative attributions about child behavior. Similarly, life stress has been shown to negatively impact parenting, largely through stress-related depression and anxiety (Simons et al, 1993; Paquette et al., 2000). Some scholars suggest that social support may help to buffer the effects of psychological distress on parenting, but very few studies have actually examined the influence of social support on the use of corporal punishment (Gershoff, 2002a). Simons et al. (1993) found that spousal support reduced harsh parenting by mothers, but social network support (from friends, family, and neighbors) had no such effect. Others suggest that social support is uniquely important for African American parents, as African Americans are less likely to be married than whites and more likely to rely on extended networks of family and friends, and/or to live in multigenerational households (Wilson, 1989).

Sociocultural Characteristics
Parental beliefs about corporal punishment seem to be one of the strongest and most reliable predictors of corporal punishment (Holden et al.,

1999). This is consistent with a view of corporal punishment as a deliberate parenting strategy that is designed to help children achieve specific socialization goals. Fox et al. (1995) found that higher maternal expectations for children were associated with greater corporal punishment. Likewise, Holden et al. found that parents who endorse corporal punishment believe it will generally have positive consequences with few negative consequences. Many studies have established a link between childhood experience of corporal punishment and endorsement of corporal punishment in adulthood (Deater-Deckard et al., 2003; Flynn, 1996; Graziano & Namaste, 1990). Ahn (1990) found that respondents were most likely to endorse what was familiar to them (e.g., Asians were far more supportive than other ethnic groups of using a wooden rod, while African Americans were more supportive of using a belt, and whites of spanking with an open hand). Interestingly, however, such beliefs are not necessarily unchanging. Some mothers become less approving of corporal punishment after having a child, largely because their child responds unfavorably to spanking (Gershoff, 2002a).

Religious beliefs also seem to influence discipline choices, although the relationship is not clear cut. A number of studies have found that, among various religious groups, conservative Protestants are the most likely to use corporal punishment, while Catholics are least likely to use it (Giles-Sims et al., 1995; Whipple & Richey, 1997; Xu et al., 2000). However, studies that go beyond religious affiliation find that religiosity (e.g., attendance at religious services or specific knowledge of religious teachings) is actually associated with less frequent corporal punishment and better parent-child relationships (Kelley et al., 1992; Wilcox, 1998). For low-income African American mothers, "Fundamentalist religious beliefs [are] related to a more child-oriented approach toward parenting" (Kelley et al., p. 574). Parental beliefs about corporal punishment likewise appear to be influenced by the region in which parents reside. Corporal punishment is viewed most favorably in the South, and least favorably in the North, after differences in race, socioeconomic status, education, and religious affiliation have been taken into account (Flynn, 1996; Giles-Sims et al., Straus & Stewart, 1999). Furthermore, higher rates of corporal punishment have been reported in rural areas than in urban ones (Giles-Sims et al.).

Some studies have found that African Americans are more likely to endorse corporal punishment than whites or Hispanics are (Ahn, 1990; Deater-Deckard & Dodge, 1997a; Heffner & Kelley, 1987). Alvy (1987) found that higher income whites tended to express ambivalence about corporal punishment, while low-income whites were more accepting of it. African Americans were the most accepting of corporal punishment, and reported using corporal punishment "in order to teach obedience to authority, appropriate social behavior, and right from wrong" (Flynn, 1996, p. 51). In contrast to this, higher income whites tended to report using corporal punishment because they were angry, or because they had run out of other options (40% of whites reported spanking in anger, as compared with 3% of African Americans). Likewise, Ahn found that of all the ethnic groups studied, whites were the most conflicted about corporal punishment, and seemed to feel a need to justify its use. Both Pinderhughes et al. (2000) and Cazenave and Straus (1990), however, found no differences between African Americans and whites in their endorsement of corporal punishment.

The evidence regarding race/ethnicity and actual use of corporal punishment is also mixed. A number of studies have found that African American parents use corporal punishment more often than white and Hispanic parents (Flynn, 1996; Smith & Brooks-Gunn, 1997; Straus & Stewart, 1999; Pinderhughes et al., 2000), while other studies have found no such difference (Hemenway et al., 1994; Ellison et al., 1999), or found that white parents spank the most (Straus, 2001). Walsh (2002) reported that African American mothers were less likely than whites to spank, but more likely to discipline severely (hit with an object). In many studies, apparent racial differences in corporal punishment become non-significant when socioeconomic status is taken into account (Day et al., 1998; Giles-Sims, et al., 1995). Pinderhughes et al. (2000) found that the effect of ethnicity on the prediction of corporal punishment was minimal, accounting for less than 2% of the variance in responses. Within the low-income subgroup, however, African American parents were more likely to report harsh parenting. Day et al. found that the mother's age, education, and psychological well-being, as well as the quality of the neighborhood of her residence, influenced the rate of spanking for white mothers but not for African American mothers.

Numerous studies have documented a relationship between low socioeconomic status and corporal punishment (Flynn, 1996; Giles-Sims et al., 1995; Gunnoe & Mariner, 1997; Kelley et al., 1992; Lareau, 2002; McLoyd, 1990; Pinderhughes et al., 2000; Simons et al., 1993; Straus & Stewart, 1999; Xu et al., 2000). Other studies, however, find no such relationship (Day et al., 1998; Mahoney, Donnelly, & Lewis, 2000; McLeod et al., 1994; Straus, 2001). Some studies even report contradictory findings, for example, Stolley and Szinovacz (1997) found that corporal punishment increased with family income, but decreased with parent education (presumably, there is a relationship of positive correlation between parent education and family income). Giles-Sims et al. found the inverse: corporal punishment increased with Aid to Families With Dependent Children (AFDC) receipt, yet was not affected by parent education. Another study found a nonlinear relationship between family income and corporal punishment, with middle-income parents (earning between $20,000 and $60,000) reporting the highest rates of corporal punishment (Wissow, 2001).

It has been argued that, as in the case of race, low socioeconomic status influences parental behavior both through increased stress and through parental beliefs. For example, Holden, Coleman, and Schmidt (1995) found that spanking was predicted both by parental endorsement of spanking and by negative mood. Similarly, Ateah and Durrant (2005) found that corporal punishment was predicted by both cognitive and affective factors (although approval of corporal punishment was the strongest predictor). This may help to explain the sometimes contradictory or complex findings regarding the role of socioeconomic status in determining parenting practices. In effect, some low-income parents may use corporal punishment because their parenting has been compromised by the heightened stress associated with poverty, while others may use corporal punishment as part of a rational strategy to prepare children for life in dangerous neighborhoods, and employment in low-status occupations. Indeed, some authors argue that the apparent importance of race in determining discipline responses is, by and large, the result of confounding race and social class; a more careful examination of attitudes and practices within social classes yields far more similarities than differences (Lareau, 2002).

CONCLUSION

The literature on corporal punishment parallels the broader literature regarding family structure effects insofar as the causes, circumstances, and consequences of corporal punishment appear to differ according to a complex interplay of multiple factors. Moreover, there is no simple dichotomy between parents who use corporal punishment and parents who do not. Finally, the discussion around corporal punishment is similarly embedded in very sensitive issues of gender, race, and class. The following chapter looks more specifically at the question of family structure and corporal punishment.

CHAPTER 3

FAMILY STRUCTURE AND CORPORAL PUNISHMENT

Corporal punishment by mothers has been linked to a variety of family characteristics, such as family structure, family stability, and quality of the spousal relationship. In particular, it is often assumed that single mothers are at higher risk of using corporal punishment than married mothers are. Research in this regard is limited, but several conceptual frameworks have been offered to explain how family structure might affect child discipline practices. Interestingly, these frameworks suggest potentially contradictory implications for the likelihood of corporal punishment. This chapter looks at the conceptual bases for the notion that family structure influences child discipline practices, reviews the relatively limited research in this area, and outlines a series of study hypotheses.

CONCEPTUAL FRAMEWORKS

Perhaps the most enduring framework used to explain family structure effects on children is referred to as the "family composition" theory or the "socialization" theory (Amato & Keith, 1991; Demo & Acock, 1996; Jeynes, 2000). Across a number of social science disciplines, including anthropology, sociology, and psychology, it is commonly assumed that a two-parent biological family conveys more child benefits than any other family structure. Particularly influential perspectives include the Freudian argument that the heterosexual married unit is critical for healthy gender identification and sexual development, and Parson's structural-functional theory that emphasizes the importance of sex role differentiation within traditional nuclear families (Demo & Acock).

Two influential contemporary proponents of the family composition perspective, Blankenhorn (1995) and Popenoe (1996), relied very heavily on the work of several evolutionary psychologists who argue that the heterosexual, two-parent family unit is biologically based and designed to maximize fitness. In effect, this perspective holds that mothers and fathers bring different innate qualities and motivations to parenting. Mothers are seen as more nurturing and relational while fathers are seen as more directive and protective. Without a father in the home, Blankenhorn (1995) argued, mothers are not able to exercise sufficient control over their children, nor to protect them adequately from outside threats. This is seen as leading to inadequate discipline and supervision, as well as to increased frustration on the part of the mother, which may result in child abuse. Furthermore, biological fathers are seen as unwilling to invest in their offspring unless they are bound by marriage, so divorced and/or surrogate fathers are seen as relatively unhelpful when it comes to parenting. Indeed, surrogate fathers are seen as having little evolutionary incentive for investing in nonrelated offspring; on the contrary, they are believed to be at high risk of mistreating such offspring. According to this perspective, therefore, one might expect to see less child discipline in single-parent families, yet potentially more child abuse in both single-parent and reconstituted families.

Less extreme theorists downplay the gender aspect of the two-parent family, but argue that two parents simply bring more resources to bear on parenting than a single parent does (Amato & Keith, 1991). This might be referred to as the "role-overload" model of parenting. Because single mothers are expected to do the work of two parents, Amato and

Keith argued, they are more likely to suffer from mental health problems such as depression and/or anxiety, and thus, to parent less effectively. According to this model, less effective parenting may take the form of increased, harsher, and more impulsive corporal punishment (Gershoff, 2002a; Giles-Sims et al., 1995; Loeber, Drinkwater, Yin, Anderson, Schmidt, & Crawford, 2000). Consequently, one might expect to see less corporal punishment by mothers in stepfamilies, since the addition of a second parent presumably reduces role overload. The same might be said for multigenerational families, in which a grandparent functions as a surrogate parent, or at least as a significant support person. Literature on the subject, however, suggests that such families may be marked by considerable conflict, which itself is believed to increase the use of corporal punishment, as shall be discussed later.

A variation on the role-overload model is the economic-stress model. According to this perspective, low-income status is associated with greater parental stress, and thus potentially compromised parenting. Indeed, this is the explanation often offered for why rates of corporal punishment appear to be higher in low-income populations than high-income populations, regardless of family structure. According to this model, never-married mothers would be at the greatest risk of using corporal punishment because they are the most likely to be poor. Similarly, divorced mothers often experience a substantial decrease in family income following divorce, so one might expect to see an increase in harsh discipline by mothers following family disruption. According to the economic-stress model, one would expect that differences in discipline practices between intact families and other family structures would be reduced or eliminated when family income is taken into account. Moreover, parenting by mothers in reconstituted and multigenerational families might be expected to look more similar to parenting in intact families than parenting in single-parent families, given the benefit of additional income.

The last framework used to explain the presumed effects of family structure on parenting looks at the stability and quality of the spousal relationship. According to this perspective, it is conflict between parents, rather than family structure per se, that is likely to increase the use of corporal punishment (Nobes & Smith, 2002). Such conflict is likely to undermine effective discipline both by increasing maternal stress and by provoking stress-related problem behaviors in children. Unstable relationships are likely to be associated with both maternal and child stress, again increasing the likelihood of harsh and impulsive discipline. Using this framework, one would expect to see higher rates of corporal punishment by mothers in high-conflict families, regardless of family structure (Hetherington, 1999). Indeed, on the one hand it could be argued that in some cases, divorce might serve to reduce corporal punishment by diminishing marital conflict. On the other hand, however, the likelihood of corporal punishment may be greater in reconstituted families because they involve complex, often conflicted relationships. Furthermore, never-married mothers and divorced mothers are more likely to have complex relationship histories with multiple partners. Thus, never-married mothers without partners might be less likely than married or divorced mothers in high-conflict or unstable relationships to use corporal punishment.

REVIEW OF THE LITERATURE

Relatively little research has been done looking specifically at the relationship between family structure and maternal use of corporal punishment. In terms of general discipline style, single motherhood has been associated with lower levels of parent-child involvement and supervision, as well as less consistent discipline (McLanahan & Sandefur, 1994). In a sample of low-income African American mothers, Coolahan et al. (2002) found that single mothers engaged both in more "active-restrictive" behaviors (similar to the authoritarian parenting style), and more "passive-permissive" behaviors (similar to the neglecting parenting style) than married mothers did. Hetherington and Kelly (2002) reported that even when the divorced women in their study tried to be authoritarian,

> they often were erratic and ineffective. Although like other authoritarians they were unloving and punitive, constantly barking out orders and criticism, they often lacked the firmness and follow-through found in most authoritarians. Their children didn't even get

the benefits of predictable, albeit predictably punitive discipline. (p. 132)

Interestingly, Nobes and Smith (2002) found that the poorest single mothers and the mothers with the most mental health problems in their sample were the least likely to use corporal punishment.

Several studies have found that single mothers and separated or divorced mothers are more likely than married mothers to use corporal punishment (Fox et al., 1995; McCabe et al., 1999; Loeber et al., 2000). Harsh discipline may also be more common in stepfamilies (Hashima & Amato, 1994; Hetherington & Kelly, 2002). Giles-Sims et al. (1995) found that, after controlling for socioeconomic status has been undertaken, married mothers and single mothers were found to be equally likely to spank, but single mothers spanked more frequently. Gelles (1989) found no difference in the rate of corporal punishment between single and married mothers, but did find a higher rate of severe corporal punishment among single mothers. Sariola and Uutela (1992) found that single mothers were actually less likely than married mothers to use corporal punishment but, again, were more likely to punish severely when they did use physical discipline. Other studies have also reported lower rates of corporal punishment by single mothers than by married mothers (Olson & Haynes, 1993), or no difference in rates by marital status (Gelles & Edfeldt, 1986; Nobes & Smith, 2002). Of course, it is important to remember that single mothers are also more likely to be low-income and to be African American than married mothers are, so findings regarding single parenthood and corporal punishment may be, in part, a reflection of different parenting norms, rather than a sign of dysfunction.

There is evidence to suggest that parents in high-conflict relationships, or relationships that involve domestic violence, are more prone to using corporal punishment (Amato & Booth, 1997; Nobes & Smith, 2002; Pinderhughes et al., 2000; Simons et al., 1993; Walsh, 2002; Xu et al., 2000). Simons et al. also found that low marital satisfaction and low spousal support were associated with greater use of corporal punishment. One study that examined child experience of corporal punishment, rather than simply maternal administration of corporal punishment, found that fathers were significantly more likely than mothers to use severe punishment, and that children in two-parent families experienced significantly higher levels of corporal punishment than children in single-parent families (Nobes & Smith). The authors postulate that in low-income populations, male partners may be more likely to bring additional stress to parenting instead of serving as a source of support. They quote Kempe and Kempe, early pioneers in the field of child abuse:

> In our experience, single parents are rather less abusive than couples, which is surprising because one would think that a spouse would provide support in the face of crises. In fact a spouse who is not supportive is worse than no spouse at all when it comes to childrearing. (Kempe & Kempe, 1978, cited in Nobes & Smith, 2002, p. 352)

Father advocates, however, claim that fathers simply have a more forceful or directive discipline style that is necessary to counterbalance the nurturing, relational style of discipline utilized by mothers (Popenoe, 1996; Pruett, 2000). Blankenhorn (1995) goes so far as to argue that paternal authority requires some element of fear or intimidation and bemoans the new "wimpy" father who tries to copy a maternal nurturing style.

Because there is evidence to suggest that corporal punishment is associated with child maltreatment, it may also be helpful to look at the literature regarding single motherhood as a risk for child maltreatment. Again, the evidence in this area is fairly limited, but many of the findings seem to parallel the findings for corporal punishment. Early research regarding child maltreatment suggested that single motherhood was strongly associated with child abuse and neglect (Caplan, Watters, White, Parry, & Bates, 1984; Daly & Wilson, 1985; Sack, Mason, & Higgins, 1985). Some studies even reported that as many as a third to a half of all children of single or remarried mothers were victims of child maltreatment (Stiffman, Schnitzer, Adam, Kruse, & Ewigman, 2002). However, these studies were methodologically compromised in many ways. For example, many studies relied on clinical (usually small and highly unrepresentative) samples, lacked any type of comparison group, and were often simply descriptive, failing to account for potential confounding factors (Gelles, 1989; Stiffman et al., 2002).

Subsequent efforts to examine the apparent relationship between single motherhood and child maltreatment more rigorously most often report no increased risk of child abuse or neglect associated with single motherhood, or an initial effect that disappears once socioeconomic status is taken into account by controlling for income, education, or TANF (welfare) receipt (Chaffin, Kelleher, & Hollenberg, 1996; Gelles, 1989; Kotch, Browne, Dufort, & Windsor, 1999; Nobes & Smith, 2002). Indeed, poverty is widely acknowledged to be a major contributor to child maltreatment (Pelton, 1991) and single mothers, especially young single mothers, are disproportionately poor. However, a limited number of studies have found a significant increase in risk associated with single motherhood (Brown, Cohen, Johnson, & Salzinger, 1998; Egan-Sage & Carpenter, 1999), although these studies still employ questionable methodologies, for example, by relying on very small samples or unsophisticated statistical analyses (e.g., bivariate associations).

A more consistent link has been found between child maltreatment and the presence of an unrelated adult (most often male) in the house, such as when the mother cohabits or remarries. Presence of an unrelated adult has been associated with an increased risk of all types of child abuse and neglect, but particularly with child death and child sexual abuse (Daly & Wilson, 1985; Fergusson, Lynskey, & Horwood, 1996; Finkelhor, Hotaling, Lewis, & Smith, 1990; Margolin, 1992; Radhakrishna et al., 2001; Stiffman et al., 2002). There also appears to be a relationship between domestic violence and risk of child maltreatment (Dubowitz, Black, Kerr, et al., 2001; Fantuzzo, Boruch, Beriama, & Atkins, 1997; McGuigan & Pratt, 2001). Such findings reinforce the perspective that interpersonal conflict, rather than single motherhood per se, puts children at risk.

It commonly is argued that father surrogates do not have the same investment, evolutionarily speaking, that biological fathers have in their offspring, and are thus more likely to harm their unrelated children, or at least to compete with them for the mother's attention and other family resources (Blankenhorn, 1995; Hetherington & Stanley-Hagan, 1999). Some critics have challenged this view, pointing to the literature on adoption, which demonstrates a strong commitment to unrelated children by adoptive parents, both mothers and fathers alike (Golombok, 1999). The distinction here may be that stepfathers or live-in partners are most often motivated by their interest in the mother, not in the children (Hetherington & Stanley-Hagan). In other words, they may become surrogate fathers by default rather than by choice, whereas adoptive parents typically are quite passionate in their desire for a child.

A mere handful of studies have attempted to directly examine how father presence and/or involvement may affect the likelihood of child maltreatment by mothers. Such studies hint at indirect and complex roles played by fathers or father figures. For example, Dubowitz et al. (2000) found that simple father presence ("father" defined as biological or surrogate) did not affect the likelihood of child neglect, but more father involvement in household tasks (possibly relieving some of the burden on the mother) and a greater sense of parenting efficacy was associated with less neglect. Interestingly, the economic contribution made by the father was not a significant factor, perhaps because poor families were disproportionately represented in their sample. In other words, the men involved probably contributed relatively little to family finances (Dubowitz et al.,). Similarly, Marshall et al. (2001) found that father presence had no direct effect on child behavioral problems in maltreated children, but also found that it was significant as an interaction term, for example, in combination with ethnicity (father presence seemed to have a moderating effect on child aggression only for African American children). In both studies, however, any such effects remained quite weak. McLanahan and Sandefur (1994) found that presence of a grandmother in the home increased child supervision, but presence of a male partner did not.

STUDY APPROACH

After reviewing the research regarding family structure effects, corporal punishment, and the linkages between the two, it is clear that any attempt to examine the relationship between family structure and maternal use of corporal punishment should strive to (1) use the ecological model to identify theoretical domains of interest; (2) move beyond marital status as a measure of family configuration; (3) attempt to differentiate corporal punishment by severity; (4) carefully consider the roles of race and socioeconomic status; and (5) explore indirect and transactional effects. This study attempts to meet each of these conditions. More detail regarding study design, participants, measures, and procedures is provided in the following chapter.

Study Hypotheses

This study is guided by two interrelated research questions:

- What relationship, if any, exists between family configuration and maternal use of corporal punishment in a low-income population?
- How do fathers, in particular, influence maternal use of corporal punishment in this population?

Figure 1 outlines the theoretical model used to guide the investigation of these questions. According to the model, the use of corporal punishment by mothers is multiply determined by complex interactions between family characteristics, maternal characteristics, child characteristics, and macro level factors such as cultural norms. Independent and dependent variables are shaded in dark gray, while control variables are shaded in light gray, and unobserved variables are left unshaded. Primary relationships tested are indicated by bold lines, secondary relationships by lighter lines, and untested relationships by dashed lines. Single arrows represent unidirectional relationships and double arrows represent bidirectional relationships.

This model postulates that family configuration may have direct and/or indirect effects on maternal use of corporal punishment. Family configuration is measured in two ways: according to *family structure* (defined by the presence or absence of a father figure), and according to *marital status*

FIGURE 1. Family structure and corporal punishment: Hypothesized relationships between study variables.

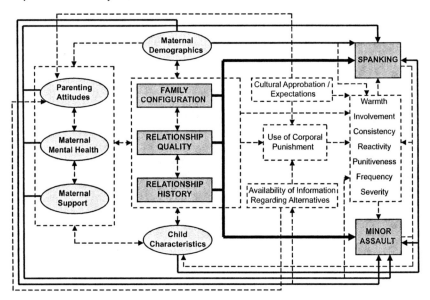

(defined by the legal relationship between adult partners). As discussed previously, however, direct effects of family configuration often have been difficult to observe, at least once income is taken into account. The prevailing wisdom is that father influence is manifested more indirectly, largely via stress on, or support for, the mother. Therefore, relationship quality and stability are also included as independent variables, according to the notion that father influence may be more readily observable in such domains. Likewise, the model includes a number of control variables known to influence maternal parenting, but also thought to be linked to father absence: maternal mental health, maternal support, and parenting attitudes. Ideally, these hypothesized interactions would have been tested statistically, but sample size did not allow for that level of analysis. Other basic control variables known to affect parenting, such as maternal demographics and child characteristics, were also included.

Using this model, a mother's use of corporal punishment is also influenced, in large part, by the view of corporal punishment held by her culture, as well as by the availability of information regarding alternative disciplinary strategies. These macro level factors are seen as mediating the influence of the family-level variables on the likelihood that a mother will respond to negative or undesirable child behavior with corporal punishment. The particular form taken by that punishment (in this case, either spanking or minor assault), as well as the relative force and frequency of corporal punishment, is seen as being determined by more proximal factors, such as maternal warmth, involvement, consistency, reactivity, and punitiveness, which are also influenced, in large part, by interactions between the other variables in the model. Because this study relied upon preexisting data, however, both these macro level variables and more proximal variables remained unobserved, and were therefore not included in the statistical analysis. Instead, a number of proxy variables were utilized. For example, perceived social support and neighborhood quality were included as potentially important extrafamilial influences, theoretically linked to cultural norms and the availability of information around parenting. The importance of religion in raising children variable might also be seen as a reflection of cultural values. Likewise, several of the parenting attitude subscales were treated as suggestive indicators of maternal warmth and consistency. Frequency and severity of spanking and minor assault were viewed as possible indicators of maternal reactivity and punitiveness.

Compelling theoretical arguments can be made for a number of seemingly contradictory predictions about potential findings. According to the conceptual frameworks described previously, the most likely finding might be that never-married and divorced mothers are more likely than always married mothers to use corporal punishment. The reasoning behind this prediction is that family disruption and/or father absence leads to decreased parenting efficacy with regard to a number of dimensions (e.g., decreased warmth, involvement, and consistency, along with increased reactivity, punitiveness, and frequency and severity of disciplinary responses), as represented in the dashed box at the far right of the diagram. This decline in parenting efficacy is believed to be mediated by financial and emotional stressors that negatively impact maternal coping and mental health.

However, this assumption is based on the notion of corporal punishment as an exclusively negative discipline practice that is indicative of compromised parenting, and maybe even abuse. As discussed in the previous chapter, it may well be the case that for some mothers, especially white middle-class mothers, the use of corporal punishment is a reflection of poor parenting, but if one takes seriously the possibility that corporal punishment represents normative—and arguably appropriate—parenting in other populations, then a "pathology" approach to predicting the use of corporal punishment is not sufficient. Assuming that family disruption reduces parental efficacy, for example, one might somewhat counterintuitively expect to see higher rates of corporal punishment by mothers in married, two-parent families, as compared to single-mother or reconstituted families. Corporal punishment in such cases may be associated with the improved maternal functioning that results from spousal support and family stability.

Even within different populations, the impetuses behind the use of corporal punishment may vary widely, with some mothers spanking out of anger, and others spanking as part of a deliberate, caring parenting strategy. According to this perspective, one might expect to see significant associations between indicators of maternal stress and corporal punishment, *as well as* between indicators of maternal efficacy and corporal punishment. Indeed, it appears from the literature on the subject that maternal stress is associated with compromised parenting at both ends of the spectrum of disciplinary tactics. In other words, mothers under stress may become more harsh in their discipline, or laxer and permissive in their discipline. If corporal punishment is a normative practice, then a permissive parenting style could be correlated with *reduced* corporal punishment. In this case, what is really neglectful parenting could paradoxically appear to be improved parenting, at least from a white, middle-class perspective.

Particularly unclear is what role fathers or surrogate father figures might play. As discussed previously, direct effects of father influence have been difficult to detect, especially in low-income populations. Many children of poor single mothers experience a series of relatively short-lived family arrangements, making "the effect of any one individual... dilute and difficult to measure" (Marshall et al., 2001, p. 291). As with prior research, it may well be that once income and race are taken into account, family configuration does not appear directly related to corporal punishment in this study. If fathers do "matter" in this population, they may play more indirect roles than direct ones, by supporting or not supporting the mother emotionally, for example, or by providing or not providing for the family financially. Therefore, it is important to look for signs of paternal influence on discipline practices in other related domains, such as relationship quality and stability.

There is compelling evidence to suggest that the instability and increased conflict associated with reconstituted families negatively affects parenting, so one might expect to see more effective child discipline by mothers in families with biological fathers than in those with surrogate fathers. Again, it is difficult to predict whether (and under what circumstances) less effective child discipline might take the form of harsher parenting (with increased likelihood of corporal punishment) or more lax parenting (with decreased likelihood of corporal punishment). The literature on the subject does indicate that children in reconstituted families are at higher risk of child abuse. In that case, one might predict that mothers in surrogate father families would be more likely to report a "high" level of spanking, or a "high" level of minor assault, assuming that more frequent corporal punishment is potentially indicative of abuse.

Finally, there is compelling evidence to suggest that patterns of family formation differ according to race and socioeconomic status, as do the precursors, characteristics, and consequences of corporal punishment on children. Therefore, one might expect to see an interactive effect between race and family structure (and/or between race and other potential antecedents of disciplinary tactics) in the prediction of the use of corporal punishment by mothers. However, because this is a uniformly low-income, high-risk sample, it may be that racial differences are less apparent than in studies with more homogenously white, middle-class samples. As a number of authors have pointed out, few studies have explored the diversity among discipline styles and strategies among poor and/or ethnic minority populations (see Ispa & Halgunseth, 2004; Kelley et al., 1992; McLoyd et al., 2007). A significant advantage to using a predominantly African American, low-income sample is that it allows for the possible detection of factors other than income or race in predicting corporal punishment.

CHAPTER 4

STUDY METHODOLOGY

STUDY DESIGN

This study employs a cross-sectional or multigroup, ex post facto design. Secondary data for the study were drawn from the "Longitudinal Studies of Child Abuse and Neglect" (LONGSCAN) (Runyan et al., 1998). LONG-SCAN is a collaborative effort of five independent, prospective, longitudinal studies designed to investigate the causes and consequences of child abuse and neglect. The five studies differ in terms of geography, specific target populations, and some research questions, yet share a core set of common "measures, definitions, training, data collection strategies, data entry, and data management" (NDACAN, 2001, p. 10). The target populations are purposely varied in their risk of child abuse or neglect, as well as the type of interventions received or not received. This approach enhances sample size and diversity, ensures that findings are not specific to one particular agency or geographical area, and allows the investigation of a wide range of precipitating factors, effects, and treatment approaches over time. The five sites are as follows: East (Baltimore), Midwest (Chicago), Southwest (San Diego), Northwest (Seattle), and South (North Carolina). The coordinating center is located at the University of North Carolina at Chapel Hill. Children are enrolled in the study at age 4 or younger, and then followed until age 20, with six comprehensive data collection points along the way.

This study utilizes the baseline data, collected at age 4, from three of the five sites: East, Midwest, and South. The decision to focus on the baseline data, rather than utilizing the longitudinal data was made by necessity; at the time of the study, only the baseline data had been released for public use. Although this study cannot capitalize on the advantages offered by a longitudinal design, the cross-sectional design still has much to offer. Such a design is appropriate for describing the characteristics and attitudes of a population, allows the simultaneous analysis of multiple variables, and may be useful in hypothesizing explanatory relationships between variables (Fortune & Reid, 1999). The main drawbacks to using a cross-sectional design are potential nonequivalence of study and comparison groups, and the difficulty of establishing causality. However, statistical techniques can be used to control for group differences and to test alternative hypotheses. Given the dearth of existing research in this area, a cross-sectional study is a useful and important first step.

The decision to use data from only three of the five sites was made after an examination of each site's sample, instrumentation, and response rates, in order to determine appropriateness to the study questions. The Northwest site was eliminated because the entire sample had been referred to Child Protective Services for suspected child abuse or neglect, potentially obscuring any distinction that might exist between child discipline and child abuse. Indeed, a preliminary analysis of the Northwest data indicated that virtually no respondent indicated spanking or otherwise hitting their child more than once in the preceding year, quite the opposite of what one might expect to find in a sample of parents referred for suspected maltreatment, as well as being significantly different from the other sites. Consequently, this sample was viewed as likely being biased. Similarly, the Southwest site was eliminated because the sample consisted only of children who had spent time in foster care.

Sample size thus was reduced in the interests of increasing the comparability of the target populations and decreasing potential response bias. Nonetheless, aggregating data across the three sites raises fundamental questions about the comparability of sites, especially considering the different target populations, geographic locations, and occasional differences in research questions (NDACAN, 2001). Therefore, careful attention is given in this study to exploring differences between the sites and the possible influence of such differences on the findings.

STUDY PARTICIPANTS

LONGSCAN is concerned primarily with child experience, so study selection criteria were based on child characteristics rather than parental characteristics. Different criteria were utilized at each site, as shall be described later. For the purposes of this study, only biological mothers of study children were included as respondents. Combining biological-mother respondents from the three sites yielded an overall sample size of 619, or approximately 91% of all respondents. The next largest category of respondents after biological mother was grandmother (4.1% of all respondents).

In the East, children were identified from a preexisting sample of children drawn from three different pediatric clinics serving an inner-city (Baltimore), low-income population ($n = 212$) (Dubowitz, Black, Cox, et al., 2001). In order to participate, children had to fall into one of two high-risk categories: failure to thrive (32.1%) or at risk of HIV infection (due to parental HIV infection and/or IV drug use) (23.1%). A comparison group without these risk factors was selected from the same clinics (44.8%).

In the South, children and mothers were recruited from a larger group of children identified as high-risk by the North and South Carolina High Priority Infant Program. High-risk children were defined as those with low birth weight (less than 2,500 grams or 5lbs, 8oz at birth), a mother aged less than 14, a birth defect, or any other serious medical problem (Kotch et al., 1999). Child subjects for LONGSCAN were randomly selected from this larger sample. Of the LONGSCAN subsample ($n = 196$), somewhat fewer than a third had been reported to Child Protective Services (CPS) by the time the child turned 4 years old.

The Midwest sample was newly recruited from a low-income, urban neighborhood in Chicago, based on referral to Child Protective Services in the past 12 months (Curtis & Schneider, 1996). Approximately 60% of children in the study met this criterion, a little less than half of whom went on to receive some kind of therapeutic services, while the other half received only public child welfare intervention. Controls were selected from the same neighborhood ($n = 211$), the only criteria being that the child had not been referred to Child Protective Services in the past 12 months, and was living below the federal poverty line.

MEASURES

The LONGSCAN Measures Committee, a subcommittee of the Coordinating Committee, was established to research, select, and in some cases, modify a core set of common measures to be implemented at each research site. Well-established, applicable measures with documented reliability and validity were located whenever possible. All instruments were pretested prior to use in the field, with a final pilot testing of the entire battery. Several instruments were developed or modified by LONGSCAN investigators specifically for this project, often in order to make them more culturally relevant (Runyan et al., 1998). As noted by the investigators, the most established measures have usually been developed using white, middle-class samples. As such, these instruments may not be as relevant to other populations, especially low-income or minority populations, as they are to white middle-class ones. Indeed, LONGSCAN investigators found that a few of the *Child Behavior Checklist* scales had low to moderate Cronbach's alphas (coefficients < .70) across LONGSCAN sites and racial groups. Nonetheless, this instrument was deemed useful for the purposes of the LONGSCAN study, with the caveat that any findings for nonwhite respondents should be viewed more cautiously.

Table 1 provides an overview of the domains, variables, and instruments relevant to this study. Further information regarding the instruments and the operationalization of each variable is provided later. Evidence regarding the psychometric properties of each instrument is

TABLE 1. Study variables according to domain.

Domain	Variable	Coding and Interpretation
Family Configuration	Family Structure	Categories constructed from responses to the Demographics instrument (Hunter et al., 2003). No father figure in home Biological father in home Surrogate father in home Mother and grandparent in home
	Marital Status of Mother	Categories constructed from responses to the Demographics instrument (Hunter et al., 2003). Never married Always married Divorced/remarried
Relationship Stability and Quality	Perceived relationship quality	Scores generated using the Autonomy and Relatedness Inventory. Recoded into dummy variable based on the median split. 0 = high quality (> 96) 1 = low quality (< 96) Instrument has 6 subscales, with scores ranging from 4 to 20. Higher scores on scales measuring positive characteristics reflect a higher degree of quality; higher scores on scales measuring negative characteristics reflect a lower degree of quality. Negative scales were reverse coded, then an overall score was obtained by summing the subscales.
	Relationship change	Categories constructed from responses to the Life Experiences Survey (LES) (Sarason, Johnson, & Siegel, 1987). 0 = no relationship change in the past year 1 = 1 or more relationship changes in the past year Possible relationship changes included: Became engaged, got married, had a break-up, became separated, divorced, got back together after break-up, had someone move in.
	Self-reported domestic violence as an adult	Response to a single item from the *History of Loss and Harm* (Hunter & Everson, 1991). 0 = not beaten as an adult 1 = beaten as an adult
Discipline Practices	Spanking	Single item (spanking) from Conflict Tactics Scale (CTS) – Caregiver to Child (Straus, 1979, as modified by LONGSCAN), recoded into dummy variable. 0 = Never or once in the past year 1 = More than twice in the past year

(continued on next page)

TABLE 1. (*continued*)

Domain	Variable	Coding and Interpretation
	High spanking	Single item (spanking) from modified CTS recoded into dummy variable. 0 = Fewer than 5 times in the past year 1 = 5 or more times in the past year
	Minor Assault	CTS – Minor Assault Scale recoded to exclude the spanking item, then scores recoded into a dummy Variable. 0 = No assaults (other than spanking) in the past year 1 = 1 or more minor assaults (other than spanking) in the past year
	High minor assault	CTS – Minor Assault Scale recoded to exclude the spanking item, then scores recoded into a dummy variable. 0 = None – 1 minor assault (other than spanking) in past year 1 = 2 or more minor assaults (other than spanking) in past year
	Psychological aggression	Scores generated using the Psychological Aggression subscale of the modified CTS. Recoded into a dummy variable based on the median split. 0 = low (< 8) 1 = high (> / = 8) Scores range from 0 to 24.
	Nonviolent discipline	Scores generated using the Nonviolent Discipline subscale of the modified CTS. Recoded into a dummy variable based on the median split. 0 = low (< 8) 1 = high (> / = 8) Scores range from 0 to 12.
Demographic Factors	Race/ethnicity	Response to a single item from the Demographics instrument (Hunter et al., 2003). 0 = white, Hispanic, and other 1 = African American
	Education	Response to a single item from the Demographics instrument (Hunter et al., 2003). 0 = high school or more than high school 1 = less than high school

(continued on next page)

TABLE 1. (continued)

Domain	Variable	Coding and Interpretation
	AFDC receipt	Response to a single item from the Demographics instrument (Hunter et al., 2003). 0 = NO 1 = YES
	Age	Response to a single item from the Demographics instrument (Hunter et al., 2003). Continuous variable.
	Number of children	Constructed from responses to the Household Composition and Family Chart (Hunter et al., 2003). 0 = 0–1 children 1 = 2 or more children
Child Characteristics	Birth weight	Response to a single item from the Perinatal Form Hunter et al., 2003). Recoded into dummy variable based on clinical cut point for low birth weight. 0 = normal birth weight 1 = low birth weight (2,500 grams or less)
	Gender	0 = male 1 = female
	Externalizing problems	Externalizing T scores generated from *Child Behavior Checklist/4–18* (Achenbach, 1991). Recoded into dummy variable according to clinical cut point. 0 = no externalizing problem (< 60) 1 = externalizing problem (> / = 60) Scores range from 30 to 100 with higher scores indicating a greater endorsement of problem behaviors. Scores of 60 or less are considered normal; 61–63 is considered borderline; scores > 63 are in the clinical range.
Maternal Mental Health	Alcohol use	Response to a single item from the Caregiver Health Form (Hunter et al., 2003). 0 = No 1 = Yes
	Depression	Scores generated using the *Center for Epidemiologic Studies-Depression Scale (CES-D)* (Radloff, 1977). Recoded into dummy variable. 0 = less than 16 1 =16 or greater Scores range from 0 to 60. Higher scores indicate greater number of depressive symptoms. Score of 16 most often used as clinical cut point.

(continued on next page)

TABLE 1. (*continued*)

Domain	Variable	Coding and Interpretation
	Psychosomatic symptoms	Scores generated using the Health Opinion Survey (HOS) (Macmillan, 1957). Recoded into a dummy variable based on the median split. 0 = low (< 27) 1 = high (27 or greater) Scores range from 20 to 60. Higher scores indicate more psychosomatic symptoms.
	Physical abuse as a child	Response to a single item from the *History of Loss and Harm* (Hunter & Everson, 1991). 0 = No 1 = Yes
Parenting Attitudes	Empathy for child	Scores generated using the Adolescent and Adult Parenting Inventory (AAPI) (Bavolek, Kline, McLaughlin, & Publicover, 1979), as modified by Lutenbacher (2001). Continuous variable with scores ranging from 5 to 35.
	Opposes corporal punishment	Scores generated using the modified AAPI. Continuous variable with scores ranging from 4 to 20.
	Appropriate expectations	Scores generated using the modified AAPI. Continuous variable with scores ranging from 8 to 40.
	Importance of religion in raising children	Response to a single item from the Demographics instrument (Hunter et al., 2003). 0 = not/somewhat important 1 = very important
Extrafamilial Influences	Perceived neighborhood quality	Scores generated using the Neighborhood Short Form (Hunter et al., 2003). Recoded into dummy variable based on the median split. 0 = low neighborhood rating 1 = high neighborhood rating Scores range from 9 to 36.
	Perceived social support	Scores generated using the Functional Social Support Scale (FSSQ) (Broadhead, Gehlbach, de Gruy, & Kaplan, 1988). Recoded into dummy variable based on the median split. 0 = low social support (< 40) 1 = high social support (> / = 40) Scores range from 10 to 50. Higher scores reflect greater perceived social support.

included whenever possible. See Hunter et al. (2003) for a full description of measures utilized by LONGSCAN. All instruments were administered during the Age 4 caregiver interview.

DEPENDENT VARIABLES

Two primary outcomes were investigated by this study: *Spanking* and *Minor Assault*. Spanking was deliberately distinguished from other types of corporal punishment (e.g., slapping or shaking) because the literature suggests that normative spanking may be qualitatively different from other types of physical punishment. Likewise, in order to capture some measure of severity, both the Spanking and Minor Assault variables were coded into "high" and "low" categories based on frequency of reported use. Reports of nonviolent discipline and psychological aggression were also examined in the bivariate analysis but were not included as separate outcome variables.

The Discipline Practices variables (nonviolent discipline, spanking, minor assault, and psychological aggression) were all derived from responses to the Conflict Tactics Scale: Caregiver to Child scales (CTS1 and CTSPC, a later revision of CTS1), as modified by LONGSCAN (Straus, 1979; Straus et al., 1998, as modified by LONGSCAN, 1991). The Conflict Tactics Scale is a well-established, widely used measure of family behaviors associated with conflict. The Caregiver to Child version focuses specifically on parental behavior toward children and is broken down into several categories, including Reasoning (later reconceptualized as Nonviolent Discipline), Psychological Aggression, and Physical Assault (divided into "minor" or "corporal punishment," and "severe"). Questions assess both occurrence and frequency: "How many times in the past year, when you have had a problem with _____, did you..." (never, once, twice, 3–5 times, more than 5 times). Internal consistency for these subscales has been shown to be moderate to low, while a number of studies have provided evidence of construct validity (Hunter et al., 2003).

In modifying the CTS: Caregiver to Child, LONGSCAN investigators selected and slightly reworded items from both the CTS1 and CTSPC and deleted others. For example, the "severe" items were deleted from the Age 4 interview instrument due to concerns about child maltreatment reporting requirements (Hunter et al., 2003). The remaining physical assault items, therefore, may be seen as falling into the categories of "minor assault" or "corporal punishment." Similarly, the highest frequency response category was changed from "more than 20 times in the past year" to "more than 5 times in the past year." Quite likely, this modification resulted in significant underestimation of the actual rates of conflict-related behaviors (Straus et al., 1998). Therefore, relatively little attention is given in this study to the absolute numbers. Also, each item assesses only respondent behavior, rather than the child's discipline experiences with a range of possible caregivers. While CTS scores are often treated as continuous variables, this study recoded the scores into a series of dummy variables (e.g., "yes/no" or "high/low"). More detail regarding this is given later. As with the original CTS: Caregiver to Child scales, internal consistency for the LONGSCAN modified subscales was moderate to low: Nonviolent Discipline (Cronbach's alpha of .49), Psychological Aggression (Cronbach's alpha of .71), and Minor Assault (Cronbach's alpha of .68) (Hunter et al.).

For the purposes of this study, the spanking item from the Minor Assault subscale was recoded into a separate variable, according to the rationale that spanking may have different consequences for children than other forms of physical discipline do, and may be more readily distinguishable from possible maltreatment (Larzelere, 2000). Responses to the spanking item were then recoded into two dummy variables: spanking (0 = 0–1 times in the past year; 1 = 2 or more times in the past year) and high spanking (0 = fewer than 5 times in the past year; 1 = 5 or more times in the past year). These cut points were made somewhat arbitrarily, since no information is available as to population norms using this modified version of the CTS.

The remaining items from the Minor Assault subscale were retained and scores were similarly recoded into two dummy variables: minor assault (0 = no minor assault in the past year; 1 = 1 or more minor assaults in the past year) and high minor assault (0 = 0–1 minor assault in the past year; $1 = 2$ or more minor assaults in the past year). Again, these cut points were established somewhat arbitrarily, but were done so according to the rationale that one would expect a lower frequency of minor assault items other than spanking, and that such behaviors might be expected to pose a higher risk of harm to the child. For example, behaviors included in the Minor Assault category include: grabbing child, shaking child, pushing or shoving child, slapping child, and throwing something at child. Although these may be considered forms of corporal punishment rather than abuse per se, for a young child (4-year-olds in this sample), the potential for injury is clearly present.

Lastly, responses to the Psychological Aggression subscale were recoded into a dummy variable (low psychological aggression/high psychological aggression) based on the median split, as were responses to the Nonviolent Discipline subscale (low nonviolent discipline/high nonviolent discipline). Psychological Aggression items included sulking or refusing to talk to child, stomping out, threatening to spank, and throwing or hitting something other than the child. Nonviolent Discipline items included talking calmly, giving a time-out, and asking for someone else's help in settling the conflict.

INDEPENDENT VARIABLES

Independent variables fell into three domains: Family Configuration, Relationship Stability, and Relationship Quality.

Family Configuration consisted of two variables: Family Structure (irrespective of marital status) and Marital Status. Ideally, these two variables would have been combined to create a constellation of family structures by marital status (e.g., "surrogate father-married" vs. "surrogate father-unmarried"), but sample size was not sufficient to do so. Instead, separate, parallel models were created to compare and contrast findings depending on whether family configuration was defined by marital status or family structure.

Relationship Stability was measured by looking at the number of relationship changes in the past year. Relationship Quality was assessed by the occurrence of domestic violence, and by scores on a Relationship Satisfaction instrument. Number of relationship changes was included because, as discussed, relationship history may actually be a more important variable than mother's relationship status at one given point in time (Ackerman et al., 2001). Both relationship quality and stability were included as possible indicators of the indirect role played by fathers in supporting mothers' direct caregiving activities (Lamb, 1997). Domestic violence was likewise included as an independent variable because interpersonal conflict, rather than family structure per se, has been shown to put children at risk (Dubowitz, Black, Kerr, et al., 2001; Fantuzzo et al., 1997; McGuigan & Pratt, 2001).

Family Configuration
The Family Structure variable was derived from the LONGSCAN-developed Household Composition and Family Chart (Hunter et al., 2003). This instrument includes a series of "yes/no" and "how many" questions regarding the presence of various family members and non-family members in the home, as defined in relation to the subject child (e.g., biological mother/father, adoptive mother/father, stepmother/father, grandmother/father, number of sisters/brothers (including half sisters/brothers), number of step sisters/brothers, number of other female/male relatives, number of other unrelated females/males).

Responses were coded into four categories: (1) no father figure in the home (no maternal spouse/partner in the home, although mother may have a partner outside the home), (2) biological father in the home (regardless of marital status), (3) surrogate father in the home (either married or unmarried), and (4) mother and grandparent in the home. In a handful of cases (< 5), mother, spouse/partner, and grandparent shared the same home. Such cases were included either in category 2 (biological father) or category 3 (surrogate father), in accordance with the main focus of this study. Likewise, adoptive fathers were categorized as biological fathers. Had sample size been larger, family structure categories would have been further broken down according to marital status, or marital status would have been included as a control variable. Given the relatively small proportion of married respondents, however, this would have made detection of statistically significant results much more difficult. Instead, a separate variable was constructed for marital status, and two sets of regressions were performed: one using family structure as a primary independent variable and the other using marital status as a primary independent variable.

Marital status was derived from responses to an item on the LONGSCAN-developed Demographics instrument (Hunter et al., 2003). Responses were coded into three categories: (1) never married, (2) always married, and (3) divorced/remarried. Had the sample size been larger, the divorced/remarried category would have been broken down into two separate categories. Given the very small proportion of divorced or remarried respondents, however, such a distinction was not possible. Again, although imperfect, this categorization has some support in the literature on the subject. Previous research suggests that rather than ameliorating the effects of divorce, remarriage itself may potentially be as harmful, or more so, than divorce (Hetherington & Stanley-Hagan, 1999). In that case, remarried respondents should not be included with always-married respondents, despite the important increase in income that accompanies remarriage (Lerman, 2002).

Relationship Stability
The relationship stability variable was constructed from responses to a series of items found in the Life Experiences Survey (LES) (Sarason et al., 1987, modified by LONGSCAN, 1991). This instrument is intended to measure both the magnitude and perception of potentially stressful life changes. The LONGSCAN version consists of 30 items that ask respondents to indicate and rate (negative/positive) life changes in the past year. Internal consistency of the original LES was moderate (Cronbach's alpha of .79), as was test-retest reliability (.63–.64). However, for the purposes of this study, only the items pertaining to relationship change were selected, and respondents' ratings of life events were disregarded. In other words, the variable constructed only reflects the occurrence of an event, not its perception. Scores were calculated by summing the number of changes, then recoded into a dummy variable: 0 = no relationship

changes in the past year, and $1 = 1$ or more relationship changes in the past year. Relationship changes included: becoming engaged, getting married, breaking up, separating, divorce, and getting back together after a break-up.

Relationship Quality

Perceived relationship quality was derived from scores on the Autonomy and Relatedness Inventory (ARI) (Schaefer & Edgarton, 1982). This instrument consists of 24 items designed to assess the quality of the respondent's relationship with his/her primary intimate. The ARI is broken down into 6 subscales: relatedness, hostile control, acceptance, detachment, control, and autonomy, so separate scores can be calculated for each scale. However, study sample size did not support including each subscale as a separate variable. For the purposes of this study, an overall score was calculated by summing scores for each subscale, as recommended by Hall and Kiernan (1992). In order to calculate a total score, the negative items on the ARI were reverse coded, then summed with the positive items. Higher scores therefore indicate a higher quality relationship. However, no established norms or cut point exist for this instrument, so scores were recoded into a dummy variable (low quality/ high quality) based on the median split.

Internal consistency of the total ARI is high (with a Cronbach's alpha of .90). The ARI is moderately but significantly correlated with the Spanier Dyadic Adjustment scale, a commonly used measure of marital satisfaction (Hall & Kiernan, 1992). In Hall and Kiernan's psychometric assessment, none of the sociodemographic factors examined (age, race, marital status, education, income, number of children, and employment status) were related to ARI score, and "the two ARI dimensions [positive and negative] were clearly discriminable in factor analyses from measures of depressive and psychosomatic symptoms" (p. 36).

The domestic violence variable was derived from responses on the *History of Loss and Harm* (Hunter & Everson, 1991). This 18-item instrument is designed to assess the respondent's lifetime experience of physical and sexual abuse, as well as separation from, or loss of, primary caregivers as a child. No information is available regarding the reliability or validity of this measure.

The occurrence of domestic violence was indicated by a "yes" response to a single item, "Since you've been an adult...have you ever been hit, slapped, beaten or pushed around by someone?" Although this question does not specifically ask about the identity of the perpetrator, subsequent questions indicate that 88% of respondents who answered "yes" were assaulted by a husband or partner, with 6% reporting assault by another family member. However, this item does not distinguish past domestic violence from present domestic violence, so it must be viewed as an imperfect indicator of current relationship quality. Because no other comparable measure was included in the LONGSCAN battery, the decision was made to include this measure in the model with this understanding of its limitations.

CONTROL VARIABLES

Control variables fell into five domains: demographics, child characteristics, maternal characteristics, parenting attitudes, and extrafamilial influences.

Research Support for Control Variables

Demographics.   Maternal age, race, education, number of children, and AFDC (welfare) receipt have all emerged as significant factors in previous studies (Giles-Sims et al., 1995). Maternal employment status was also considered as a control variable but preliminary analyses revealed no significant associations of interest so it was dropped in the interest of parsimony.

Child Characteristics.   Child gender was included as a control variable because some studies suggest that boys are at higher risk of harsh discipline than girls are, although findings are mixed (Giles-Sims et al., 1995). Child age was not included as a control variable because children in the sample were supposed to be approximately 4 years old at the time of baseline data collection. In actuality, about a third of the sample was aged 5–6 years old at the time of baseline data collection, so differences in age could potentially bias findings. Preliminary analyses, however, did not reveal any significant associations with the outcome variables. Moreover, theoretically, it is reasonable to assume that discipline practices might be similar across this age range. Child race also was not included as a control variable because in the vast majority of cases, child race was congruent with maternal race. In about 40 cases, child race was either different from maternal race, or was described as "mixed," but this population was not big enough to examine separately. Most of these cases involved a white or Hispanic mother with a child of mixed race.

Child birth weight was included as a control variable for two reasons: Firstly, a number of studies have suggested that child difficulty or vulnerability (such as an irritable temperament or presence of a disability at birth) may elicit harsh treatment by parents (Fox et al., 1995). Low birth weight, especially in prematurely born children, may be a characteristic of children especially likely to exhibit difficult behaviors. Secondly, the South site specifically recruited mothers of low-birth-weight infants, so a sizeable proportion of the sample fell into this category, potentially biasing the findings. Child externalizing behavior was included as a control variable for reasons discussed previously: externalizing behavior itself may elicit harsh treatment by parents, as well as possibly resulting from harsh treatment by parents. Many researchers today believe that a complicated, bidirectional relationship exists between externalizing behavior and corporal punishment (Deater-Deckard & Dodge, 1997a).

Maternal Mental Health.   Many studies have linked substance abuse with potentially harmful parenting behaviors (Chaffin et al., 1996). Alcohol use was included here as a proxy for possible substance abuse. Similarly, maternal depression and psychological disturbance may be associated with compromised parenting (Kotch et al., 1999). Finally, a childhood history of child abuse has been associated with a higher risk for harsh parenting (Whipple & Richey, 1997).

Parenting Attitudes.   As discussed previously, one of the most robust findings from the literature on corporal punishment is that parenting attitudes play a large role in determining the discipline choices made by parents (McLoyd et al., 2007). In order to examine the influence of other variables, therefore, one must control for parenting attitudes.

Extrafamilial Influences.   In accordance with the ecological model, an attempt was made to account for two factors outside the family that might impact child discipline: social support and neighborhood quality. Previous research indicates that social support may play an important role in moderating maternal stress, providing parenting information, and encouraging more positive parenting (Kotch et al., 1999). Other research suggests that potentially harmful parenting may be concentrated in certain geographical areas, or "high-risk" neighborhoods that provide little support to parents trying to parent effectively (Coulton, Korbin, & Su, 1999).

Operationalization of Control Variables
Demographics.   A number of variables were derived from the LONGSCAN-developed Demographics Form (Hunter et al., 2003), including maternal age, race, educational status, and AFDC (welfare) receipt. The race variable was recoded into two categories: African American and white (with white defined as the reference group). The number of respondents in other categories—Hispanic (5.7%), mixed race (1.3%), Native American (.5%), and other (.6%), for example—was too small to create separate categories, but elimination of such cases from the sample was seen as undesirable. Instead, they were included in the "white" category. Although imperfect, this categorization has some support in the literature on the subject; previous research suggests that Hispanic mothers (by the far the largest proportion of these non-African American/nonwhite race categories) may be more similar to white mothers than to African American mothers in terms of corporal punishment (Flynn, 1996; McLeod et al., 1994).

AFDC (welfare) receipt was simply coded as a dummy variable, with "no" defined as the reference group. Maternal age was treated as a continuous variable. Maternal education was coded as a dummy variable, with "high school or more than high school" defined as the reference group. The "number of children" variable was derived from the Household Composition and Family Chart (Hunter et al., 2003). Stepsiblings and half siblings were included in the total, according to the rationale that caregiving responsibility would be more salient than biological relation.

Child Characteristics.   Child birth weight was derived from the LONGSCAN developed Perinatal Form (Hunter et al., 2003), a brief instrument that asks about prematurity, neonatal hospitalization, services received, and so forth. Weight at birth (in grams) was recoded into a dummy variable (low birth weight/not low birth weight) according to the established clinical cut point for low birth weight ($</=2,500$ grams, or 5lbs, 8oz).

The Externalizing Problems variable was derived from scores on the Externalizing scale of the *Child Behavior Checklist/4–18 (CBCL)* (Achenbach, 1991). The *CBCL* is a standard instrument used in research regarding children's characteristics and behaviors. Its psychometric properties have been well studied and established. Cronbach's alpha for the Externalizing Problems scale was .93 for both boys and girls and "Evidence for content, construct, and criterion-related validity is well documented" (Hunter et al., 2003, p. 4). The Externalizing Problems scale combines two measures: Delinquent Behavior and Aggressive Behavior. A cut point of 63 is typically used to identify clinically significant problems, while scores of 60–63 are considered borderline. For the purposes of this study, scores on the Externalizing Problems scale were recoded into a dummy variable based on the cut point of 60.

Maternal Mental Health.   The maternal depression variable was derived from scores on the *Center for Epidemiologic Studies-Depression Scale (CES-D)* (Radloff, 1977). This is a longstanding, widely used screening tool for depression with high internal consistency (Cronbach's alpha of .85–.90, depending on the study) and moderate test-retest reliability (Radloff, 1977). Furthermore, the *CES-D* discriminates well between the clinical and general population, and is moderately correlated with other measures of depression. Higher scores on the *CES-D* reflect more symptoms of depression, with the cut point of 16 commonly used to identify clinical depression. For the purposes of this study, *CES-D* scores were recoded into a dummy variable (depressed/not depressed) using the cut point of 16.

A measure of "neurotic" symptomology or mental disorder was derived from scores on the Health Opinion Survey (HOS) (MacMillan, 1957). This 20-item scale assesses psychosomatic symptoms in the respondent (e.g., rapid heartbeat, upset stomach, dizziness, nervousness). Butler and Jones (1979) reported acceptable internal consistency for the HOS but also suggest that the instrument may fail to discriminate between physical and psychological symptomology. Likewise, Tousignant, Denis, and Lachapelle (1974) argued that the HOS screens for physical, rather than mental, disorders, as well as failing to distinguish between transitory stress and chronic psychological disturbance. Thus, although higher scores on the HOS are thought to reflect greater psychological disturbance, a more conservative interpretation may simply be that higher scores reflect stress on the respondent, whether manifested physically and/or psychologically, or temporary or chronic in nature. Little evidence exists to suggest what an appropriate cut point might be, so scores were recoded into a dummy variable (low symptoms/high symptoms) based on the median split. Some studies have used 32 as the clinical cut point (Hunter et al., 2003), which is close to the median value of 27 used in this study.

The "alcohol use" variable was derived from responses to a single "yes/no" item on the LONGSCAN-developed Caregiver Health Scale (Hunter et al., 2003): "Do you now drink or have you ever drunk alcoholic beverages?" Although an alcohol abuse screening tool was administered as part of this measure, too few respondents met the criteria for being at risk of an alcohol problem to include it as a variable. Furthermore, nonresponse was high on questions regarding substance abuse treatment. Nonetheless, substance use itself arguably puts a parent at risk of less effective parenting, and respondents with a problem may be more likely to endorse alcohol use than items more suggestive of addiction.

Indeed, it has been argued by many that even the established cut point for the CAGE (Mayfield, McLeod, & Hall, 1974), the extensively used alcohol screening tool included in the LONGSCAN battery, is set too high to accurately detect a significant proportion of alcohol problems, particularly in women (Bradley, Boyd-Wickizer, Powell, & Burman, 1998; Midanik, Zahnd, & Klein, 1998; Zeiler, Nemes, Holtz, Landis, & Hoffman, 2002). Thus, although alcohol use itself certainly cannot be treated as a proxy for substance abuse, it remains a variable of interest.

Physical abuse as a child was derived from the previously described responses to the *History of Loss and Harm* (Hunter & Everson, 1991). For the purposes of this study, the experience of physical abuse as a child was indicated by a "yes" response to a single item: "When you were a child or teenager...were you ever physically hurt by a parent or someone else...like hit, slapped, beaten, shaken, burned, or anything like that?" As with any self-report measure that relies on retrospective recall, responses to the question about physical abuse history may be subject to lapses or distortions in memory. Previous research comparing adult recall to administrative records suggests that when childhood abuse is misremembered, most often it is underreported (Widom & Shepard, 1996). Furthermore, the acts that are defined as "abuse" by the researcher may not be defined thus by the respondent. Interpretation of findings requires an acknowledgement of such limitations.

Parenting Attitudes. The parenting attitudes variables were derived from scores on the Adolescent and Adult Parenting Inventory (AAPI), as modified by Lutenbacher (Bavoleket al., 1979; Lutenbacher, 2001). The original AAPI (Bavolek et al., 1979) is a 32-item inventory intended to identify parents at high risk of child abuse or neglect. The inventory is divided into four subscales: Inappropriate Expectations, Lack of Empathy, Value of Corporal Punishment, and Role Reversal. Higher scores are thought to indicate more positive parenting attitudes, while lower scores suggest relatively poor parenting. Scores on the Lack of Empathy subscale best discriminate known child abusers from nonabusive parents (Bavolek, 1984). Test-retest reliability over a 1-week period was .76 and

Cronbach's alphas for the subscales were adequate (.69–.86) (Bavolek, 1984). The instrument has received extensive use in studies of child abuse and neglect.

Despite its widespread use, concerns have been raised regarding the appropriateness of the AAPI to various populations. The AAPI was tested on adolescents in Utah and Idaho, and then on a small sample of college students in Chicago. In addition to these concerns, some have questioned aspects of Bavolek's factor analysis (e.g., the decision to use a lower than recommended cut point for retention of items, and the inclusion of items that loaded on multiple factors) (Lutenbacher, 2001). When Lutenbacher tested the psychometric properties of the AAPI in a sample of low-income single mothers using a factor-loading cut point of .40 (compared with .20 in Bavolek's original study), only 19 of the original 32 items were retained. Furthermore, a three-factor model was shown to be more appropriate than Bavolek's four-factor model, with many of the Inappropriate Expectations and Role Reversal items loading onto the same factor. Cronbach's alphas for the modified scales fall in the same range as for the original four subscales.

Considering the characteristics of the LONGSCAN sample, the decision was made to use Lutenbacher's (2001) modified AAPI rather than the original. The data were recoded in accordance with Lutenbacher's three-factor model (whose factors are Lack of Empathy, Value of Corporal Punishment, and Inappropriate Expectations (M. Lutenbacher, personal communication, September 24, 2004). Variable names were changed to Empathy for Child, Opposes Corporal Punishment, and Appropriate Expectations. Scores for each subscale were included as separate, continuous variables. According to Lutenbacher (2001), lower scores indicate more problematic parenting. In the case of the Opposes Corporal Punishment subscale, however, it must be noted that opposition to corporal punishment does not necessarily indicate superior parenting. As discussed earlier, endorsement of corporal punishment actually may represent a normative (and appropriate) parenting value in some cultures. Thus, this study does not interpret scores on the Opposes Corporal Punishment subscale as being reflective of healthy, as opposed to dysfunctional, parenting, but rather simply as being indicative of differences in opinion.

The final parenting attitude variable, Importance of Religion in Raising Children, was derived from an item on the Demographics instrument (Hunter et al., 2003). Responses to the question, "How important are your religion or spiritual beliefs in the way you raise your child(ren)?" were recoded into a dummy variable: "not/somewhat important" and "very important."

Extrafamilial Influences. Perceived neighborhood quality was derived from scores on the LONGSCAN developed Neighborhood Short Form (Hunter et al., 2003). This instrument consists of 9 items designed to measure neighborhood safety, self-image, and availability of social support, with higher scores indicating a higher neighborhood rating. Internal consistency for this measure was adequate, with a Cronbach's alpha for the total score of .87 (Hunter et al., 2003). Scores were recoded into a dummy variable (low neighborhood rating/high neighborhood rating) based on the median split.

Perceived social support was derived from scores on the Functional Social Support Scale (FSSQ), as modified by LONGSCAN (Broadhead et al., 1988, modified by Hunter et al., 2003). This 10-item (originally 8-item) instrument is designed to measure support in three areas: confidant support, affective support, and instrumental support. The authors of the original FSSQ report test-retest reliability after 2 weeks of .66. Sex, marital status, and age were not correlated with FSSQ scores, but whites did score significantly higher than other groups on the Confidant Support subscale. Adequate internal consistency was demonstrated for the Confidant Support and Affective Support subscales, but only one item loaded onto the Instrumental Support factor ("help around the house"), suggesting that this dimension was in need of further development. Likewise, only the Confidant Support and Affective Support subscales were significantly correlated with other commonly used measures of social support such as the Social Contacts subscale of the Rand Social Activities Questionnaire; Instrumental Support was only associated with "socialized with other people" (Broadhead et al., 1988). Therefore, LONGSCAN investigators added two additional items in an effort to strengthen the Instrumental Support subscale. Internal consistency for the LONGSCAN modified version was good, with a Cronbach's alpha of .80–.93, depending upon race of respondents, study sites, and data collection point (Hunter et al., 2003).

For the purposes of this study, only a total social support score was calculated, due, in part, to concerns about the Instrumental Support sub-scale, as well as to limited sample size. Higher scores are thought to reflect greater perceived social support on the part of the respondent, but no established norms or cut points exist. Thus, scores were recoded into a dummy variable (low support/high support) based on the median split.

PROCEDURES

Because this study is a secondary analysis of existing data, no primary data collection was conducted by the author. Instead, a brief description of LONGSCAN's data collection procedures is provided as follows.

Data collection procedures varied somewhat between sites, in terms of timing of interviews, specific contact procedures, and interview loca-tion, for example, especially in the case of the two preexisting research studies (the East and the South). However, efforts were made to ensure consistency, particularly for the LONGSCAN baseline data collection at age 4. Data were collected through in-person interviews with the respondent-caregiver when the study child was approximately 4 years old, and via administrative record review. Interviews were conducted by trained interviewers and lasted about 2 hours. In some cases, data were collected using paper and pencil booklets; in other cases A-CASI or "computer-assisted interviews" were conducted. Interviews were conducted in Spanish for Spanish-speaking respondents but respondents speaking languages other than English or Spanish were screened out of the study (Runyan et al., 1998). Data collection was (and is) managed by the LONGSCAN Coordinating Center (CC), including development of interview protocols, training of project coordinators, ongoing technical assistance, and centralized data entry and maintenance:

> The CC provides the sites with data collection software that includes built-in checks, skip patterns, and within- and across-instrument consistency checks. To ensure the quality of the data, the CC conducts double entry verification, assessments of inter-observer reliability and site visits. Sites send their raw data files to the CC on an established schedule. The CC, in turn, regularly distributes datasets to the sites...The CC also checks data for consistency across forms and time points. Periodically, reports of data inconsistencies and errors are sent to each site with a request to correct these errors. (NDACAN, 2001, p. 21)

Various efforts were made at each site to track and retain study participants, including the annual gathering of contact information: the sending of birthday or holiday cards, newsletters, or other updates from the projects; the provision of small stipends (e.g., $25 per interview) and/or gifts; the hosting of annual get-togethers; and the review of public databases. Childcare during caregiver interviews was provided when possible.

Human Subjects
This study uses existing, publicly available data. As such, the LONGSCAN baseline dataset has been stripped of all names and any other identifying information such as birth dates, addresses, and so forth. Such research is exempt from the full human subjects review process by the University of California, Berkeley, Committee for the Protection of Human Subjects (CPHS). This study was granted exemption on August 30, 2003. Although the dataset is publicly available and contains no identifying information, the study involves both vulnerable populations and sensitive information, prompting extra precautions on the part of the Investigators. Therefore, the LONGSCAN dataset can only obtained from the National Data Archive on Child Abuse and Neglect. In order to gain access to the data, one must submit documentation of human subjects approval from an institutional review board registered with the U.S. Office for Human Research Protections, and pay a fee of $75.

In terms of LONGSCAN's informed consent procedures and protection of human subjects, appropriate steps were taken in all regards. A special committee within the Coordinating Committee was established specifically to examine human subjects concerns. Balancing confidentiality and child safety with trying to encourage subject participation and full disclosure, is a complicated ethical challenge for research such as this. On the one hand, there may be a greater likelihood that some participants will be scared off entirely, or that some participants will hold back important information, potentially biasing the findings. On the other hand, researchers have a moral obligation to protect the children involved in their research.

LONGSCAN investigators gave particular attention to processes for informing parents (and children, at later data collection points) about requirements to report suspected child abuse or neglect (Knight et al., 2000). As mentioned previously, in some cases, modifications were made to study instruments in order to avoid possible disclosures of maltreatment. At certain sites, some instruments were not used at all, due to concerns on the part of the institutional review boards about the reporting of child maltreatment. Prior to consenting to participation, parents at each site were given the chance to examine the instruments that would be administered to their children. Likewise, parents were assured that their decision to participate or not to participate would have no bearing on the services or benefits their family was currently receiving. Incentives for participation—usually a $25 check—were modest, in order to avoid unintentional financial coercion.

APPROACH TO DATA ANALYSIS

Data analysis proceeded from simple to complex, beginning with univariate analyses, followed by bivariate analyses, and culminating in the multivariate analyses. All statistical analyses were conducted using SPSS Version 11.5 (September 6, 2002). The first step was to summarize the data, one variable at a time, beginning with the demographic characteristics of the sample (both maternal and child). Due to the methodological issues involved in aggregating data across sites, demographic characteristics were further broken down according to site. Due to the potentially significant role of race in parenting and discipline, as suggested by the literature on the subject, demographic characteristics were also analyzed separately according to race (African American/white). Next, frequencies were calculated for each of the dependent, independent, and control variables, again with separate frequencies calculated according to site and race. Differences according to site, race, and family configuration were tested for statistical significance through a series of bivariate analyses, including cross tabulations (chi-square tests), correlations, t-tests, and/or ANOVAs (depending on the types of variables being compared).

The next step was to begin exploring potential relationships between variables. First, each of the independent variables was run against the 4 outcome variables in order to test for possible effects. To investigate whether significant associations seemed to hold across sites, these analyses were performed both on the combined sample, and separately, according to site. Although not every independent variable was significantly associated with every outcome variable at each of the sites, there was sufficient consistency among sites to proceed.

However, the descriptive analyses did reveal a number of significant differences among respondents according to site that could potentially bias the findings. Several LONGSCAN investigators have included study site as a control variable in order to account for such site differences (Dubowitz, Black, Cox, et al., 2001; Litrownik, Newton, Hunter, English, & Everson, 2003). In this study, it was found that including study site obscured the role of race, due, in large part, to the preponderance of African American subjects in the East site (93%). In other words, the East variable was functioning, in part, as a proxy for race. Considering the apparent importance of race to the issue of child discipline, this was deemed unacceptable and study site variable was dropped from the model. Another approach might have been to include interaction terms for those variables significantly associated with site, but preliminary analyses demonstrated that sample size was not sufficient; cell size was reduced to the point that any significant effects likely would be undetected and/or estimates of effect size would be unacceptably inaccurate.

At the same time, it must be recognized that, in reverse, the race variable may also serve in part as a proxy for the East site, so excluding the study site variable is an imperfect solution. In any case, it is not clear what controlling for site would mean for the findings. It is not known which characteristics of particular sites might be responsible for influencing the findings—it could be differences in the target population, slight variations in study procedures, unique features of the geographic location, recent developments in the policy environment, and so forth. At least using this approach, one can control for known differences between the samples, such as racial composition or low birth weight status. Of course, interpretation of findings must then include a careful consideration of interrelationships between study site and variables in the model, as well as a very conservative approach to generalizing findings.

The next step was to identify potential indirect relationships between the independent variables and the outcome variables by testing for apparent moderator effects at the bivariate level. First, each of the variables, both independent and control, was run against each of the outcome variables separately according to race. Next, a number of theoretically relevant variables were run against each of the outcome variables separately according to family structure and marital status (for example, depression and spanking according to family structure). Preliminary analyses, however, indicated that sample size probably was not sufficient to support the inclusion of multiple family structure or marital status interaction terms, due to the large number of categories and relatively small number of respondents in some of the categories (e.g., divorced/remarried mother and multigenerational family structure).

Likewise, Menard (2002) cautioned in particular against the overfitting of logistic regression models: "There is a real danger of...building in components that really capture random variation, rather than systematic regularities in behavior (p. 90). Although it is sometimes recommended that all potential interactions be included when testing for interactions, Menard (2002) argued that this approach greatly increases the risk of a Type I error, and advises only including interaction terms for which there is compelling theoretical support. Taking such considerations into account, the decision was made to focus exclusively on race interactions, while relying on a main effects approach for the family composition and relationship quality variables. No effort was made to explore relationships between control variables (maternal depression and perceived social support, for example) because such relationships were deemed peripheral to the focus of this study.

The final step was to construct a series of logistic regression models using the 4 dummy outcome variables: Spanking, High Spanking, Minor Assault, and High Minor Assault. Each regression was run separately according to family structure and according to marital status. In addition to the independent and control variables described previously, a series of race interaction terms was added to each model, including race interacted with each independent and control variable. A 2-step process was employed for running the regressions themselves. Firstly, an automated, backward, stepwise logistic regression was run on the saturated model, whereby one variable is removed at a time from the model, based on a cut-off point of $p < .05$, until the best fit is achieved. "Computer-controlled" stepwise regression is a commonly used technique for exploratory research (Menard, 2002). However, such an approach is compromised insofar as it is not theory driven, it capitalizes on chance, and it minimizes investigator discretion in assessing model fit. In this case, for example, a number of important control variables were removed from the model because they did not meet the cut off for statistical significance. Likewise, borderline findings of potential interest were excluded.

Therefore, a second regression was performed whereby variables were removed manually, one at a time, by the investigator, while desired control variables were retained. In general, a liberal approach to significance testing was followed, in accordance with the exploratory nature of this study. Statistical significance was established at $p < .05$ level, but "borderline" findings are also included when $.05 < p < .10$. In some cases, findings that only approached significance ($p > .10$) were included to demonstrate the direction of a suggestive relationship, for example, when a variable seemed to act in an opposite direction for African Americans than it did whites or Hispanics. Although using a more liberal criterion for statistical significance increases the possibility of finding relationships that do not really exist, Menard (2002) argued that the standard cut off of .05 is too stringent for exploratory stepwise regressions. To avoid excluding potentially important variables, he recommends using a cut off of $p = .15–.20$. A core group of control variables was retained in every model, regardless of statistical significance: maternal age, maternal race, AFDC (welfare) receipt, child birth weight, child gender, and number of children.

Model specification and interpretation was made more challenging by the inclusion of the race interaction terms. In many cases, an interaction term would only be borderline significant or approaching statistical significance. Sometimes an interaction term would be significant only when another interaction term was included, or would become nonsignificant when another interaction term was included. Jaccard (2001) noted that logistic regression with multiple interaction terms may result in "seeming 'anomalies'" such as these (p. 65). The decision to include or drop an interaction term may not be straightforward and depends in large part on theoretical considerations and overarching patterns in the data.

In an effort to corroborate or reject the relationships suggested by the interaction terms, separate regressions were run according to race. The results were compared in order to identify variables that looked significant for one group but not for the other. Variables that appeared significant for whites but not for African Americans were given particular weight, considering the much smaller sample size for whites. In other words, a variable might be significant for African Americans but not quite significant for whites simply due to the smaller number of whites than African Americans in the sample. Where appropriate, findings from the separate analyses are presented in the chapter entitled "Results," alongside findings from the combined analyses. At the same time, simply "eyeballing" apparent differences between coefficients in the separate analyses according to race is not sufficient: "Formal interaction analysis through product terms in a single equation is preferable because it provides a means of formally testing the difference between logistic coefficients" (Jaccard, 2001, p. 17).

Because the sites differed significantly in their relative proportions of African Americans to whites, final models were also run separately according to site, in order to make sure that apparent race interactions were not, in fact, site interactions. One such case was identified. Race x neighborhood rating emerged as significant in a number of models, but separate analyses according to race indicated that neighborhood rating was really only significant in the South, and there was no sign of an interactive effect according to race. Neighborhood rating appeared to be highly significant for both African Americans and whites. The reason for this difference is unclear, yet might be linked to regional differences between the sites. Both the East and the Midwest samples were drawn from large, urban areas, while the South sample had a substantial rural population. In any event, the decision was made to drop the race x neighborhood rating term from those models.

Three indicators were used to assess model fit, as suggested by Menard (2002): the percentage correctly predicted by the model, the Hosmer and Lemeshow test, and the log-likelihood test. Final models maximized the percentage correctly predicted, passed the Hosmer and Lemeshow test ($p > .05$), and minimized the -2 log-likelihood value. Finally, a series of diagnostic procedures were performed on the final models to make sure the basic assumptions of logistic regression were being met. Three procedures were performed, as recommended by Menard (2002): (1) a test for Collinearity (VIF > 4), (2) identification and deletion of studentized residuals less than -3 and greater than $+3$, and (3) identification and deletion of leverage values 3 times the expected value (average) of $(k +1)/N$. No problems with collinearity were detected. All VIF statistics were less than 4 except for those associated with the interaction terms, which is customary and unproblematic (Jaccard, 2001). In a few of the regressions, a handful of extreme outliers (e.g., 2 or 3) were identified and deleted. No formal test for nonlinearity was performed, although inclusion of interaction terms is a kind of test in itself. Taken together, these findings suggest that the final models presented are adequate.

Odds ratios and confidence intervals (95%) were calculated by SPSS for each of the predictor variables. The odds ratio (OR) compares the probabilities of a given outcome for two groups (assuming a dummy predictor variable); if the OR is equal to 1, there is no relationship between group membership and the outcome variable. However, when findings are only borderline significant or approaching significance, as is the case for some of the estimates reported here, the confidence interval may contain 1. If the OR is greater or less than 1, one may say an association exists between the predictor and the outcome variables. In other words, membership in one group, as compared to the other, either increases or decreases the likelihood of the specified outcome. The confidence interval (CI) provides a range of possible values for the true effect size, conveying a sense of the relative accuracy of estimates produced by the model. Wider confidence intervals indicate greater uncertainty about the accuracy of the estimate.

In the cases of interactions, the odds ratios calculated by SPSS cannot be interpreted in the same manner. Because the relative odds differ according to the groups being compared, the odds ratios for the interaction term and the odds ratios for the focal independent variables included in that term have no stand-alone meaning. Thus, odds ratios for respective groups must be calculated by hand (or the baseline group must be redefined and the regression rerun on the computer). Similarly, the confidence intervals calculated by SPSS for the interaction terms and associated focal independent variables are not useful for interpretation. However, because the terms in an interaction are not independent, calculation of meaningful confidence intervals is a very cumbersome process (Jaccard, 2001).

For this reason, this study reports only confidence intervals for the main factors not associated with an interaction term. In the cases of interaction terms, the p-value is relied upon for evidence of a differential effect. Odds ratios for the relative groups were calculated by hand using coefficients from the model that combined all respondents. These odds ratios are reported in the text, accompanied by supporting evidence from the separate regressions according to race, including the confidence intervals calculated by SPSS. Although certainly not a perfect measure, this approach provides another clue to the relative accuracy of the odds ratios calculated for the focal independent variables according to race (the moderator variable).

CHAPTER 5

RESULTS

SAMPLE DESCRIPTION

The total number of respondents in the final sample was 619, all of whom were birth mothers of LONGSCAN study children. The sample was predominantly African American, with a little more than two-thirds of the sample identifying as African American and the remaining 30% identifying as white, Hispanic, or Other (22% Caucasian, 6% Hispanic, 2% Other). The majority of mothers were 20–29 years old, with about a third in the 30–49 age range. Almost half of the respondents had three or more children. The sample was largely poor with almost two-thirds of respondents receiving AFDC. A little more than half (54%) had completed high school.

About two-thirds of mothers in this sample had never been married (63%), with a fifth having been continuously married, and less than a fifth (17%) having divorced or remarried. Family structure was more widely distributed. The largest percentage of respondents reported no father figure (including boyfriends) in the home (39%), followed by respondents living with the biological father of their child (28.3%).

The third largest group consisted of mothers and children living with a grandparent (19.6%). Finally, 13% of respondents reported a stepfather or mother's partner in the home. However, more than two-thirds of all mothers indicated that they were involved with someone they considered to be a spouse or life partner.

Differences According to Site

A number of significant differences according to site were identified (see Table 2). As mentioned previously, the East sample was composed almost entirely of African Americans (93%), while 61% of respondents were African American in the South sample, and 56% were African American in the Midwest sample ($\chi^2 = 85.6$, $p = .000$). Respondents in the East were also more likely to receive AFDC than the other two sites ($\chi^2 = 38.0$, $p = .000$). The samples differed with regard to age, with respondents being significantly younger in the South than in the East or Midwest ($F = 9.35$, $p = .000$). Respondents in the South were also significantly more likely than respondents in the other sites to have three or more children ($\chi^2 = 23.5$, $p = .000$). No differences according to site were noted with regard to family structure, but respondents in the South were significantly more likely to be married ($\chi^2 = 28.5$, $p = .000$), and there was some evidence to suggest that respondents in the Midwest were less likely to report having a spouse or partner, although this finding did not reach the level of statistical significance ($\chi^2 = 5.7$, $p = .06$).

Child Characteristics

In terms of the study children, the sample is evenly split with regard to gender. Somewhat less than a quarter (23%) of children were of a low birth weight, as compared to the national rate of 7.7% (Polhamus et al., 2004). In this sample, African American children were more likely to be of low birth weight than white children were ($\chi^2 = 2.86$, $p = .09$), which also reflects national trends (the proportion of children born with a low birth weight is 11.8% for African Americans, 7.1% for whites,

TABLE 2. Maternal demographics according to study site.

	East (n = 212)	South (n = 196)	Midwest (n = 211)	Total (N = 619)
	%	%	%	%
Race**				
African American	92.9	60.7	55.5	70.0
White, Hispanic, and other	6.6	39.3	44.1	29.7
Age**				
18–19	0.5	1.5	0.5	0.8
20–29	51.9	68.4	56.4	58.6
30–49	37.7	22.4	37.9	33.1
> / = 50	0.0	0.0	0.0	0.0
Marital Status**				
Never married	72.6	49.0	64.5	62.8
Always married	11.8	28.6	19.9	20.0
Divorced or remarried	14.6	22.4	14.7	17.1
Family Structure				
No father figure in home	41.0	34.7	41.2	39.1
Bio father in home	25.0	29.1	30.8	28.3
Step/partner in home	10.4	16.8	11.8	12.9
Mother and grandparent	23.6	19.4	15.6	19.6
Has Spouse or Partner				
Yes	70.1	71.8	61.1	67.5
No	29.9	28.2	38.4	32.4
Number of Children**				
1	21.3	19.9	14.7	18.6
2	33.6	44.4	25.6	34.2
3 or more	45.0	35.7	59.2	47.0
Education				
High school and beyond	57.8	56.4	47.9	54.0
Less than high school	42.2	43.2	51.7	45.7
Receipt of AFDC**				
Yes	78.3	49.5	67.3	65.4
No	21.7	50.5	32.2	34.4
Neighborhood Rating				
Low	50.5	43.4	47.9	47.3
High	41.0	48.0	40.8	43.1

(continued on next page)

TABLE 2. (continued)

	East (n = 212)	South (n = 196)	Midwest (n = 211)	Total (N = 619)
	%	%	%	%
Religious Affiliation*				
Catholic	10.4	3.1	17.5	10.5
Protestant/Christian	43.3	62.8	39.8	48.5
No religion	33.5	29.1	38.4	33.9
Other religion	12.3	5.1	3.8	7.1

Note. Percentages do not always total 100% due to missing values.
*Significant at the $p < .05$ level. **Significant at the $p < .01$ level.

TABLE 3. Child characteristics according to study site.

	East (n = 212)	South (n = 196)	Midwest (n = 211)	Total (N = 619)
	%	%	%	%
Gender				
Male	54.2	44.9	46.9	48.8
Female	42.9	55.1	51.7	49.8
Low Birth Weight**				
Yes	17.9	32.1	18.0	22.5
No	79.7	65.3	80.1	75.3
Externalizing behavior				
Clinical range	27.4	26.0	23.7	25.7
Normal range	69.8	74.0	74.9	72.9

Note. Percentages do not always total 100% due to missing values.
*Significant at the $p < .05$ level. **Significant at the $p < .01$ level.

and 5.3% for Hispanics). Study children from the South were significantly more likely to have been born with a low birth weight than children from the other sites were ($\chi^2 = 15.8$, $p = .000$).

A little more than a quarter (26%) of study children had externalizing problems in the borderline to clinical range. In the general preschool-aged child population, 3% to 6% of children are estimated to have externalizing behavior problems (Achenbach & Edelbrock, 1981), but among low-income children, the prevalence seems to be closer to 30% (Fell, Walker, Severson, & Ball, 2000; Gross, Sambrook, & Fogg, 1999).

Differences According to Race
Some significant differences in respondent characteristics also emerged according race: On the one hand, African American respondents were significantly more likely than white respondents to report receiving AFDC (χ^2 = 36.89, p = .000), and to give their neighborhood a low rating (χ^2 = 19.99, p = .000). On the other hand, African American respondents were more likely than white respondents to have completed high school (χ^2 = 5.95, p = .015). African American respondents were also significantly more likely to never have been married, whereas white respondents were more likely to always have been married or to have divorced or remarried (χ^2 = 114.02, p = .000). Moreover, African American respondents were significantly more likely to report no father figure in the home, or to report a mother and grandparent in the home, while white respondents were more likely to report a biological or surrogate father in the home (χ^2 = 65.21, p = .000). White respondents were also significantly more likely than African American respondents were to report having a spouse or intimate partner (χ^2 = 13.64, p = .000).

Relationship History and Quality
Somewhat fewer than half of the respondents reported no relationship changes in the past year, while roughly a quarter reported one change, and another quarter reported two or more changes. The most common type of change was breaking up (25.4% of respondents reporting this change), followed by reuniting (17%), and getting engaged (16.2%). A little less than a twentieth of the sample reported getting married in the past year; fewer still reported getting divorced (2.7%).

More than a third of the respondents reported a history of domestic violence in adulthood. This is roughly equivalent to the estimated lifetime prevalence of domestic violence in the U.S. female population (Collins,

TABLE 4. Maternal demographics according to race.

	African American (n = 433)	White (n = 184)	Total (N = 619)
	%	%	%
Age			
18–19	2.8	2.2	2.6
20–29	62.3	69.0	64.3
30–49	35.0	28.8	33.1
> / = 50	0.0	0.0	0.0
Marital Status**			
Never married	75.5	32.1	62.8
Always married	10.6	41.8	20.0
Divorced or remarried	13.4	26.1	17.1
Family Structure**			
No father figure in home	46.0	23.4	39.1
Biological father in home	19.9	47.8	28.3
Stepfather or partner in home	11.1	17.4	12.9
Grandmother/Grandfather in home	22.9	11.4	19.6
Has Spouse or Partner**			
Yes	63.0	78.3	67.5
No	37.0	21.7	32.4
Number of Children			
1	19.6	15.8	18.6
2	32.3	38.6	34.2
3 or more	47.8	45.7	47.0
Education*			
High school and beyond	57.3	46.7	54.0
Less than high school	42.5	53.3	45.7
Receipt of AFDC**			
Yes	73.2	47.8	65.4
No	26.8	52.2	34.4
Neighborhood Rating**			
Low	53.8	32.6	47.3
High	38.3	54.3	43.1
Religious Affiliation**			
Catholic	5.5	22.3	10.5
Protestant/Christian	50.6	43.5	48.5
No religion	34.6	32.1	33.9
Other religion	9.2	2.2	7.1

Note. Percentages do not always total 100% due to missing values.
*Significant at the $p < .05$ level. **Significant at the $p < .01$ level.

TABLE 5. Relationship history and quality according to race.

	African American (n = 433)	White (n = 184)	Total (N = 619)
	%	%	%
Number of Relationship Changes in Past Year**			
No changes	42.3	57.1	46.7
1 change	30.7	21.2	27.9
2 or more changes	26.1	21.2	24.6
Type of Change			
Engagement	15.9	16.3	16.2
Marriage	3.7	7.1	4.7
Breakup**	31.9	10.4	25.4
Type of Change			
Separation	7.9	10.9	8.7
Divorce	2.1	4.3	2.7
Being reunited**	19.6	11.4	17.1
Moving in	12.0	16.8	13.4
Perceived Quality of Current Relationship			
Low quality	46.5	43.4	44.4
High quality	52.8	53.7	53.5
Domestic Violence			
Yes	35.3	41.3	37.0
No	64.0	58.2	62.4

Note. Percentages do not always total 100% due to missing values.
*Significant at the $p < .05$ level. **Significant at the $p < .01$ level.

Schoen, Duchon, Simantov, & Yellowitz, 1999), but, considering the relatively young age of the sample, this rate of reported domestic violence may be high. There were no significant differences in relationship history or perceived relationship quality according to study site. However, there were some differences by race: White respondents were significantly more likely to report no relationship changes in the past year ($\chi^2 = 11.5$, $p = .003$). African American respondents were significantly more likely than white respondents were to report a breakup ($\chi^2 = 30.83$, $p = .000$) or a reunion ($\chi^2 = 5.87$, $p = .015$).

Maternal Mental Health and Victimization History

A little more than a third of the respondents met the clinical cut point for depression, as compared to the much lower U.S. prevalence (at any one point in time) of 6.5% for women (National Institute of Mental Health, 2001). Other studies suggest that African American women and single mothers (especially nonwhite single mothers) are at higher risk for depression than white women and married mothers are (Brown & Moran, 1997; Gazmararian, James, & Lepkowski, 1995; Wang, 2004). One recent study found that 40% of African American single mothers on welfare experienced clinical depression during a 2-year period (Coiro, 2001). Similarly, in this sample, African American respondents were significantly more likely than white respondents were to meet the clinical cut point for depression ($\chi^2 = 4.11$, $p = .043$). African American

TABLE 6. Maternal mental health and history of victimization according to race.

	African American (n = 433)	White (n = 184)	Total (N = 619)
	%	%	%
Depression*			
Clinically depressed	37.9	28.8	35.1
Not depressed	61.7	69.0	64.0
Psychosomatic Symptoms			
Low	51.7	47.3	50.4
High	47.1	51.6	48.5
Alcohol Use			
Yes	56.6	62.5	58.5
No	43.4	37.5	41.5
Physical Abuse as a Child**			
Yes	18.3	37.5	24.0
No	80.7	62.0	75.2
Perceived Social Support*			
Low	53.8	43.5	50.7
High	45.0	56.0	48.1

Note. Percentages do not always total 100% due to missing values.
*Significant at the $p < .05$ level. **Significant at the $p < .01$ level.

respondents were also more likely than whites respondents were to report a low level of social support ($\chi^2 = 5.9$, $p = .015$).

Close to a fifth (18.7%) of respondents reported experiencing physical abuse as a child, with white respondents being significantly more likely than African American respondents to report a history of physical abuse as a child ($\chi^2 = 25.71$, $p = .000$). No differences were found according to race in rates of alcohol use or levels of psychosomatic symptoms.

Parenting Attitudes

Average scores for each subscale of the Adult and Adolescent Parenting Inventory (AAPI) (as modified by Lutenbacher, 2001) are presented in Table 7. Because this study uses the modified version of the AAPI, no normative data exist for the purposes of comparison.

Several significant differences emerged according to both race and site. On the one hand, white respondents were significantly more likely than African American respondents were to oppose corporal punishment ($t = 5.36$, $p = .000$), and expressed a higher level of empathy ($t = 5.95$, $p =.000$) and more age-appropriate expectations for children ($t = 7.8$, $p = .000$). On the

TABLE 7. Parenting attitudes according to race.

	African American (n = 433)	White (n = 184)	Total (N = 619)
Opposes Corporal Punishment**			
Mean score (Range 4–20)	13.3	14.7	13.7
Empathy for Child**			
Mean score (Range 7–35)	24.5	27.0	25.3
Age-Appropriate Expectations**			
Mean score (Range 8–40)	28.3	32.0	29.4
Importance of Religion in Raising Children*			
Not/somewhat important	42.5	51.1	45.4
Very important	56.6	48.4	54.1

Note. Percentages do not always total 100% due to missing values.
*Significant at the $p < .05$ level. **Significant at the $p < .01$ level.

other hand, African American respondents were significantly more likely than white respondents were to say that religion was very important to parenting ($\chi^2 = 3.72, p = .05$).

Respondents in the Midwest site were significantly more likely than respondents from the other two sites were to oppose corporal punishment ($F = 15.29, p = .000$), and expressed a higher level of empathy ($F = 27.8, p = .000$) and more age-appropriate expectations for children ($F = 26.53, p = .000$), perhaps because the Midwest site had the highest proportion of white respondents. Respondents in the South were significantly more likely than other respondents were to say that religion was very important to parenting ($\chi^2 = 11.1, p = .004$).

Discipline Practices
About a fifth of the sample reported never spanking their child or spanking their child once in the past year. As discussed previously, this is consistent with previous research which indicates that spanking is a widespread parenting behavior (Straus & Stewart, 1999). Indeed, in this study, too few respondents (69, or 11.2%) reported never spanking their child to include "never spank" as a separate category. However, almost 40% of respondents reported a high level of spanking (as defined by the median split).

In contrast to spanking, a little less than half (46%) the respondents reported never perpetrating a minor assault upon their child. Examples of a minor assault include slapping, shaking, grabbing, pushing, and throwing something at the child. Percentages reporting specific types of minor assault can be found in Table 8. Less than a third (31%) of respondents reported a high level of minor assaults. Because this study uses the LONGSCAN modified version of the CTS (Straus, 1979), no normative data exists for the purposes of comparison, but findings from a 1995 Gallup survey that included the CTSPC likewise indicate a lower prevalence rate for minor assault, compared to spanking (Straus et al., 1998). For example, only 9% of respondents reported shaking a child in the past year, while 4.6% reported slapping on the face, head, or ears. Compared to those figures, the proportion of respondents reporting such behaviors in this sample appears to be high: 17.1% reporting shaking

TABLE 8. Discipline practices.

Discipline Practice	%
Never spanked	11.2
Spanked once	8.9
Spanked five or more times	39.2
No minor assault	46.0
Threw something at child	4.3
Grabbed child	50.7
Shook child	17.1
Pushed/shoved child	7.0
Slapped child	9.3
Two or more minor assaults	31.0

a child, and 9.3% reporting slapping a child in the past year (although the slapping item included in the LONGSCAN modified CTS did not specify where on the body, so this may well include slaps to the hand or arm).

Although it is not the focus of this study, it should be noted that virtually all respondents also reported using nonviolent methods (talking calmly, time-out, etc.) as well as psychological aggression (yelling, threatening, insulting, etc.) in disciplining their child. For the purposes of comparison according to race, these two discipline categories were coded into dummy variables (low/high) based on the median split.

A number of differences in discipline behaviors were identified according to site. Respondents in the Midwest were significantly less likely than respondents in the other two sites were to report any of the discipline practices (see Table 9). Respondents in the East were significantly more likely than respondents in the South or Midwest were to report minor assault ($\chi^2 = 53.33$, $p = .000$), while respondents in the South were significantly more likely to report a high level of spanking ($\chi^2 = 39.11$, $p = .000$), as well as a high level of minor assault ($\chi^2 = 42.84$, $p = .000$).

A number of significant differences in discipline practices also emerged according to race. On the one hand, white respondents were significantly more likely than African American respondents were to report

TABLE 9. Discipline practices according to study site.

Discipline Strategy	East (n = 212) %	South (n = 196) %	Midwest (n = 211) %	Total (N = 619) %
Spanking**				
Low	15.6	8.1	36.0	20.1
Medium/High	84.4	91.9	63.5	79.7
High Spanking**				
Low/Medium	60.4	45.4	75.4	60.5
High	39.6	54.6	24.2	39.2
Minor Assault**				
No incidents	27.4	49.0	62.0	46.0
1 or more	72.6	51.0	38.0	53.7
High Minor Assault**				
None/Low	52.6	45.4	80.6	68.9
High	46.9	54.6	19.0	30.8

Note. Percentages do not always total 100% due to missing values.
*Significant at the $p < .05$ level. **Significant at the $p < .01$ level.

a high use of nonviolent discipline ($\chi^2 = 28.3$, $p = 00$). On the other hand, African American respondents were significantly more likely to report both minor assault ($\chi^2 = 19.49$, $p = .000$) and high minor assault ($\chi^2 = 14.97$, $p = .000$). There were no significant differences by race in regard to self-reported rates of spanking or psychological aggression.

Differences According to Family Structure
A large number of bivariate associations were identified between family structure and the other variables included in the models (see Table 11 for a summary of findings). Respondents who reported the biological father of their child(ren) in the home were also significantly less likely than other respondents were to receive AFDC ($\chi^2 = 68.28$, $p = .000$), and were more likely to give their neighborhood a high rating. Respondents with no father figure in the home were significantly more likely than other respondents were to give their neighborhood a

TABLE 10. Discipline practices according to race.

Discipline Strategy	African American (n = 433) %	White (n = 184) %	Total (N = 619) %
Nonviolent Discipline**			
Low use	53.4	29.9	46.2
High use	46.4	70.1	53.6
Psychological Aggression			
Low use	53.1	52.2	52.8
High use	46.4	47.8	46.8
Spanking			
Low	18.6	23.9	20.1
Medium/High	81.4	75.5	79.7
High Spanking			
Low/Medium	62.2	56.5	60.6
High	37.8	42.9	39.2
Minor Assault**			
No incidents	40.4	59.8	46.0
1 or more	59.6	40.2	53.7
High Minor Assault**			
None/Low	64.5	79.9	68.9
High	35.3	19.6	30.8

Note. Percentages do not always total 100% due to missing values.
*Significant at the $p < .05$ level. **Significant at the $p < .01$ level.

low rating ($\chi^2 = 39.11$, $p = .000$). Mothers with a surrogate father to their child(ren) in the home were significantly less likely than other mothers were to have completed high school, while mothers with no father figure in the home were less likely than mothers with a biological father or a grandparent in the home to have completed high school ($\chi^2 = 17.45$, $p = .001$).

Respondents with the biological father in the home were significantly less likely than other respondents to report a relationship change in the past year ($\chi^2 = 34.69$, $p = .000$). Both mothers with a biological father of their child(ren) in the home, and mothers living with a grandparent,

TABLE 11. Differences according to family structure.

	No Father Figure in Home (n = 242) %	Biological Father in Home (n = 175) %	Surrogate Father in Home (n = 80) %	Mother and Grandparent in Home (n = 121) %	Total (N = 619) %
Education**					
High school	49.6	60.6	38.0	63.3	54.0
Less than HS	50.0	38.9	62.0	36.7	45.7
AFDC Receipt**					
Yes	78.1	40.6	70.0	73.6	65.4
No	21.9	58.9	30.0	26.4	34.4
Neighborhood Rating**					
Low	61.6	32.0	44.3	43.3	47.3
High	30.6	60.0	41.8	45.8	43.1
Relationship Change**					
No change	39.3	65.1	34.2	43.0	46.7
1 or more	60.3	34.9	64.6	57.0	53.0
Perceived Social Support**					
Low	42.1	57.1	52.5	57.5	50.7
High	55.8	42.3	47.5	41.7	48.1
Depression*					
Yes	41.3	28.5	36.7	30.8	35.1
No	57.4	70.9	62.0	68.3	64.0

Alcohol Use					
Yes	64.0	58.9	62.5	44.6	58.5
No	36.0	41.1	37.5	55.4	41.5
Physical Abuse as a Child					
Yes	21.5	24.6	39.2	18.3	24.0
No	77.3	75.4	59.5	80.8	75.2
Domestic Violence					
Yes	44.2	26.9	55.0	25.8	37.0
No	54.5	73.1	45.0	74.2	62.4
Nonviolent Discipline					
Low	53.7	38.3	26.3	55.4	46.2
High	45.9	61.7	73.7	44.6	53.6
Maternal Age					
Mean	28.8	29.0	26.0	26.7	28.1
Empathy for Child					
Mean score	24.1	26.7	26.0	25.0	25.3
Age-Appropriate Expectations					
Mean score	28.2	30.9	30.1	29.1	29.4

Note. Percentages do not always total 100% due to missing values.
*Significant at the $p < .05$ level. **Significant at the $p < .01$ level.

were significantly less likely to report a history of domestic violence in adulthood, whereas mothers with a surrogate father to their child(ren) in the home were more likely than other mothers were to report such a history ($\chi^2 = 31.33$, $p = .000$). No significant differences were found in perceived relationship quality according to family structure.

In terms of mental health, both mothers with the biological father of their child(ren) in the home and mothers living with a grandparent were significantly less likely than other mothers were to report clinical depression ($\chi^2 = 9.03$, $p = .029$). Respondents living with a grandparent were significantly less likely than other respondents were to report drinking alcohol ($\chi^2 = 13.2$, $p = .004$). Mothers without a father figure in the home were significantly more likely than other mothers were to report a high level of perceived social support ($\chi^2 = 11.55$, $p = .009$). Respondents living with a surrogate father figure to their child(ren) were significantly more likely than other respondents to report having experienced physical abuse as a child ($\chi^2 = 13.7$, $p = .004$).

Regarding parenting attitudes, mothers without a father figure in the home reported a significantly lower level of empathy for children than other mothers did, with mothers living with the biological father of their child(ren) reporting the highest levels ($F = 11.59$, $p = .000$). Moreover, respondents with no father figure in the home reported the lowest level of age-appropriate expectations for children ($F = 9.12$, $p = .000$). Mothers with a surrogate father to their child(ren) in the home were also most likely to report a high level of nonviolent discipline, while mothers without a father figure in the home, and mothers living with a grandparent, were more likely to report low use of nonviolent discipline ($\chi^2 = 27.13$, $p = .000$). No differences in spanking or minor assault were found according to family structure at the bivariate level.

Differences According to Marital Status
Bivariate associations according to marital status are summarized in Table 12. Many of the differences according to marital structure were similar to the aforementioned differences according to family structure, if one equates "no father figure" with "never married," "biological father"

TABLE 12. Differences according to marital status.

	Never Married (n = 386) %	Always Married (n = 123) %	Divorced or Remarried (n = 106) %	Total (N = 619) %
AFDC Receipt**				
Yes	77.0	26.8	68.9	65.4
No	23.0	73.2	31.1	34.4
Neighborhood Rating**				
Low	52.6	29.3	49.1	47.3
High	38.3	63.4	38.7	43.1
Relationship Change**				
No change	45.3	69.9	24.5	46.7
1 or more	54.3	30.1	74.5	53.0
Depression**				
Yes	35.9	23.8	46.2	35.1
No	63.0	76.2	52.8	64.0
Psychosomatic Symptoms*				
Low	52.8	53.7	39.6	50.4
High	47.2	45.5	59.6	48.5
Physical Abuse as a Child**				
Yes	17.7	29.3	41.5	24.0
No	81.5	70.7	56.6	75.2

(continued on next page)

TABLE 12. (continued)

	Never Married (n = 386) %	Always Married (n = 123) %	Divorced or Remarried (n = 106) %	Total (N = 619) %
Domestic Violence**				
Yes	31.5	31.7	64.8	37.0
No	67.7	68.3	34.9	62.4
Importance of Religion in Raising Children*				
Not/Somewhat important	48.7	36.6	55.9	45.4
Very important	50.0	63.4	44.1	54.1
Nonviolent Discipline**				
Low	52.3	39.0	35.8	46.2
High	46.4	61.0	64.2	53.6
Maternal Age**				
Mean	27.3	29.6	29.4	28.1
Empathy for Child**				
Mean score	24.3	27.1	26.6	25.3
Opposes Corporal Punishment*				
Mean score	13.5	13.8	14.3	13.7
Age-Appropriate Expectations**				
Mean score	28.4	31.2	30.8	29.4

Note. Percentages do not always total 100% due to missing values.
*Significant at the *p* < .05 level. **Significant at the *p* < .01 level.

with "always married," and "surrogate father" with "divorced/remarried." Again, no differences in relationship quality were found according to marital status. Divorced/remarried mothers were significantly more likely than other respondents were to report a history of domestic violence in adulthood ($\chi^2 = 0.28$, $p = .000$). Divorced/remarried respondents were significantly more likely than other respondents were to report symptoms of depression that met the clinical cut point ($\chi^2 = 13.15$, $p = .001$), as well as a high level of psychosomatic symptoms ($\chi^2 = 6.01$, $p = .049$). Divorced/remarried mothers were also significantly more likely than other respondents were to report a childhood history of physical abuse, while always single mothers were the least likely category (in terms of marital status) to report such a history ($\chi^2 = 28.57$, $p = .000$).

Always-married respondents were significantly more likely than other respondents were to assert that religion is very important to parenting, while divorced/remarried respondents were the category (in terms of marital status) the least likely to endorse this view ($\chi^2 = 6.61$, $p = .037$). Always-married respondents also expressed significantly higher levels of empathy for children ($F = 22.79$, $p = .000$) and age-appropriate expectations for children ($F = 16.7$, $p = .000$) than other respondents did, whereas never-married respondents scored the lowest in these regards. However, divorced/remarried respondents were significantly less likely than other respondents were to endorse corporal punishment ($F = 3.4$, $p = .034$). Never-married mothers were significantly less likely than other mothers were to report a high level of nonviolent discipline ($\chi^2 = 10.94$, $p = .000$). No differences in psychological aggression, spanking, or minor assault were found according to marital status at the bivariate level.

BIVARIATE ASSOCIATIONS WITH DISCIPLINE PRACTICES

Spanking

A number of variables were significantly associated with the "spanking" outcome variable. Mothers who reported spanking were significantly younger than other mothers were ($t = 2.34$, $p = .02$), and had

TABLE 13. Variables associated with spanking.

	No/Low Spanking (n = 125)	Medium/High Spanking (n = 493)	Total (N = 619)
	%	%	%
Number of Children**			
1–2	38.7	56.4	52.8
More than 2	60.5	43.6	47.0
Psychosomatic Symptoms*			
Low	59.7	48.4	51.4
High	38.7	50.8	48.5
Alcohol Use**			
Yes	45.6	61.9	58.5
No	54.4	38.1	41.5
Beaten as Adult*			
Yes	28.2	39.0	37.0
No	70.2	60.6	62.4
Relationship Change**			
No change	58.4	43.9	46.7
1 or more changes	41.6	55.7	53.0
Child Externalizing Behavior**			
Yes	10.5	29.1	25.7
No	87.9	69.5	72.9
Maternal Age*			
Mean age	29.2	27.8	28.1
Opposes Corporal Punishment**			
Mean score	14.9	13.4	13.7

Note. Percentages do not always total 100% due to missing values.
*Significant at the $p < .05$ level. **Significant at the $p < .01$ level.

fewer children ($\chi^2 = 12.07$, $p = .001$). In terms of parenting attitudes, spanking was positively associated with the endorsement of corporal punishment ($t = 5.4$, $p = .000$). Both alcohol use ($\chi^2 = 11.56$, $p = .001$) and psychosomatic symptoms ($\chi^2 = 5.52$, $p = .019$) were associated with an increased likelihood of spanking. Similarly, respondents who reported a relationship change during the past year ($\chi^2 = 8.69, p = .003$) were significantly more likely than other respondents were to report spanking, as were respondents with a history of domestic violence in adulthood ($\chi^2 = 4.61, p = .032$). Finally, spanking was significantly associated with child externalizing behavior ($\chi^2 = 18.1, p = .000$). Neither family structure nor marital status was significantly associated with spanking.

High Spanking
Mothers who reported a high level of spanking were also younger, more likely to use alcohol, and more likely to endorse corporal punishment than other mothers were (see Table 14). As in the prior analysis, high spanking was also positively associated with child externalizing behavior. Psychosomatic symptoms, domestic violence, and number of relationship changes, however, were not significantly associated with high spanking. There was some evidence to suggest that physical abuse as a child was associated with high spanking, but this finding did not reach the level of statistical significance ($\chi^2 = 3.22, p = .073$). Neither family structure nor marital status was significantly associated with high spanking.

Minor Assault
Alcohol use, psychosomatic symptoms, domestic violence, relationship change, endorsement of corporal punishment, and child externalizing behavior were all significantly associated with minor assault by the respondent. Maternal age and number of children, however, were not related to minor assault. A number of additional variables emerged as significant in relation to minor assault. African American respondents were more likely than white respondents were to report a minor assault against their child ($\chi^2 = 19.55, p = .000$). Mothers who reported a minor assault were more likely than other mothers were to express a lower level of empathy for children ($t = 3.44, p = .001$), and less age-appropriate expectations ($t = 4.16, p = .000$). Finally, low perceived relationship quality was also associated with an increased likelihood of minor assault

TABLE **14.** Variables associated with high spanking.

	No/Low/Medium Spanking (*n* = 376)	High Spanking (*n* = 242)	Total (*N* = 619)
	%	%	%
Alcohol Use**			
Yes	52.4	68.2	58.5
No	47.6	31.8	41.5
Child Externalizing Behavior**			
Yes	18.2	36.4	25.7
No	80.7	61.6	72.9
Maternal Age*			
Mean	28.5	27.4	28.1
Opposes Corporal Punishment**			
Mean score	14.2	12.9	13.7

Note. Percentages do not always total 100% due to missing values.
*Significant at the *p* < .05 level. **Significant at the *p* < .01 level.

($\chi^2 = 5.03$, $p = .025$). There was some evidence to suggest that physical abuse as a child was associated with minor assault, but this finding did not reach the level of statistical significance ($\chi^2 = 3.56$, $p = .059$). Neither family structure nor marital status was significantly associated with minor assault.

High Minor Assault
High minor assault was significantly associated with all of the variables described above for minor assault (in the same direction), as well as with an additional variable: respondents reporting receipt of AFDC were more likely than other respondents were to report a high level of minor assault ($\chi^2 = 6.6$, $p = .01$). There was some evidence to suggest that mothers who indicated a strong belief in the role of religion in parenting were less likely than other respondents were to report a high level of minor assault ($\chi^2 = 3.17$, $p = .075$), and that respondents were more likely to report a high level of minor assault against a male child than against a female

TABLE 15. Variables associated with minor assault.

	No Minor Assault (*n* = 285)	Minor Assault (*n* = 332)	Total (*N* = 619)
	%	%	%
Race**			
White	38.6	22.2	29.7
African American	61.4	77.2	70.0
Psychosomatic Symptoms**			
Low	58.1	44.1	51.4
High	40.5	55.0	48.5
Alcohol Use**			
Yes	51.0	65.0	58.5
No	49.0	35.0	41.5
Domestic Violence*			
Yes	31.3	41.7	37.0
No	67.3	58.0	62.4
Relationship Quality*			
Low	38.9	48.0	44.4
High	60.0	48.9	53.5
Relationship Change*			
No change	52.3	42.0	46.7
1 or more changes	47.7	57.4	53.0
Child Externalizing**			
Yes	14.1	35.1	25.7
No	84.9	63.1	72.9
Empathy for Child**			
Mean score	26.0	24.6	25.3
Opposes Corporal Punishment**			
Mean score	14.4	13.1	13.7
Age-Appropriate Expectations**			
Mean score	30.4	28.5	29.4

Note. Percentages do not always total 100% due to missing values.
*Significant at the *p* < .05 level. **Significant at the *p* < .01 level.

TABLE 16. Variables associated with high minor assault.

	None/Low Minor Assault (n = 426)	High Minor Assault (n = 191)	Total (N = 619)
	%	%	%
Race**			
White	34.5	18.9	29.7
African American	65.5	80.0	70.0
AFDC Receipt**			
Yes	62.4	72.6	65.4
No	37.6	26.8	34.4
Depression*			
Yes	32.5	40.5	35.1
No	66.6	58.4	64.0
Psychosomatic Symptoms**			
Low	54.4	42.4	51.4
High	44.2	57.6	48.5
Alcohol Use*			
Yes	55.4	65.4	58.5
No	44.6	34.6	41.5
Domestic Violence*			
Yes	34.4	42.4	37.0
No	64.7	57.6	62.4
Relationship Quality**			
Low	40.1	53.3	48.9
High	58.4	43.8	48.0
Importance of Religion in Raising Children*			
Not/Somewhat important	42.4	50.0	45.4
Very important	56.7	48.9	54.1
Child Externalizing**			
Yes	19.1	39.4	25.7
No	79.8	58.4	72.9
Empathy for Child*			
Mean score	25.5	24.7	25.3
Opposes Corporal Punishment**			
Mean score	14.0	12.9	13.7
Age-Appropriate Expectations**			
Mean score	29.7	28.6	29.4

Note. Percentages do not always total 100% due to missing values.
*Significant at the $p < .05$ level. **Significant at the $p < .01$ level.

child (χ^2 = 3.25, p = .072), but neither of these findings reached the level of statistical significance. Neither family structure nor marital status was significantly associated with high minor assault.

CONSTRUCTING THE MULTIVARIATE MODELS

The bivariate analysis is the first step toward establishing a possible relationship between the independent variables and the outcome variables. The findings described previously provide initial support for a hypothesis of an association between relationship stability and quality and corporal punishment, at least with regard to the spanking, minor assault, and high minor assault outcome variables (none of these variables emerged as significant for high spanking). However, neither of the family composition variables (family structure and marital status) emerged as significant in association with any of the four discipline outcomes. This would seem to indicate that family composition is not relevant to the likelihood of physical discipline.

However, when examining the association between family composition and corporal punishment separately by race, a number of significant differences were identified. For example, never-married white respondents were significantly less likely than always-married and divorced/remarried white respondents were to report spanking (p = .015), whereas no such relationship existed for African Americans at the bivariate level. Always-married white respondents were also more likely than never-married and divorced/remarried white respondents were to report a minor assault (p = .05) or a high level of minor assault (p = .08), but this did not hold true for African Americans. Instead, divorced/remarried African American respondents were significantly more likely than always-married and never-married African American respondents were to report a high level of minor assault (p = .09). Similarly, white respondents with the biological father of their child(ren) in the home were more likely than other white respondents were to report a minor assault (p = .10) or a high level of minor assault (p = .08), whereas African Americans with a surrogate father to their child(ren) in the home were more likely than other African American respondents to report a high level of minor assault (p = .10).

These findings provide support for the notion that the relationship between family composition and child discipline practices is a complex one, influenced in part by race. Identification of seemingly differential effects such as these also helps to explain why family composition does not appear significant in the analyses that combine both African Americans and whites. In some cases, the influence of family composition may be cancelled out because the effects tend to occur in different directions, or the mechanism by which family structure influences child discipline varies according to race.

The same appeared to be true for some of the control variables, with a number of variables emerging as significant for one racial/ethnic group but not for the other. Nonetheless, it is important to reiterate that simply due to the large proportion of African Americans in this sample, it is likely that some variables might appear significant for African Americans but fail to reach the level of statistical significance for whites. Indeed, all but two of the variables that were significant for one racial/ethnic group but not the other were significant for African Americans but not for whites. Thus, no attempt was made to single out particular variables that appeared to have differential effects according to race at the bivariate level. Rather, every independent and control term was interacted with race for formal testing in the multivariate regressions.

The following two sections present the findings from these multivariate regressions. The first presents the spanking and high spanking models, and the second presents the minor assault and high minor assault models. Four models are presented for each outcome variable. The first of these includes all respondents and controls for family structure; the second includes all respondents and controls for marital status; the third model selects only respondents currently in a relationship and controls for family structure; while the last model selects respondents currently in a relationship and controls for marital status.

MULTIVARIATE ANALYSES: SPANKING AND HIGH SPANKING

A series of logistic regression analyses were conducted using the spanking outcome variables, "spanking" and "high spanking." To construct the spanking variable, responses were coded into two categories: 0 = spanked 0–1 times in the past year, and 1 = spanked 2 or more times in the past year. This question refers only to the respondent's behavior and not to the child's discipline experiences with all the adults during his or her life.

SPANKING

Family Structure Model

The first spanking analysis included family structure as the family configuration predictor variable. Table 17 presents findings from the final model. As described in the chapter entitled "Study Methodology," three criteria were used to evaluate the fit of the final model: accuracy of prediction, the Hosmer and Lemeshow test, and the –2 log-likelihood value. The model presented here passes the Hosmer and Lemeshow test, maximizes accuracy of prediction, and minimizes the –2 log-likelihood value. Furthermore, the confidence intervals for the point estimates (odds ratios) are relatively narrow, indicating an acceptable degree of precision in the estimates. Diagnostics revealed one residual outlier + / – 3 standard deviations (case # 519), and one case (case #50) with a suspiciously high leverage statistic (> .09). Both were deleted from the analysis. A test for multicollinearity revealed no problems. All VIF statistics < 4 except for those associated with the interaction terms, which is customary and unproblematic (Jaccard, 2001).

Independent Variables

Family Structure. Controlling for all other variables in the model, the odds of spanking were lower for mothers without a father figure in the home, as compared to mothers with the biological father of their child(ren) in the home (OR = 2.04: 95% CI = .1.04, 4.00)[2], and as compared to multigenerational families (OR = 1.95: 95% CI = .95, 4.03). Similarly, the odds of spanking were lower for mothers living with a surrogate father figure to their child(ren) in the home, as compared to mothers with the biological father of their child(ren) in the home (OR = 2.36: 95% CI = .97, 5.75), and as compared to multigenerational families (OR = 2.25: 95%

TABLE 17. Logistic regression analysis: Family structure and likelihood of spanking.

N = 564 (55 missing cases)	B	p-value	Odds Ratio	95.0% CI for OR Lower	Upper
Maternal Age	−.050	.024	1.05	1.007	1.10
Race	−.097	.810			
Education	−.454	.079	1.57	.95	2.61
AFDC Receipt	.032	ns			
Number of Children	−.805	.002	2.24	1.35	3.70
Low Birth Weight	.114	ns			
Child Gender	−.345	ns			
Child Externalizing Behavior	1.018	.006	2.77	1.35	5.69
Alcohol Use	.835	.001	2.30	1.39	3.81
Empathy for Child	.099	.003	1.10	1.03	1.18
Opposes Corporal Punishment	−.329	.000	1.39	1.25	1.55
Psychosomatic Symptoms	.694	.016	2.00	1.14	3.52
Maternal Depression	−.456	.133	1.58	.87	2.87
Domestic Violence	.651	.025	1.92	1.09	3.39
Perceived Social Support	−.545	.209			
No Father Figure in Home	−.714	.038	2.04	1.04	4.00
Surrogate Father Figure in Home	−.859	.060	2.36	.97	5.78
Mother and Grandparent in Home	−.046	ns			
Race × Social Support	.994	.060			
CONSTANT	5.292	.000			
Mother and Grandparent as Baseline:					
No father figure in home	−.668	.071	1.95	.95	4.03
Surrogate father in home	−.813	.088	2.25	.89	5.75
Biological father in home	.046	ns			
Percentage Correctly Predicted	83.2				
Hosmer and Lemeshow Test	$\chi^2 = 9.05$ (df = 8), p = .34				
−2 Log Likelihood	441.54				

CI = .89, 5.75). Subsequent analyses were conducted using each of the family structure categories as the reference group, but no other significant findings emerged.

Domestic Violence. Report of domestic violence in adulthood almost doubled the odds of spanking (OR = 1.92: 95% CI = 1.09, 3.39).

Relationship Stability. Relationship change was not a statistically significant predictor of spanking and was dropped from the final model.

Perceived Relationship Quality. Since this analysis applied to all respondents, irrespective of relationship status, inclusion of the relationship variable was not appropriate. Subsequent analyses were conducted with respondents in relationships in order to examine the influence of relationship quality on spanking. Findings from these analyses are presented in a subsequent section.

Control Variables
Demographics. Greater maternal age decreased the odds of spanking (OR = 1.05: 95% CI = 1.007, 1.10), as did having more than two children (OR = 2.24: 95% CI = 1.35, 3.70). Not completing high school also decreased the odds of spanking (OR = 1.57: 95% CI = .95, 2.61). AFDC receipt was not significantly associated with spanking. Race was likewise not a significant predictor of spanking in the model, with or without interactions.

Child Characteristics. In this analysis, child externalizing behavior almost tripled the odds of spanking (OR = 2.77: 95% CI = 1.35, 5.69). Neither child gender nor low-birth-weight status was a significant predictor of spanking but both were retained as control variables.

Maternal Mental Health. Both alcohol use (OR = 2.30: 95% CI = 1.39, 3.81) and high psychosomatic symptoms (OR = 2.00: 95% CI = 1.14, 3.52) increased the odds of spanking. There was some evidence to suggest that maternal depression decreased the odds of spanking (OR = 1.58: 95% CI = .87, 2.87), but this finding did not reach the level of statistical significance (p = .13). Perceived social support was significant in interaction with race, as shall be discussed later. Maternal history of child physical abuse was not a significant predictor of spanking and was dropped from the model.

Parenting Attitudes.   A 1-unit increase in the Empathy for Child score increased the odds of spanking by a factor of 1.10 (95% CI = 1.03, 1.18). A 1-unit increase in the Opposes Corporal Punishment score decreased the odds of spanking by a factor of 1.39 (95% CI = 1.25, 1.55). Neither Age-Appropriate Expectations nor belief in the importance of religion to raising children was significantly associated with spanking so both were dropped from the model.

Extrafamilial Influences.   Neighborhood rating did not emerge as a significant predictor of spanking and was therefore dropped from the final model.

Interaction Term

In Table 17, no odds ratios are presented for the interaction term, as the relative odds of spanking must be calculated separately for each group, depending upon which group is selected as the baseline or reference group. Similarly, the odds ratios for the focal independent variables that make up the interaction term cannot be considered in isolation from the interaction term. Instead, the odds ratios that correspond with four different comparisons are presented in the text below: (1) African American with focal variable/African American without focal variable; (2) white with focal variable/white without focal variable; (3) African American with focal variable/white with focal variable; and (4) African American without focal variable/white without focal variable.

To clarify the nature of the interaction, a series of separate regressions were run according to race (see Table 18). These findings are included solely for the purpose of corroboration. To ensure greater accuracy, the

TABLE **18.** Family structure and likelihood of spanking: Separate regressions according to race.

	White N = 169 (15 missing)					African American N = 396 (37 missing)				
	B	p-value	OR	95% CI for OR		B	p-value	OR	95% CI for OR	
Social Support	−.528	.25	1.69	.68	4.22	.426	.20	1.53	.80	2.97

odds ratios presented in the text were calculated using coefficients from the logistic regression that included all respondents, rather than the coefficients generated in the separate regressions. Therefore, slight deviations may be observed between the odds ratios reported in the text and those presented in Table 18.

Race x Social Support. Perceived social support seemed to act in opposite directions for African Americans and whites. For African Americans, a high level of perceived social support increased the odds of spanking (OR = 1.57), as compared to African Americans with a low level of perceived social support. For whites, a high level of social support decreased the odds of spanking (OR = 1.72), as compared to whites with a low level of perceived social support. Comparison of the odds of spanking for African Americans and whites with the same level of social support revealed that the odds of spanking for African Americans with a high level of perceived social support were 2.45 times higher than the odds for whites with a high level of social support. However, the odds of spanking for African Americans with a low level of social support were 1.10 times lower than the odds for whites with a low level of social support.

Although these findings did not reach the level of statistical significance in the separate regressions, the interaction term was significant in the main model and inclusion of the interaction term enhanced overall fit. Nonetheless, this finding must be considered somewhat speculative.

Marital Status Model

The second logistic regression analysis included marital status as the family configuration predictor variable, with "spanking" as the outcome variable. Controlling for all other variables in the model, the odds of spanking were lower for never-married mothers, as compared to always-married mothers ($p = .048$; OR = 2.26: 95% CI = 1.007, 5.05). The odds of spanking for divorced/remarried mothers also appeared to be lower than the odds for always married mothers, but this finding did not reach statistical significance ($p = .21$). These findings are similar to the findings for family structure, if one equates "no father figure" with "never married" and "surrogate father" with "divorced/remarried." The "race x social support" interaction term was not statistically significant when controlling for marital status as opposed to family structure ($p = .15$), although it tended in the same direction. Finally, maternal depression, which only approached significance in the family structure analysis, became less significant ($p = .17$). Otherwise, effect sizes for the marital status and family structure models were similar in magnitude and tended in the same direction.

Relationship Quality

The final two Spanking analyses focused only on respondents in current relationships, first including family structure as the family configuration variable and then marital status. The primary reason for conducting these separate analyses was to examine the potential role of relationship quality in predicting spanking behavior. Perceived relationship quality was not significantly associated with spanking.

HIGH SPANKING

Next, a series of logistic regression analyses were conducted using the "high spanking" outcome variable. Responses were coded into two categories: 0 = spanked fewer than 5 times in the past year, and 1 = spanked 5 or more times in the past year.

Family Structure Model

The first analysis included family structure as the family configuration predictor variable. Table 19 presents findings from the final model. The model presented below satisfies the criteria for model fit, and diagnostic testing revealed no problems. However, it should be noted that that the percentage predicted correctly is somewhat low (67.8%) and the –2 log-likelihood value is high (695.54), an indication that this model may not have as much predictive power as the spanking model. Indeed, far

TABLE 19. Logistic regression analysis: Family structure and likelihood of high spanking.

N = 590 (29 missing cases)	B	p-value	Odds Ratio	95.0% CI for OR Lower	Upper
AFDC Receipt	–.117	.598			
Race	–.350	.119	1.42	.91	2.20
Education	–.226	ns			
Maternal Age	–.037	.038	1.04	1.002	1.08
Number of Children	–.166	ns			
Low Birth Weight	.101	ns			
Child Gender	–.078	ns			
Child Externalizing Behavior	.851	.000	2.34	1.55	3.55
Alcohol Use	.670	.001	1.96	1.33	2.87
Opposes Corporal Punishment	–.210	.000	1.23	1.15	1.33
Age-Appropriate Expectations	.067	.002	1.07	1.03	1.11
No Father Figure in Home	.061	ns			
Surrogate Father Figure in Home	.332	ns			
Mother and Grandparent in Home	.052	ns			
CONSTANT	1.282	.136			
Percentage Correctly Predicted	67.8				
Hosmer and Lemeshow Test	$\chi^2 = 8.87$ (df = 8), p = .35				
–2 Log Likelihood	695.54				

fewer variables than in the Spanking analysis emerged as significant in this analysis, suggesting that there may be some important omitted variables. Interestingly, a few race interactions approached significance. For example, race x neighborhood rating was significant at the $p = .113$ level, but rendered the model a poor fit when included (the model failed the Hosmer and Lemeshow test).

Independent Variables

Family Structure.   When all other variables in the model were controlled for, family structure was not significantly associated with high spanking, unlike the findings for spanking.

Domestic Violence.   Also unlike the findings for spanking, domestic violence was not significantly associated with high spanking, and was therefore dropped from the model.

Relationship Change.   Number of relationship changes was not a statistically significant predictor of high spanking and was therefore dropped from the final model.

Control Variables

Demographics.   Greater maternal age decreased the odds of high spanking (OR = 1.04: 95% CI = 1.002, 1.08). There was some evidence to suggest that the odds of high spanking for African Americans were lower than the odds for whites (OR = 1.42: 95% CI = .91, 2.20), although this finding did not reach the level of statistical significance ($p = .119$), and became clearly nonsignificant when marital status, rather than family structure, was controlled for. No other demographic variables were significant.

Child Characteristics.   In this analysis, child externalizing behavior more than doubled the odds of high spanking (OR = 2.34: 95% CI = 1.55, 3.55).

Maternal Mental Health.   As in previous analyses, maternal alcohol consumption increased the odds of high spanking (OR = 1.96: 95% CI =

1.33, 2.87). However, neither maternal depression nor psychosomatic symptoms was significantly associated with high spanking. Both variables were therefore dropped from the final model.

Parenting Attitudes.   As in previous analyses, a 1-unit increase in the Opposes Corporal Punishment score decreased the odds of high spanking by a factor of 1.23 (95% CI = 1.15, 1.33). Unlike the spanking analysis, however, the Empathy for Child score was not associated with high spanking. However, a 1-unit increase in the Age-Appropriate Expectations score increased the odds of high spanking by a factor of 1.07 (95% CI = 1.03, 1.11).

Extrafamilial Influences.   Neighborhood rating was not a significant predictor of high spanking and was therefore dropped from the model. Social support was no longer significant in association with race.

Marital Status Model
The next logistic regression analysis included marital status as the family configuration predictor variable, with "high spanking" as the outcome variable. When all other variables in the model were controlled for, marital status was found not to be significantly associated with high spanking. However, there was some evidence to suggest that marital status might influence high spanking differentially according to race. For example, race x never-married approached significance (p = .15) when included in the model. Separate regressions according to race seemed to support this finding (see Table 20). For whites only, the odds of high spanking seemed to be lower for never-married respondents than for always-married respondents.

Otherwise, the same control variables that were significant in the Family Structure model were significant in this model, with the exception of race. Controlling for marital status rather than family structure, race was no longer significantly associated with high spanking. Effect sizes were quite similar in magnitude and tended in the same direction.

TABLE 20. Logistic regression analysis: Marital status and high spanking—Separate regressions according to race.

	White N = 176 (8 missing)				African American N = 409 (24 missing)			
	B	p-value	OR	95% CI for OR	B	p-value	OR	95% CI for OR
Always married as baseline								
Never Married	−.958	.05	2.60	1.00 6.80	.072	.85	1.08	.50 2.31

Relationship Quality

The final two High Spanking analyses focused only on respondents in current relationships, first including family structure as the family configuration variable, and then marital status. Again, relationship quality was not a significant predictor of high spanking, but was included in the model as a control variable.

THE ROLE OF RACE IN SPANKING

Because race is included in a number of interaction terms in these analyses, it has no stand-alone meaning as a main factor, making the influence of race on the likelihood of spanking more challenging to ascertain. In some of the analyses, race was borderline significant or approaching significance in models without interaction terms, but became nonsignificant when interaction terms were introduced. Similarly, when comparing the relative odds of spanking for African Americans and whites, depending upon the other factors included in the interaction terms, there was no consistent pattern of one race/ethnicity being at higher risk of spanking. Finally, race never emerged as significant predictor when only respondents with a spouse or partner were selected. Taken together, these findings suggest that race plays an indirect role in determining spanking behavior, rather than direct one.

TABLE **21.** Summary of findings: Spanking and high spanking.

	Spanking	High Spanking
Family Structure	Odds for no father figure and surrogate father figure < odds for biological father in home	ns
	Odds for no father figure and surrogate father figure < odds for multigenerational family	
Marital Status	Odds for never married < odds for always married	ns
	Some evidence that odds for divorced/remarried < odds for always married	Some evidence that for whites only, odds for never married < always married
Relationship Quality	ns	ns
Domestic Violence	Increased odds	ns
Relationship Change	ns	ns
Demographics	Greater maternal age decreased odds	Greater maternal age decreased odds
	Having more than 2 children decreased odds	
Child Characteristics	Externalizing behavior increased odds	Externalizing behavior increased odds
Maternal Mental Health	Alcohol use and psychosomatic symptoms increased odds	Alcohol use increased odds
	Suggestion that maternal depression decreased odds	
Parenting Attitudes	Opposition to corporal pun ishment decreased odds	Opposition to corporal pun ishment decreased odds
	Greater empathy for children increased odds	More age-appropriate expectations of children increased odds
Extrafamilial Influences	For African Americans, high social support seemed to increase the odds, while for whites, high social sup port decreased the odds	ns

MULTIVARIATE ANALYSES: MINOR ASSAULT AND HIGH MINOR ASSAULT

A series of logistic regression analyses were run on all respondents using the minor assault outcome variables, "minor assault" and "high minor assault." To construct the minor assault variable, responses were coded into two categories: 0 = no minor assault in the past year, 1 = 1 or more minor assaults in the past year. Behaviors included in the Minor Assault category included: grabbing child, shaking child, pushing or shoving child, slapping child, and throwing something at child.

MINOR ASSAULT

Family Structure Model
The first analysis included family structure as the family configuration predictor variable. Table 22 presents findings from the final model. This model passes the Hosmer and Lemeshow test, maximizes accuracy of prediction, and minimizes the –2 log-likelihood value. The confidence intervals for the point estimates (odds ratios) are relatively narrow, indicating an acceptable degree of precision in the estimates. Diagnostic testing revealed no outliers or suspiciously high leverage values. A test for multicollinearity revealed no problems. All VIF statistics < 4, except for those associated with the interaction terms. However, it should be noted that that the percentage predicted correctly is somewhat low (66.9%) and the –2 log-likelihood value is high (676.00), suggesting that this model may have limited predictive power.

Independent Variables
Family Structure.   When all other variables in the model were controlled for, the odds of minor assault were found to be significantly lower for respondents without a father figure in the home (OR = 2.19: 95% CI = 1.32, 3.65) and for respondents with a surrogate father to their child(ren) in the home (OR = 1.94: 95% CI = 1.006, 3.77) than for respondents with the biological father of their child(ren) in the home. There was

TABLE 22. Logistic regression analysis: Family structure and likelihood of minor assault.

N = 571 (48 missing cases)	B	p-value	Odds Ratio	95.0% CI for OR Lower	95.0% CI for OR Upper
Maternal Age	−.006	ns			
Race	1.024	.000	2.75	1.74	4.47
Education	−.389	.052	1.47	1.00	2.18
AFDC Receipt	−.161	ns			
Number of Children	.020	ns			
Low Birth Weight	−.384	.092	1.47	.94	2.29
Child Gender	−.461	.015	1.58	1.09	2.30
Child Externalizing Behavior	1.076	.000	2.93	1.81	4.75
Alcohol Use	.537	.006	1.71	1.17	2.51
Opposes Corporal Punishment	−.075	.049	1.08	1.00	1.16
Age-Appropriate Expectations	−.048	.030	1.05	1.005	1.10
Psychosomatic Symptoms	.449	.040	1.57	1.02	2.41
Depression	−.324	.157	1.38	.88	2.16
Physical Abuse as a Child	.377	.130	1.46	.89	2.38
Domestic Violence	.643	.003	1.90	1.24	2.93
No Father Figure in Home	−.784	.003	2.19	1.32	3.65
Surrogate Father Figure in Home	−.666	.048	1.94	1.006	3.77
Mother and Grandparent in Home	−.458	.123	1.58	.88	2.83
CONSTANT	2.156	.017			
Percentage Correctly Predicted	66.9				
Hosmer and Lemeshow Test	$\chi^2 = 8.44$ (df = 8), p = .39				
−2 Log Likelihood	676.00				

also evidence to suggest that the odds of minor assault were lower for respondents in a multigenerational family than for other respondents (OR = 1.58: 95% CI = .88, 2.83), but this finding did not reach the level of statistical significance ($p = .12$).

Domestic Violence. Domestic violence almost doubled the odds of minor assault (OR = 1.90: 95% CI = 1.24, 2.93).

Relationship Change. Number of relationship changes was not a statistically significant predictor of minor assault and was therefore dropped from the final model.

Control Variables

Demographics. The odds of minor assault for African American respondents were found to be 2.75 times higher (95% CI = 1.74, 4.47) than the odds for white respondents, when the other variables in the model were controlled for. The odds of minor assault were lower for mothers who had not completed high school than for those who had (OR = 1.47: 95% CI = 1.00, 2.18). Neither receipt of AFDC, maternal age, nor number of children was a significant predictor of minor assault.

Child Characteristics. Child externalizing behavior almost tripled the odds of minor assault (OR = 2.93: 95% CI = 1.81, 4.75). The odds of minor assault were about 1 and a half times lower (OR = 1.58: 95% CI = 1.09, 2.30) for girls than for boys. Finally, the odds of minor assault were about 1 and a half times lower for children of low-birth-weight status than for other children (OR = 1.47: 95% CI = .94, 2.29).

Maternal Mental Health. As in previous analyses, maternal alcohol consumption was found to increase the odds of minor assault (OR = 1.71: 95% CI = 1.17, 2.51). A high level of psychosomatic symptoms also significantly increased the odds of minor assault (OR = 1.57: 95% CI = 1.02, 2.41). Maternal history of physical abuse as a child also increased the odds of minor assault (OR = 1.49: 95% CI = .88, 2.51), although this finding only approached significance (p = .13). Finally, there was a suggestion that maternal depression decreased the odds of minor assault, but this finding did not reach the level of statistical significance (p = .157). Nonetheless, the variable was retained because it enhanced model fit and was consistent with the earlier spanking analysis.

Parenting Attitudes.   A 1-unit increase in the Opposes Corporal Punishment score decreased the odds of minor assault by a factor of 1.08 (95%
CI = 1.00, 1.16). A 1-unit increase in the Age-Appropriate Expectations
score likewise decreased the odds of minor assault by a factor of 1.05
(95% CI = 1.005, 1.10). Empathy for children and beliefs about the
importance of religion in raising children were not significant to the odds
of minor assault, and were therefore dropped from the final model.

Extrafamilial Influences.   Neither neighborhood rating nor perceived
social support was a significant predictor of minor assault, so both were
dropped from the model.

Marital Status Model
The next analysis replaced family structure with marital status as the
family configuration variable. When other variables in the model were
controlled for, the odds of minor assault for both never-married respondents (p = .016; OR = 2.02: 95% CI = 1.14, 3.60) and divorced/remarried
respondents (p = .028; OR = 2.08: 95% CI = 1.08, 4.02) were found to
be lower than the odds for always-married respondents were. This is
comparable to the findings for family structure, if one equates "never
married" with "no father figure" and "divorced/remarried" with "surrogate father." All the other variables that were significant in the family
structure model were significant in marital status model, with the exception of maternal depression, which became less significant (p = .21). In
general, effect sizes were quite similar in magnitude and tended in the
same direction.

Relationship Quality
The final two Minor Assault analyses focused only on respondents currently in relationships, first including family structure as the family configuration variable, and then marital status. Again, perceived relationship
quality was not significantly associated with minor assault, but was retained
in the model for theoretical purposes.

HIGH MINOR ASSAULT

A second series of logistic regressions were performed using the High Minor Assault outcome variable. Responses were coded into two categories: 0 = 0–1 minor assaults in the past year, and 1 = 2 or more minor assaults in the past year.

Family Structure Model

The first analysis included family structure as the family configuration predictor variable. Table 23 presents findings from the final model. The model presented below passes the Hosmer and Lemeshow test, maximizes accuracy of prediction, and minimizes the –2 log-likelihood value. This model appears to be a slightly better fit than the minor assault model, with a higher percentage correctly predicted (72.8%), and a lower –2 log-likelihood value (617.38). The confidence intervals for the point estimates (odds ratios) are relatively narrow, indicating an acceptable degree of precision in the estimates. Diagnostic testing revealed no outliers or suspiciously high leverage values. A test for multicollinearity revealed no problems. All VIF statistics < 4, except for those associated with the interaction terms.

Independent Variables

Family Structure. The odds of high minor assault were lower for respondents with no father figure in the home (OR = 2.29: 95% CI = 1.20, 4.39) and for respondents living with a grandparent (OR = 2.39: 95% CI = 1.14, 4.98), as compared to respondents with a surrogate father to their child(ren) in the home. For African Americans only, the odds of high minor assault were also lower for respondents with a biological father in the home, as compared to respondents with a surrogate father in the home (OR = 2.51). For whites only, the odds of high minor assault were lower for respondents with no father figure in the home (OR = 3.78) and for respondents in a multigenerational family (OR = 3.85), as compared to respondents with the biological father of their child(ren) in the home, although the latter finding only approached significance (p = .13 for race x multigenerational family).

TABLE 23. Logistic regression analysis: Family structure and likelihood of high minor assault.

N = 586 (33 missing cases)	B	p-value	Odds Ratio	95.0% CI for OR Lower	Upper
Maternal Age	.024	ns			
Race	.087	.819			
Education	−.369	ns			
AFDC Receipt	.297	ns			
Number of Children	−.088	ns			
Low Birth Weight	−.372	.129	1.45	.90	2.35
Child Gender	−.593	.003	1.81	1.22	2.68
Child Externalizing Behavior	.798	.001	2.22	1.41	3.49
Alcohol Use	.288	.171	1.33	.88	2.02
Opposes Corporal Punishment	−.095	.006	1.10	1.03	1.18
Psychosomatic Symptoms	.280	.194	1.32	.87	2.02
Physical Abuse as a Child	.455	.155	1.58	.84	2.95
Relationship Change	.334	.114	1.40	.92	2.11
Importance of Religion in Raising Children	−.469	.024	1.60	1.06	2.40
No Father Figure in Home	−1.330	.032			
Surrogate Father in Home	−.438	.421			
Mother and Grandparent in Home	−1.298	.114			
Race × No Father Figure	1.426	.037			
Race × Surrogate Father Figure	1.350	.048			
Race × Multigenerational Family	1.347	.130			
CONSTANT	−.393	.609			
Surrogate Father as Baseline:					
Race	1.467	.000			
No father figure in home	−.830	.012	2.29	1.20	4.39
Biological father in home	.458	.318			
Multigenerational family	−.870	.021	2.39	1.14	4.98
Race × Biological father	−1.380	.008			
Percentage Correctly Predicted	72.8				
Hosmer and Lemeshow Test	$\chi^2 = 6.75$ ($df = 8$), $p = .56$				
-2 Log Likelihood	617.38				

Comparing the odds of high minor assault for African Americans and whites across the same family structure, one finds that the odds of high minor assault are higher for African American respondents with no father figure in the home than for white respondents with no father figure in the home (OR = 4.54); a similar relationship holds true for African Americans and whites in a multigenerational family structure (OR = 4.20). However, the odds of high minor assault are almost the same for African American and white respondents with the biological father of their child(ren) in the home (OR = 1.09).

Domestic Violence.   Domestic violence was not a significant predictor of high minor assault and was therefore dropped from the model.

Relationship Change.   There was a suggestion that having one or more relationship changes in the past year increased the likelihood of high minor assault, but this finding did not reach the level of statistical significance (p = .114). The variable was retained because it improved model fit and tended toward significance.

Control Variables
Demographics.   None of the demographic variables were significant predictors of high minor assault.

TABLE 24. Logistic regression analysis: Family structure and likelihood of high minor assault—Separate regressions by race.

	White N = 170 (14 missing)				African American N = 397 (36 missing)			
	B	*p*-value	OR	95% CI for OR	B	*p*-value	OR	95% CI for OR
Biological Father as Baseline:								
No father figure	−1.62	.017	5.05	1.33 19.23	.088	.780	1.09	.59 2.03
Surrogate father	−.344	.563	1.41	.44 4.52	.804	.063	2.24	.96 5.22
Multigeneration	−1.44	.109	4.20	.73 24.39	.071	.848	1.07	.52 2.22

Child Characteristics. As with the Minor Assault analysis, child externalizing increased the odds of high minor assault, while low-birth-weight status decreased the odds of high minor assault. Furthermore, the odds of high minor assault were lower for girls than they were for boys.

Maternal Mental Health. Maternal alcohol use ($p = .17$), psychosomatic symptoms ($p = .19$), and physical abuse as a child ($p = .16$) were all positively associated with high minor assault, but none of these variables reached the level of statistical significance. They were retained in the model because they tended toward significance, were consistent with prior analyses, and improved model fit.

Parenting Attitudes. A 1-unit increase in the Opposes Corporal Punishment score decreased the odds of high spanking by a factor of 1.10 (95% CI = 1.03, 1.18). Belief that religion is very important to raising children decreased the odds of high minor assault (OR = 1.60: 95% CI = 1.06, 2.40).

Extrafamilial Influences. Neither neighborhood quality nor perceived social support was a significant predictor of high minor assault, so both were dropped from the model.

Marital Status Model
The next analysis replaced family structure with marital status as the family configuration variable. When all other variables in the model were controlled for, the marital status variables were found not to be significant predictors of high minor assault when included simply as main factors. However, as with the family structure analysis, marital status was significant in interaction with race. For example, being single (never married) decreased the odds of high minor assault for whites (OR = 2.40), when compared to always-married white respondents, but the same relationship did not hold true for African Americans. The interaction term "race x never married" was significant at the $p = .027$ level. Similarly, when

compared to always-married respondents, being divorced decreased the odds of high minor assault for white respondents (OR = 3.14), but increased the odds for African American respondents (OR = 2.66). The interaction term "race x divorced/remarried" was significant at the p = .003 level. Separate analyses according to race seemed to confirm these findings (see Table 25). These findings are comparable to the findings for family structure, if one equates "never married" with "no father figure," and "always married" with "biological father in the home." All the other variables that were significant in the family structure model were also significant in marital status model. In general, effect sizes were quite similar in magnitude and tended in the same direction.

Relationship Quality

The final two High Minor Assault analyses focused only on respondents currently in relationships, first including family structure as the family configuration variable, and then marital status. A low relationship rating increased the odds of high minor assault (OR = 1.56: 95% CI = .95, 2.55).

THE ROLE OF RACE IN MINOR ASSAULT

In contrast to the spanking analyses, race emerged as a significant predictor of minor assault in these analyses, both as a main factor, and in

TABLE 25. Logistic regression analysis: Marital status and high minor assault—Separate regressions by race.

	White N = 170 (14 missing)				African American N = 395 (38 missing)			
	B	p-value	OR	95% CI for OR	B	p-value	OR	95% CI for OR
Always Married as Baseline:								
Never married	−1.141	.050	3.13	1.002 9.80	.563	.189	1.76	.76 4.07
Divorced/ Remarried	−1.333	.038	3.79	1.08 13.33	1.060	.034	2.89	1.08 7.70

TABLE 26. Summary of findings: Minor assault and high minor assault.

	Minor Assault	High Minor Assault
Family Structure	Odds for no father figure (FF), surrogate father figure, and multigenerational family structure < odds for biological father in home	Odds for no FF and multigenerational family < odds for surrogate father For African Americans (AA) only, odds for biological father also < odds for surrogate father For whites only, odds for no FF and multigenerational family < odds for biological father
Marital Status	Odds for never married and divorced/remarried < odds for always married	For whites only, odds for never married and divorced/remarried < odds for always married For AA only, odds for divorced/remarried > odds for always married
Domestic Violence	Domestic Violence increased odds	*ns*
Relationship Change	*ns*	Relationship change increased the odds
Relationship Quality	*ns*	Low quality relationship increased the odds
Demographics	No high school diploma increased odds Being AA increased odds.	*ns*
Child Characteristics	Externalizing increased odds Being a girl decreased odds Low-birth-weight status decreased odds	Externalizing increased odds Being a girl decreased odds Low-birth-weight status decreased odds
Maternal Mental Health	Alcohol use increased odds Psychosomatic symptoms increased odds Suggestion that history of physical abuse as a child increased odds	Alcohol use increased odds Suggestion that history of physical abuse as a child increased odds
Parenting Attitudes	Opposition to corporal punishment decreased odds More age-appropriate expectations decreased odds	Opposition to corporal punishment decreased odds Belief in the importance of religion to raising children decreased odds
Extrafamilial Influences	*ns*	*ns*

interaction with family structure and marital status. Although in some analyses race influenced the likelihood of minor assault differentially according to family configuration, race also seemed to exert an effect above and beyond these indirect relationships. When comparing the odds of minor assault according to race across family configurations, the odds of minor assault were consistently higher for African American respondents than for white respondents.

ENDNOTE

1. Statistical significance was established at p < .05 level, but borderline findings were are also included when .05 < p < .10. In some cases, findings that
   only approached significance (p > .10) were included to demonstrate the
   direction of a suggestive relationship.

CHAPTER 6

DISCUSSION

The purpose of this study was to investigate the possible relationship between family structure and the use of corporal punishment in a sample of low-income, predominantly African American mothers. Based on the literature on the subject, a number of study hypotheses were generated:

- Indicators of parental stress as well as of parental warmth would be associated with maternal use of corporal punishment.
- If corporal punishment were normative for this population, maternal use of corporal punishment would be more likely in married, two-biological-parent families.
- Higher, potentially problematic levels of corporal punishment by mothers would be observed in surrogate-father families.
- Father influence would be more likely to operate indirectly rather than directly, as well as manifest in variables such as relationship quality or domestic violence.
- The prediction of corporal punishment by mothers might vary in some instances according to race.

Findings regarding each hypothesis are discussed here. It should be noted that spanking was almost universally reported in this sample and more than half of the respondents also reported other minor assaults such as shaking, slapping, and pushing. This is consistent with prior research, which indicates widespread use of corporal punishment in American families.

PRIMARY STUDY FINDINGS

Finding #1: Motivations for Using Corporal Punishment Are Mixed

It was hypothesized that indicators of poor parenting, as well as indicators of effective parenting, would predict maternal use of corporal punishment. This hypothesis was confirmed by the spanking analyses. For example, spanking was associated with risk factors such as maternal anxiety (psychosomatic symptoms), alcohol use, and so forth, but was also associated with greater maternal empathy, more age-appropriate child expectations, higher income, and for African Americans, greater social support. This supports the notion that some mothers may be spanking out of stress, while others are spanking more "rationally" (or that the same individual may have multiple motivations for spanking). This is consistent with prior research showing high levels of spanking in the context of both nurturing and rejecting parent-child relationships (Thompson et al., 1999; Wissow, 2001). Without more sophisticated measurement strategies, it is difficult to differentiate a potentially appropriate spanking response from an out-of-control response. This finding may help explain the many inconsistencies in the literature on the subject.

In the case of minor assault, however, there seemed to be a more straightforward pattern of association with likely indicators of compromised parenting. For example, having more age-appropriate expectations of children *decreased* the odds of minor assault (whereas it increased the odds of spanking). This was especially true regarding the high minor assault outcome. For example, a number of likely risk factors, such as AFDC receipt, a history of abuse as a child, poor relationship quality, and relationship change, were all associated with an increased likelihood of high minor assault by mothers, but not with minor assault or spanking. Some unique findings also emerged regarding the relationship between family structure and high minor assault, which shall be discussed later. Thus, there is reason to think that minor assault may be more stress driven than spanking is. High minor assault in particular may more closely resemble physical abuse than it does normative discipline.

Finding #2: Corporal Punishment by Mothers Is More Likely in Families With a Biological Father in the Home; Higher Levels of Corporal Punishment Are More Likely in Families With a Surrogate Father Figure

It was hypothesized that if corporal punishment represented normative discipline in the sample population, then maternal use of corporal punishment would be most likely in the more "traditional" family structures. This was confirmed in the case of spanking: The odds of spanking were significantly higher for respondents who resided with the biological father of their child(ren) than they were for respondents with no father figure or with a surrogate father to their child(ren) in the home. The presence of a grandparent in the home was also associated with an increased likelihood of spanking, which is consistent with the notion that multi-generational families can compensate for father absence. This may also help to explain the finding that social support increased the likelihood of spanking for African American mothers, if social support from extended family helps to mitigate the negative effects of father absence on child discipline. African Americans in this sample were more likely than whites to report a multigenerational family structure.

However, the odds of minor assault were also significantly higher for respondents living with the biological father of their child(ren) than they were for respondents with other family structures (including the multigenerational family structure). This finding is more difficult to interpret. On the one hand, it could mean that, like spanking, minor assault is also a normative discipline practice in this population, and is thus more likely to occur in intact families. On the other hand however, as discussed previously, there is also evidence to suggest that minor assault is more stress driven than spanking is. In that case, one might expect to see a *reduced* likelihood of minor assault in two-biological-parent families. The case may be, as Nobes and Smith (2002) argued, that male partners of low-income mothers sometimes put additional stress on mothers, rather than relieving the stress of poverty. Thus, the two-biological-parent family may provide greater structure and more consistent discipline for children than other family structures do, but also potentially expose them to a higher level of physical punishment by mothers.

Some different findings emerged with regard to high levels of both spanking and minor assault. For example, high spanking was not predicted by family structure or by marital status. This finding may be interpreted in several ways: It could be that high spanking is a distinct phenomenon, which is less related than lower levels of spanking to family composition, and might be better predicted by unidentified factors not included in the model. Indeed, according to the indicators of model fit used to evaluate each model, this model seemed to have relatively weak predictive power. Alternatively, it could be that the cut off used in this study to differentiate high spanking from spanking simply does not reflect a substantive difference in behavior.

Family structure, by contrast, was a significant predictor of high minor assault, although there were some differences according race. For African American mothers, the odds of high minor assault were significantly higher for mothers with surrogate fathers to their child(ren) in the home than they were for all other family structures (mothers with the biological father of their child(ren) in the home, mothers without a father figure in the home, and mothers in multigenerational families). These findings suggest that for African Americans, high minor assault may be distinct from lower levels of minor assault, and probably does not represent normative discipline. Instead, high minor assault may be an indicator of corporal punishment that is approaching physical abuse, a view consistent with the literature on the subject that shows an increased risk to children living with unrelated adult males. Indeed, one study using an expanded dataset from the South site found that children living in homes with a surrogate father were at twice the risk of having a maltreatment report than children living either in two-biological-parent or single-mother families were (Radhakrishna et al., 2001). In that study, however, it was not clear whether the mothers or the surrogate fathers were the alleged perpetrators (records available for review did not include that level of detail).

For whites, mothers with a surrogate father to their child(ren) in the home were also more likely to report minor assault than mothers with no father figure in the home or mothers in multigenerational families were. However, there was no difference in the likelihood of high minor assault between mothers with the biological father of their child(ren) in the home and mothers with a surrogate father to their child(ren) in the home. Similarly, mothers with no father figure in the home and mothers in multigenerational families were less likely than mothers with the biological father of their child(ren) in the home were to report a high level of minor assault. It appears that for low-income whites, having the biological father of one child(ren) in the home does not serve as a protective factor against potential abuse by mothers, as seems to be the case for African American mothers. This difference might be explained by the fact that African American women are much less likely than white women are to live with the biological father of their child(ren). In effect, there may be something qualitatively different about a two-biological-parent family structure for low-income African Americans and low-income whites. For African American women, coresidence with and/or marriage to the biological father of their child(ren) may be an indication of a particularly strong relationship. As Edin and Kefalas (2005) argued, African American women may "have a higher standard for marriage than whites" (p. 213).

Taken together, the findings for spanking and minor assault suggest that the relationship between family structure and corporal punishment is quite complex, varying according to race, relationship status, and the relative severity of punishment. For African American mothers in this sample, it appears that the two-biological-parent family structure and the multigenerational family structure may provide the most consistent discipline with the lowest risk of abuse, while single-mother families may be at risk of neglecting discipline, and surrogate-father families at risk of potential abuse. For low-income white mothers, the two-biological-parent family configuration may likewise provide more structure, but may also run the risk of exposing children to higher levels of physical discipline by mothers than other family configurations do. Mothers living with surrogate father figures may be less likely to discipline than other mothers are, yet more likely to use severe physical punishment. Single motherhood without cohabitation seems to offer children some protection from higher levels of physical punishment, but may also be associated with reduced structure or maternal involvement, something which can be equally as detrimental to child well-being as physical abuse is, or more so (Baumrind, 1997). For whites in this sample, the multigenerational family structure seemed to be the best option for consistent discipline with the lowest risk of abuse.

The importance of the multigenerational family structure to low-income whites might come as a surprise, given the popular association of multigenerational families with African American culture. Indeed, in this sample, African American mothers were significantly more likely than white mothers were to live in multigenerational families. However, it is well known that families also tend to "double up" in times of economic stress. Cohen and Casper (2002) found that even African American and Latino families were much less likely to be multigenerational as income increased. In the middle-class population, white multigenerational families are formed largely through divorce. One study, for example, found that almost a third of divorced white single mothers had lived with their parents at some point (Jayakody, 1998). In this sample, however, 71% of white mothers living in multigenerational families had never been married, and such mothers were significantly younger than mothers living in other family structures. This suggests that for poor whites, multigenerational families probably provide many of the same functions and supports commonly associated with the African American multigenerational family.

**Finding #3: Father Presence Has a Direct Effect on Maternal
Use of Corporal Punishment as Well as an Indirect One**

It was hypothesized that father influence might be more apparent in the
indirect measures of relationship quality and stability than in family
structure, per se. This hypothesis was not generally supported, although
indirect influences were apparent in addition to the family structure
effects previously discussed. For example, domestic violence emerged
as an important predictor of corporal punishment in a majority of the
analyses. However, perceived relationship quality and relationship stability were significant only with regard to high minor assault. Given that
only a little more than a quarter of mothers in this study were living with
the biological father of their child(ren), it may be the case that relatively
unstable, low-quality relationships are more commonplace in this population than stable, high-quality ones are. In that case, coresidence with
the biological father of one's children may be a more salient indicator
of relationship quality and stability than maternal self-report. It is also
important to remember that relatively few potential interactions were
investigated. For example, it would have been interesting to explore the
impact of relationship quality and/or relationship change on measures of
maternal mental health such as psychosomatic symptomology and alcohol use, but sample size did not allow for such analyses.

Consequently, this study offers relatively little in the way of explanations of the mechanisms by which father presence might influence
maternal use of corporal punishment. Of course, mothers living with the
biological father of their child(ren) reported significantly more family
income than any other family structure. Indeed, three-quarters of the
mothers from this sample who were living with the biological father of
their child(ren) reported incomes greater than $10,000 per year. This
might not sound like much, but considering that more than half of the
total sample reported incomes of less than $10,000 per year, it represents
a significant economic advantage. Cohabiting mothers reported the next-
highest level of income, with somewhat less than two-thirds reporting
incomes of over $10,000 per year. Less than a third of mother-headed
households (those with no partner present) reported family incomes of

over $10,000 per year, while the same proportion reported incomes of less than $5,000 per year. This is consistent with McLanahan and Sandefur's (1994) claimed that differences in income between family structures account for a substantial proportion (perhaps even the majority) of effects attributed to family structure.

At the same time, it should be noted that there was nothing in this study to suggest that biological fathers were more involved in child discipline than other father figures were. Because this study reports only maternal behavior, there is no way of knowing the nature or extent of paternal involvement in disciplinary episodes. It was *mothers*, not fathers, who reported spanking more in homes with biological fathers. Other research indicates that mothers and fathers are equally likely to use corporal punishment, although fathers may spank less frequently simply because they are less involved in day-to-day discipline (Feldman & Wentzel, 1990; Flynn, 1996; Straus, 2001). This would appear to contradict Blankenhorn's (1995) assertion that fathers serve as the strict disciplinarians in families, while mothers fulfill a more nurturing role. The finding that a multigenerational family structure might serve to ameliorate the effects of single parenthood on child discipline likewise undermines the notion that a "strong" male figure is necessary for effective child discipline.

Indeed, this study suggests that father presence does not always exert a positive influence on child discipline. At least for whites, it appears that harsh physical punishment by mothers, or even abuse, may be more likely when a father figure (either biological or surrogate) is in the home. For African Americans, the presence of a biological father also seems to increase the likelihood of harsh physical punishment by mothers, although it may decrease the likelihood of actual maltreatment. As discussed previously, these findings may reflect the reality that poor, unemployed fathers may sometimes cause stress, rather than providing assistance. Furthermore, if one assumes some level of father involvement in child discipline, it would be reasonable to believe that children in families with a father figure may be experiencing significantly higher levels of corporal punishment than children in single parent families. In fact, one study that examined child experience of corporal punishment, rather than simply maternal administration of corporal punishment, found that fathers were significantly more likely than mothers were to use severe punishment, and that children in two-parent families were much more likely to experience corporal punishment than children in single parent families were (Nobes & Smith, 2002).

This study is also consistent with the literature on the subject that shows an elevated risk for both African American and white children living with surrogate father figures. Again, the mechanism underlying this apparent risk is not clear. Some argue that surrogate father figures simply have little evolutionary incentive to invest in unrelated offspring and are therefore more likely themselves to become perpetrators than biological fathers are (Blankenhorn, 1995; Popenoe, 1996). Others point out that reconstituted families are likely to be more complex and more conflicted than other families are, both characteristics which may be associated with child maltreatment by mothers as well as surrogate fathers (Hetherington & Kelly, 2002). Finally, some argue that mothers in reconstituted families are likely to possess certain characteristics that predispose them to interpersonal conflict and lead to poor choices in mates (Radhakrishna et al., 2001). This notion is supported by findings from the bivariate analysis which indicated that respondents living with a surrogate father were significantly more likely than other children were to report physical abuse as a child, as well as domestic violence as an adult.

Finding #4: In a Uniformly Low-Income Sample, Race Still Is Salient to the Prediction of Corporal Punishment

It was hypothesized that in a uniformly low-income sample, racial and income differences in maternal use of corporal punishment might be less apparent, allowing other salient variables to emerge. Findings provided partial support for this hypothesis. A number of studies have found that psychosocial variables such as mental health, social support, and so forth, are linked with child disciplinary strategies for whites but not for African Americans (Day et al., 1998). In this study, however, a large number of such variables were significant for African American and white mothers alike.

This notwithstanding, some differences according to race were still observed. As discussed previously, race clearly interacted with family structure in the prediction of corporal punishment by mothers. In addition, however, the likelihood of minor assault was uniformly higher for African American than it was for white mothers, although there was no apparent difference in the likelihood of spanking according to race. This finding could be interpreted in a number of ways: There is evidence to suggest that minor assault—although perhaps relatively common among low-income African American mothers—is not necessarily "normative," if normative represents a deliberate approach to child discipline, rather than a reactive one. Therefore, the higher likelihood of minor assault for African American mothers than white mothers could be a sign that low-income African American mothers are experiencing a higher level of stress than low-income white mothers. This interpretation is consistent with the literature on the subject, and with findings from this study indicating a higher rate of depression and anxiety among African American mothers than among white mothers (Coiro, 2001; Wang, 2004). Indeed, in this sample, African American respondents were significantly more likely than white respondents were to report depression.

Alternatively, this finding could simply reflect a different set of parenting values among African American mothers than among white mothers. According to this study, African American mothers scored consistently "lower" on each of the parenting attitude measures than white mothers did. In other words, the African American mothers in this sample expressed higher acceptance of corporal punishment, lower empathy for children, and less age-appropriate expectations for children the white mothers did. This is consistent with other studies showing a less child-centered orientation toward child rearing among African Americans than among whites (Kelley et al., 1992). However, maternal depression is also associated with less child-centered parenting, so the issue may be one not so much of race, per se, but rather of mental health (Simons et al., 1993). Another possibility might be that greater cultural acceptance of physical discipline creates a climate in which inhibitions against assault or abuse are reduced. In other words, distressed mothers might be more likely to act on aggressive impulses in a culture that believes a certain level of physical force with children is necessary (Straus, 2000). Indeed, Crouch and Behl (2001) found that high stress was associated with child physical abuse when mothers strongly endorsed corporal punishment, but no such association existed for mothers who did not believe in corporal punishment.

MEASURES OF FAMILY COMPOSITION

In order to better distinguish between subtypes of single mothers, this study included family structure as the primary measure of family configuration, rather than marital status. As discussed previously, most of the literature regarding single motherhood has relied upon marital status as a measure of family structure, yet pathways to unmarried motherhood are diverse and highly influenced by race and class. For example, in this study, married respondents were significantly more likely to be white than to be African American, as well as more likely to live in the South than live in the other regions. Furthermore, close to two-thirds of the sample had never been married. Grouping all of those mothers into one category might obscure significant variations in their living arrangements, in particular, the roles of nonbiological and/or nonresidential father figures. It was believed that using family structure as a measure of family configuration (defined largely by the presence or absence of a father figure in the home) rather than marital status would allow for the detection of more subtle effects.

To test the hypothesis that findings might differ according to the operationalization of family composition, all analyses were run twice, first according to family structure, and then according to marital status. Contrary to expectations, the results were quite similar in most cases, with the exception of the findings regarding the multigenerational family structure, for which there is no comparable marital status. How can this finding be explained? At least for this sample, there seemed to be substantial overlap between the family structure categories and the marital status categories. For example, the biological-father family structure overlapped in large part with the "always married" marital status. Less than a third of respondents with the biological fathers of their child(ren) in the home were unmarried. Similarly, the "no father figure" category overlapped with the "never married" category. Almost 80% of the respondents living without a father figure in the home had never been married. If the biological-father family structure is roughly equivalent to the always-married status and the no-father-figure structure is roughly equivalent to the never-married category, then similar findings would be expected whichever measure of family composition was used. The similarity of findings for the surrogate-father family structure and the divorced/remarried marital status is more difficult to explain, as the overlap between the two categories was much smaller, especially for African American respondents. It may be the case that being divorced and having a surrogate father figure to one's child(ren) in the home are somewhat independent of one another, yet exert effects in the same direction.

It is not clear whether the apparent equivalence of family structure and marital status in this study is indicative of less diversity in family configuration than initially expected. It may be the case that less common family configurations simply occurred at too low a rate to significantly influence the findings. Had the sample size been larger, more specific subcategories could have been developed, perhaps allowing for the detection of more subtle differences between family structure and marital status. In particular, one might expect to find differences according to race with regard to the measure of family composition used. Because African American women are significantly less likely than white women are to marry, it is reasonable to speculate that marital relationships may be qualitatively different for African Americans and whites. Indeed, findings from this study seem to point in that direction.

CONTROL VARIABLES

Although not the main focus of this study, a brief review of findings regarding the influence of control variables is worthwhile, especially considering the dearth of information about factors other than race and class which influence corporal punishment in the sample population.

Child Characteristics

As expected, there was a significant association between child externalizing behavior and maternal use of corporal punishment in every analysis, no matter how corporal punishment was defined. Because this is a cross-sectional study, however, it cannot be said with certainty whether child externalizing behavior causes corporal punishment, or whether it is a consequence of it. Most authors today believe that the relationship is bidirectional (Parke, 2002). Other research suggests that the relationship may be bidirectional for white children, but not for African American children. In other words, child misbehavior may be associated with spanking for both African American and white children, but spanking itself may be more likely to cause problem behavior for white children than for African American children (Whaley, 2000). This debate is likely to continue unresolved for some time.

Child gender and birth weight were not significant in either of the spanking analyses, but both emerged as significant in the minor assault analyses. The finding that mothers were less likely to engage in minor assault behaviors with girls than they were with boys is consistent with the literature on the subject (Giles-Sims et al., 1995). The finding that low-birth-weight status was associated with a reduced risk of minor assault is inconsistent with some studies demonstrating increased risk for vulnerable children (Fox et al., 1995), but, as discussed previously, the literature is equivocal in this regard.

Maternal Demographics

Greater maternal age was associated with a reduced likelihood of spanking, a finding consistent with the literature that shows greater use of corporal punishment among younger mothers than among older ones (Giles-Sims et al., 1995). Larger family size was also associated with a decreased likelihood of spanking by mothers, a finding inconsistent with research showing increased risk with larger family size (Giles-Sims et al.,

1995). However, this may simply reflect the reality that older mothers tend to have more children. Alternatively, using the notion of corporal punishment as normative discipline, one might argue that poor mothers with more children are likely to become overwhelmed and thus discipline less frequently than other mothers do. Neither maternal age nor family size was associated with minor assault, again suggesting that minor assault behaviors are distinct from spanking. Similarly, having less than a high school education was associated with an increased likelihood of minor assault, but not with spanking.

Maternal Mental Health
Although the measure of potential substance abuse used in this study was very crude (a simple "yes/no" answer to a question about alcohol use), it is interesting to note that maternal alcohol use emerged as a significant predictor in every analysis. Other studies have reported similar findings (Walsh, 2002). Because the measure is so broadly defined, one really cannot speculate as to the possible nature of alcohol use in this sample. However, it does seem reasonable to postulate that even moderate alcohol use by mothers may be associated with more reactive or more impulsive parenting, as alcohol is known to affect mood and to loosen inhibitions.

Maternal psychosomatic symptomology likewise increased the odds of both spanking and minor assault, a finding consistent with research suggesting that distressed mothers are likely to be more irritable and reactive with their children than other mothers are (Simons et al., 1993). Psychosomatic symptomology was not a significant predictor of either high spanking or high minor assault, although it did approach significance in both of these analyses. It is possible that the association between psychosomatic symptomology and high spanking and/or high minor assault was simply weaker than the association with the lower levels of spanking and minor assault, or that cell size was reduced to the point where detection of a statistically significant effect was made more difficult. Both high spanking and high minor assault (and especially the latter) were relatively rare outcomes and far fewer variables emerged as significant in these analyses, especially when interaction terms were included.

Maternal depression seemed to be weakly associated with a decreased likelihood of spanking, a finding seemingly inconsistent with the literature on the subject. It is difficult to know how to interpret this finding. Perhaps if spanking is normative in this population, the lethargy often associated with depression might result in a reduction of appropriate child discipline. However, this tendency in the data did not reach the level of statistical significance, and was not observed for any of the other analyses, so it may be of no importance. Alternatively, maternal depression may not have emerged as significant simply because it overlapped, in large part, with reported psychosomatic symptomology in this sample: Approximately 80% of depressed respondents also reported a high level of psychosomatic symptomology. Still, no problem with multicollinearity was detected in the logistic regression, suggesting that the two instruments used do measure independent phenomenona, and it is known that depression and anxiety commonly cooccur (Hirshfeld, 2001). It may be the case that psychosomatic symptomology is a more sensitive measure of maternal distress for this sample than it is for the general population. Clinical research suggests that African Americans are more likely than whites are to "somaticize," or experience and label psychological distress as bodily symptoms (Dinges & Dana, 1995).

Maternal history of abuse as a child was not relevant to spanking but was weakly associated with both minor assault and high minor assault. This may be another indication that minor assault is more closely linked to child abuse than to spanking, as literature suggests that a history of abuse during childhood may increase the odds of perpetrating child abuse as an adult (Kolko, 2002).

Parenting Attitudes

As in previous studies, in this study, parenting attitudes were found to be important predictors of corporal punishment. Not surprisingly, maternal views on corporal punishment influenced the likelihood of reporting corporal punishment in virtually every analysis; the more respondents opposed the use of corporal punishment, the less likely they were to report using it. However, the relationships between the other measures of parenting attitudes and reported corporal punishment were more complex. In the case of spanking, for example, empathy for children was associated with higher odds of spanking by mothers, while age-appropriate expectations were associated with more frequent spanking. These findings may seem counterintuitive unless one views spanking as a normative discipline practice used in the context of a warm, yet demanding parent-child relationship.

As discussed previously, these relationships seemed to shift when minor assault was the outcome variable. Empathy was no longer a significant predictor, and age-appropriate expectations were associated with a *decrease* in minor assault by mothers. Religious beliefs also emerged as a significant protective factor in the minor assault analyses, with strong belief in the importance of religion to raising children being associated with lower odds of high minor assault by mothers. This is somewhat inconsistent with prior research showing a higher incidence of corporal punishment among religious conservatives, but is consistent with research demonstrating a more child-centered parenting style among highly religious African Americans (Kelley et al., 1992; Xu et al., 2000).

Extrafamilial Influences
Two measures of extrafamilial influence were included in this study: perceived social support and perceived neighborhood quality. Previous research indicates that social support may help ameliorate the relationship between maternal stress and compromised parenting, although spousal support usually emerges as more important (Kotch et al., 1999; Simons et al., 1993). Some authors argue that social support is more important to African American mothers than it is to white mothers, perhaps partly because African American families are more likely than white families are to be headed by a single mothers (Wilson, 1996). In this study, social support seemed to influence the likelihood of maternal use of corporal

punishment differentially according to race, with greater social support increasing the odds of spanking for African Americans, but decreasing them for whites. As with other findings, the finding regarding African Americans makes sense if one treats spanking as normative discipline. Support from friends and family could help single African American mothers maintain a structured family life with more consistent child discipline. Since social support apparently reduces the odds of spanking for white mothers, this finding also suggests that whites may be more prone than African Americans are to spank out of stress, an interpretation that is supported by the literature on the subject (Ahn, 1990; Alvy, 1987; Flynn, 1996).

Perceived neighborhood quality was not significant as a main factor in any of the analyses. Other studies have likewise concluded that among uniformly low-income populations, micro level factors may emerge as more important than macro level factors. For example, Marshall, English, and Stewart (2001) found that neighborhood violence and neighborhood socioeconomic status only accounted for 3% of the variance in predicting child behavior problems, whereas factors such as peer relationship and parental warmth accounted for 27% of the variance. This is one of the rationales for focusing on a high-risk sample: research that relies on predominantly white, middle-class samples may underestimate the influence of micro level factors for low-income groups if they are dwarfed by larger differences in race and income.

As discussed in the chapter entitled "Study Methodology," race x neighborhood rating emerged as significant in a number of models, but separate analyses according to race indicated that neighborhood rating was really only significant in the South, and that there was no evidence of an interactive effect according to race. Neighborhood rating appeared to be highly significant for both African American and white mothers. The reason neighborhood rating was only significant in the South is unclear, yet it might be linked to regional differences between the sites. Both the East and the Midwest samples were drawn from large, urban areas, while the South sample had a substantial rural population. In any event, the decision was made to drop the "race x neighborhood rating" term from those models where it appeared significant.

IMPLICATIONS FOR POLICY AND PRACTICE

The Role of Family Structure

Findings from this study suggest that family structure does indeed influence the likelihood of maternal use of corporal punishment in a low-income, high-risk sample, but that the relationship is far from straight-forward and appears to vary according to race, relationship status, and severity of punishment. As Wissow (2001) noted, "This diversity of contexts suggests why it may be difficult...to develop consistent profiles of parents who use spanking" (p. 127). To further complicate matters, it is not clear what the impact of corporal punishment (or a lack thereof) might be from one family to the next. Judging from the literature on the subject, the effects of corporal punishment seem to depend, in large part, on the specific context. Given these complex scenarios, it is hard to make clear-cut, global policy or practice recommendations regarding the role of family structure in corporal punishment. There are, however, several suggestive patterns in the findings that can be used to inform cautious speculation about more or less effective policy approaches.

For example, it seems clear from this study, as well as from the findings from a number of other studies, that single-parent status does not automatically put mothers at higher risk of using corporal punishment, or of using more severe corporal punishment. Indeed, single mothers in this sample were consistently less likely than mothers living with the biological father of their child(ren) or mothers living in multigenerational families were to use corporal punishment. This could be interpreted to mean that single mothers are less violent toward their children than other mothers are, but given the seemingly normative status of corporal punishment in low-income and/or African American communities, it may be more likely that single mothers are simply using less discipline.

A lack of child discipline may be equally as troubling as the possible excessive use of corporal punishment, or even more so. In fact, emotional neglect has been found to be a better predictor than harsh punishment of externalizing behaviors in children, remaining significant even after harsh punishment has been controlled for (Baumrind, 1997). As Straus (2001) noted, this finding may partially explain why corporal punishment looks relatively benign, or even beneficial, for minority children: "Corporal punishment may not be good for children but failure to properly supervise and control is even worse" (p. 199). In that case, children might be better off in a two-biological-parent family or multigenerational family than in a single-mother family because their mothers spank *more* often, rather than less often, than single mothers do.

At first blush, these findings might be seen as providing support for policies aimed at preserving the two-parent family structure, such as the Bush administration's "Healthy Marriage Initiative." This initiative, included in the welfare reform reauthorization bill, is attempting to influence marriages rates as well as marriage quality among the poor, through funding for various marriage promotion education activities and marital counseling at the community level. Proponents of these efforts argue that fathers in married-couple relationships are essential to assuring the well-being of children, women, men themselves, and overall social stability (Blankenhorn, 1995; Popenoe, 1996). This study suggests that father presence may indeed be associated with more effective maternal disciplinary behavior. However, it is not clear whether marriage promotion among the poor is the best approach to encouraging effective child discipline.

First of all, an acknowledgement of the cultural context of corporal punishment should not be construed as blanket approval for corporal punishment in low-income or ethnic minority communities. At the most basic level, simply demonstrating that corporal punishment does not harm low-income children is not sufficient. In order for corporal punishment to be recommended, there should be some evidence of *benefit* (Gershoff, 2002b). The number of studies showing neutral or possibly beneficial outcomes of corporal punishment for low-income and African American children remains relatively small. As demonstrated by this study and many others, there also is reason to believe that some proportion of corporal punishment in such communities is stress driven, and is thus likely to be more impulsive and reactive—both characteristics of discipline that are associated with negative child effects—than "controlled." Some corporal punishment may be severe enough to pose a risk of child abuse, which is clearly associated with child harm.

Findings from this study and others suggest that children raised in families with surrogate father figures may be at particular risk of overly harsh or abusive physical punishment (Daly & Wilson, 1985; Radhakrishna et al., 2001; Stiffman et al., 2002). For poor white mothers, it also appears that coresidence with the biological father of their child(ren) may be associated with a greater likelihood of abusive behavior, while for African American mothers, it may encourage higher levels of corporal punishment. This presents a conundrum: Low-income, mother-headed (no-partner) families may be less likely to provide appropriate structure and discipline for children than two-biological-parent families are, but they also offer a greater degree of safety from harsh punishment or abuse; two-biological-parent families may provide greater structure, yet be at higher risk of harsh punishment or even child maltreatment. In that case, one cannot say with certainty that either family structure is "better" for children than the other. The only thing that seems less equivocal is the risk posed by surrogate father figures: mothers living with surrogate fathers seem to be more lax than other mothers are when it comes to discipline, yet more likely to use excessive force when they do punish. This finding is consistent with other research showing a greater likelihood of externalizing problems among children raised in cohabiting families and stepfamilies (Ackerman et al., 2001; Jeynes, 2000). This suggests that, if anything, an anticohabation message might be of greater benefit to children than a promarriage message.

The problem is that the mechanisms by which father presence influences child discipline by the mother are not well understood. Marriage proponents argue that marriage raises living standards for women and children, reducing stress on mothers and bringing increased stability and security. Even cohabation may convey significant financial benefit to single mothers and children (Lerman, 2002). It seems reasonable to expect that mothers will function more effectively as disciplinarians under such conditions. However, poor-quality or transitory relationships are unlikely to benefit children, even if such relationships result in a higher living standard for the family. Moreover, in many cases, marriage does not result in financial security for poor women and children, because poor women are likely to marry poor men, who are often unemployed or only able to obtain low-income jobs (Gadsen, 1999). Poor fathers or father figures may cause stress rather than provide assistance: "If the male figure is not providing economic or social support to an already deprived household, then he could be an additional burden on the already stressed mother" (Radhakrishna et al., 2001, p. 287). Similarly, if poor women have to depend on male partners for economic support, it may be harder for them to protect themselves or their children from violence (Edin & Lein, 1997).

Other studies indicate that early ("shotgun") marriages are more likely to fail than later marriages are, resulting in increased family conflict and instability (Ludtke, 1997). This may help to explain the discrepancy in risk for high minor assault this study found between African American and white mothers living with the biological father of their child(ren). Because whites are more likely than African Americans are to marry, there may be a higher proportion of unstable or conflictual marriages among poor white mothers than among African American mothers. Similarly, a much higher percentage of unplanned or nonmarital pregnancies result in marriage for whites than do for African Americans (Mauldon, 1998). "Consequently, we walk a thin line when we attempt to promote matrimony as a public good if many or most marriages turn out to be unstable or conflict-ridden" (Frank Furstenburg, quoted in Ludtke, 1997, p. 424). In some cases, stable, single motherhood, or perhaps single parenting within a multigenerational family setting, may be a better option for protecting children from overly harsh punishment or abuse than an unstable marriage is. Even recommending marriage for low-income African Americans—the group most likely to benefit from marriage, according to this study—might not be a good idea, if African American women are already self-selecting out of dysfunctional relationships. Indeed, African

American mothers in this study were not only significantly less likely than white mothers were to marry, but were also significantly less likely to cohabit. Scott et al. (2001) found that many welfare-reliant African American women worried that marriage, or even involvement in a relationship, would not be in their children's best interests, given the pool of apparently unacceptable mates and their prior negative experiences with men.

Edin and Kefalas' (2005) longitudinal, ethnographic study of 162 low-income African American, Hispanic, and white mothers in urban Philadelphia suggested that far from disparaging marriage, poor mothers actually hold it in high regard. It is precisely because they believe that the fathers of their children (and sometimes they themselves) are not ready for the commitment, that they choose to postpone marriage (rarely do they abandon the notion entirely). Edin and Kefalas (2005) argued that low-income women have, in many ways, adopted the same high expectations of marriage as middle-class women have, and are therefore marrying later and perhaps less frequently; the difference is that for poor mothers, marriage is decoupled from the decision to have a child. Choosing to have children before marriage may be difficult for middle-class Americans to understand, yet the decision to postpone marriage to the father can be viewed as quite rational, when one considers the widespread problems of drug and alcohol abuse, domestic violence, infidelity, and criminal activity among poor men: "Indeed, it is hard to envision any type of social program that would, or even should, motivate couples to wed in the light of such serious problems" (Edin & Kefalas, 2005, p. 214).

On a more pragmatic level, it is not clear whether the "Healthy Marriage Initiative" will be very effective. As many have argued, it seems unlikely that posting billboards and handing out pamphlets will do much to change deeply personal decisions that are usually considered outside the purview of public policy (Berrick, 2005). Others argue that the intended audience is likely to be relatively unreceptive to arguably middle-class models of "talk therapy" (Cherlin, 2003). Over the past decade, similar psychoeducational interventions (ranging from premarital counseling to divorce education programs for parents) designed to prevent divorce or to mitigate the effects of postdivorce family conflict have proven relatively ineffectual (Emery, 2001).

Furthermore, in a recent national poll, only 3% of respondents agreed that promoting marriage should be a goal of the welfare system, demonstrating that the Bush administration is grossly out of step with public opinion on this issue (Lake, Snell, & Kolling, 2002). As feminists point out, turning back the clock on the family is not only impossible, but arguably undesirable. The "breakdown" of the traditional family has liberated all parties involved, and paved the way for gender equality and greater diversity of family forms (Stacey, 1998). Indeed, it is unclear why government intervention in this case is specifically aimed at the poor, despite the fact that single motherhood has increased among all groups in society, affecting children of various socioeconomic backgrounds. Ethically, it is difficult to argue that public policy should be used to "coerce" a particular group into marriage. The welfare system has long been faulted for its efforts to regulate the lives of women receiving public assistance, in particular with regard to their relationships with men (Frame, 1999).

Given the fact that neither marriage nor cohabitation is a panacea, the next logical step might be to put into place some kind of comprehensive income support for poor single mothers and their children and/or for poor multigenerational families involved in raising children. Greater economic stability and security would likely enhance parenting by single mothers, while decreasing the pressure to cohabit or to enter into dysfunctional marriages. It appears that poor single mothers may be at particular risk of perpetrating child neglect, and consequently of child welfare involvement. Contrary to popular perception, child neglect cases actually make up the vast majority of child welfare caseloads (U.S. Department of Health and Human Services, 2002). As Radhakrishna et al. (2001) argued, "Rather than penalizing or stigmatizing single mothers, providing greater services to them…may reduce the risk of child maltreatment reports" (p. 287). Such support might also help single mothers already struggling with dysfunctional relationships to gain more independence and better protect their children. Unfortunately, such a proposal seems farfetched, at least for now, especially when one considers the climate of welfare reform and the current state of the economy. Perhaps even more so than economic hardship, nonmarital childbearing, and, to a lesser extent, divorce, are considered by many Americans to be personal decisions—or more to the point, moral failures—making public support very unlikely (Nordlinger, 1998).

Another, possibly more realistic approach to encouraging effective child discipline by low-income mothers might be to shift the focus from marriage back to premarital childbirth. Levin-Epstein (2005) argued that the recent preoccupation with marriage has obscured the crucial role that could be played by sexuality education and family planning. According to Levin-Epstein (2005), the abstinence-unless-married approach taken under TANF may actually undermine the formation of high-quality, lasting first marriages. Without access to reliable information and birth control, young women are more likely to engage in unprotected sex, and consequently to bear a child at a younger age and outside of marriage. Young, unmarried mothers are 40% less likely to ever marry than other women are, and those that do are more likely to divorce, as well as to have another closely spaced child (Levin-Epstein, 2005). All of these factors are associated with higher rates of poverty and worse outcomes for children. Comprehensive sexuality education programs are demonstrated to be effective both in delaying sexual activity and in reducing teen pregnancy (Levin-Epstein, 2005). Including such a curriculum instead of, or alongside, the abstinence curriculum currently in place could well increase the number of high-quality, lasting first marriages by empowering young women to be more in control of their fertility.

According to Edin and Kefalas'study (2005), however, most young, low-income women did have information about, and access to, birth control. Most of the premarital pregnancies that occurred seemed to fall somewhere in between planned and accidental. Edin and Kefalas (2005) argued that for poor women, having children "early" is more rational than it appears because their earning potential is so low to begin with, early childbearing does not significantly affect their prospects, and indeed, may be viewed as far more meaningful work than a low-quality service job. The problem is that early childbearing is associated with detrimental outcomes for children, a reality that is not well understood in low-income communities, where good parenting is liable to be defined simply as feeding and clothing a child, keeping a roof over his or her head, and "being there" (Edin & Kefalas, 2005). The young mothers in Edin and Kefalas' study (2005) were quite confident in their parenting abilities, even at ages as young as 14. Therefore, another way to influence child outcomes in low-income single-mother families might be to provide greater education regarding child development, and a renewed commitment to early childhood programs such Head Start. As some commentators have noted, the whole movement to bring greater awareness of the importance of the period from birth to age 3 ironically seems to have resulted in the rapid expansion of products and services aimed primarily at *affluent* families, rather than at disadvantaged families, the original target of such efforts (Warner, 2005).

Corporal Punishment and Effective Discipline
Findings from this study suggest that corporal punishment may be a normative disciplinary practice among low-income mothers. Other studies have found benign or even positive effects of corporal punishment for low-income and/or African American children. Such findings would appear to contradict the almost axiomatic belief among many child advocates that corporal punishment universally indicates dysfunctional parenting, and is likely to result in considerable child harm. Thus, corporal punishment may warrant reexamination as a disciplinary technique, especially among low-income and ethnic minority groups.

Nonetheless, there is still cause for concern. The evidence regarding the effects of corporal punishment is inconclusive, although certainly weighted toward the negative as the frequency and severity of punishment increases. Similarly, even if corporal punishment is normative in some communities, it is clear that it can be used punitively and with too much force under conditions of stress. It is also most likely to be used during the toddler and preschool years when young children are most vulnerable to physical injury. Finally, as Lareau (2002) argued, an orientation toward authority may be counterproductive to economic success and social mobility in a society that values independence and self-initiative above all else. The poor and working-class children in Lareau's study (2002) did not assert themselves or negotiate their environments with the same skill, and to the same advantage, that the middle- and upper-class children did. In that case, a more egalitarian parent-child relationship might benefit poor children in the long run.

The question remains how best to influence disciplinary behavior by American parents. A number of child advocates have called for the banning of corporal punishment in the United States (Straus, 2000). The United Nations Committee on the Rights of the Child has condemned corporal punishment of children as incompatible with basic rights to bodily integrity and dignity. Corporal punishment has been outlawed in 23 (largely European) countries (Global Initiative to End All Corporal Punishment of Children, 2007). Although it is possible for parents to be criminally prosecuted under such laws, the intent is not punitive, and very few prosecutions have occurred (Durrant, 2000). Instead, these bans were conceived as more of a public marketing campaign, designed to change attitudes around corporal punishment, as well as to provide parents with information regarding alternative strategies for discipline and with social services available for support.

There is very little evidence regarding the impact of such bans on the use of corporal punishment. The most evidence comes from Sweden, where the ban has been in place since 1979. It is difficult to gauge changes in public attitudes, as the questions used in surveys over the years have changed. Depending upon which question is used, an argument can made that public support for corporal punishment has decreased (Durrant, 1999) or increased slightly (Larzelere & Johnson, 1999). As of 1994, a little more than half of those surveyed indicated complete opposition to all physical discipline, but a substantial proportion still agreed that corporal punishment was sometimes necessary, or would be used when they were angry enough (Larzelere & Johnson, 1999). Similarly, most Swedish youths today report never having experienced corporal punishment;

of those who do report corporal punishment, most say they were hit only once or twice (Durrant, 1999). This is in contrast to near universal use of corporal punishment by Swedish mothers in the 1950s (Durrant, 1999). However, one study that compared rates of corporal punishment in the generation preceding the ban with rates of corporal punishment 15 years after the ban found only a modest decrease in use (32% in 1994 versus 34% in the generation preceding the ban) (Statistics Sweden, 1996, cited in Larzelere, 2000). In other words, the use of corporal punishment had probably decreased significantly prior to the ban.

It is also unclear how the decline in corporal punishment has affected rates of child abuse in Sweden. Paradoxically, there was a dramatic increase in criminal physical abuse of children under 7 years old during the period from 1981 to 1994, and the rate of out-of-home removal of children increased by 7% from 1982 to 1995 (Wittrock, 1995, cited by Larzelere, 2000). There are a variety of possible explanations for such trends, but Larzelere and Johnson (1999) speculated that decreased use of spanking may actually contribute to the escalation of disciplinary interactions, thus increasing the likelihood of an angry or impulsive response by the parent. Earlier studies found roughly equivalent or even higher rates of child abuse in Sweden following the ban than they did in the United States at the same time (but with higher rates of spanking in the United States), although the circumstances may have changed since then (Gelles & Edfeldt, 1986). Perhaps most discouragingly, almost half of the so-called "support and care" preventive measures offered to families under the spanking ban were actually out-of-home removal (Larzelere, 2004), arguably a very "punitive" outcome for legislation originally intended to help parents.

It is important to remember, however, that these bans have been driven primarily by an expanding notion of children's universal rights, rather than by evidence that corporal punishment is harmful to children (Bussman, 2004). Indeed, many believe that the debate surrounding corporal punishment should be influenced as much by values as it is by evidence, given the weighty moral and ethical issues involved in inflicting physical pain on the most vulnerable, powerless group in society (Straus, 2001).

Clearly, it is not enough to argue that corporal punishment is effective. Moreover, as many commentators have pointed out, this type of violence is no longer permitted against women or even animals, so why should children not be similarly protected? Gershoff (2002b) argued that the bar should be set very high in order to justify using physical force against children: corporal punishment must be shown not only to be harmless, but to exert a *positive* effect on child outcomes—more positive than the effects of alternative disciplinary tactics that do not involve physical pain.

There are, however, several problems with the child rights position. Firstly, the notion of children's rights within families, although extremely important, is complicated by the fact that children are dependents, not peers. Even parents committed to nonviolence do, and must, routinely "coerce" their children, especially small children, in order to keep them safe and healthy. In many cases, physical coercion may be involved, for example, strapping an unwilling toddler into a car seat, or holding down a wriggling child in order to change a diaper. Many parents in the United States strongly believe that corporal punishment falls into the same category of parenting practices as these examples do, and the evidence is not clear whether they are wrong, at least in the case of mild, instrumental spanking. Condemning corporal punishment according to values alone begs the question: Whose values count? If working-class and/or some ethnic minority groups prefer corporal punishment to a reasoning style of discipline, does that mean they have the wrong parenting values? This is a very touchy and complicated question. It is one thing to say that disadvantaged groups in society are under stress that may negatively affect parenting (a seemingly sympathetic response), but another thing altogether to imply that one culture's normative approach to child discipline is inherently dysfunctional, or even unethical.

Some authors argue that the overrepresentation of African American children in the public child welfare system can be explained, in part, by different views on corporal punishment held by white social workers and African American parents (Mosby et al., 1999). Several studies have shown that social workers are likely to treat corporal punishment as confirmation of inappropriate parenting (Cox & Ephross, 1998; Siegel,

1994). Ashton (2001) found that entry-level social service workers were more likely to make a report of suspected child maltreatment if they disapproved of corporal punishment. Mosby et al. (1999) found that white social service workers were reluctant to participate in a pilot program to use African American elders as parenting mentors because

> they would reinforce the 'wrong' parenting styles...They considered [support for corporal punishment to be] evidence that, as a community, African Americans did not have proper parenting skills, rather than as evidence that the preferences of the community were different but equally appropriate. (p. 451)

Chibnall et al. (2003) likewise found that African American child welfare caseworkers perceived their white colleagues as being racially biased when it came to distinguishing physical discipline from physical abuse in African American families.

Whether these differences in attitudes result in the inappropriate removal of African American children from their families is unclear. The literature on the subject is inconsistent in this regard, with some studies finding apparent evidence of racial bias at various decision points within the public child welfare system (referral, investigation, substantiation, out-of-home placement, and reunification), but others finding no such evidence, especially when risk factors other than race are taken into account (Ards, Chung, & Myers, 1999; Derezotes, Poertner, & Testa, 2005; Eckenrode, Powers, Doris, Munsch, & Bolger, 1988). Rolock and Testa (2005) found that white caseworkers were more likely to substantiate cases than African American caseworkers were, and were particularly likely to substantiate physical abuse allegations, but were not more likely to substantiate cases involving African American children than they were those involving white children.

Given such concerns, an educational approach to minimizing the potential dangers of corporal punishment seems preferable to a legislative approach. A ban on corporal punishment would likely be viewed by poor and minority groups as a particular assault on their culture and preferred parenting style. It is no secret that the public child welfare system—correctly or not—is already perceived by many poor people as racist and punitive. The example of Sweden suggests that a ban on corporal punishment might indeed be associated with increased out-of-home placement of children, since dollars for preventative services always seem to be in short supply. In any case, it seems unlikely that corporal punishment could be banned in the United States any time in the near future, given the support for corporal punishment among the population, as well as the enduring hostility to government intrusion into the family arena.

The challenge to using an educational approach in this case is that the message is complex and not necessarily amenable to sound bites and sloganeering; for example, a simple "don't spank" message runs the risk of backfiring in communities where spanking is the primary form of child discipline. Automatically equating corporal punishment with inappropriate parenting, or even child abuse, is likely to alienate potential audiences of an anticorporal punishment message. Contrary to the model that sees the use of corporal punishment as "just a failure to understand 'proper parenting,'" the literature on the subject suggests that beliefs about corporal punishment tend to be deeply and sincerely held, and thus quite resistant to change (Mosby et al., 1999, p. 451). Similarly, a clear distinction is made in the African American community between appropriate and excessive physical discipline (discipline, not punishment, is the preferred terminology) (Kelley et al., 1992). Mosby et al.'s (1999) elders defined appropriate discipline as a consistent, immediate response (spanking) combined with "teaching" (reasoning) and respectful language—but noted that all children are different, so different discipline strategies may be needed from one child to the next. Apart from the spanking, this does not sound altogether different from what the experts might recommend.

Whaley (2000) argued that culturally competent parenting instruction needs to explore the functional significance of corporal punishment before arriving at any conclusions regarding the appropriateness of the approach. If corporal punishment is what he calls "parent centered," that is, overly focused on obedience to the parent at the expense of the child's own needs, then it should be treated as problematic. However, if corporal punishment is "child centered," or designed to help children learn how to regulate themselves and become socially responsible adults, there may be less cause for concern. Alternative disciplinary approaches still can and should be introduced for the simple reason that excessive reliance on any one approach is likely to be less effective and potentially more harmful than using a range of approaches is (Larzelere, 2000). Encouraging parents to try alternative disciplinary approaches and perhaps decrease their use of corporal punishment is likely to be more successful when preexisting beliefs about corporal punishment are treated with respect and empathy (Davis, 1999). For example, several studies suggest that African American parents are open to using "response cost" (taking away privileges) as an alternative to corporal punishment (Kelley et al., 1992; Whaley, 2000).

Larzelere (2000) recommended using the metaphor of a parenting "toolbox." According to this metaphor, spanking is one possible tool among many other, potentially useful tools for child discipline. For all parents, regardless of whether they use corporal punishment or not, discipline is most likely to be effective when it is delivered early in an interaction, consistently, calmly, and with an explanation. The actual choice of disciplinary strategy (time-out, spanking, verbal reprimand, response cost, etc.), should be flexible and responsive, customized to the particular circumstances and the unique characteristics of any given child. It could be added that spanking is not necessary because other techniques work equally as well; given the potential for harm, the most prudent path might be to avoid it. However, for parents who do choose to use corporal punishment, guidelines can be offered to maximize effectiveness and minimize harm:

1. Don't use with children under 2 or with teenagers.
2. Give a single warning before spanking.
3. Keep it mild in nature: One or two light spanks on the bottom with an open hand.
4. Don't use it when feeling excessively angry or out of control.

5. Combine with reasoning.
6. Do it in private (avoid public shaming).

> Try another strategy when mild spanking doesn't work—don't escalate the spanking. (Larzelere, 2000, pp. 215–216)

To this list one might also add, "Don't spank under the influence of drugs or alcohol." Although this message is probably too complex for a brief television or radio spot, it could be developed as a print advertisement and/or a handout to be distributed by health care professionals, educators, and other social service workers. In Sweden, for example, the government sent every family a booklet on child discipline following passage of the spanking ban (Straus, 2001). Of course, positive parenting messages are already out there, but as Straus (2001) noted, any mention of spanking is usually avoided—or at the most, spanking is sort of vaguely discouraged in passing—leaving parents with little guidance in this regard.

A number of studies suggest that many parents who believe in corporal punishment still try to avoid using it (Straus, 2001). Indeed, considering the fact that daily frustration with young children is almost universally reported (89% of mothers in one study), it is clear that most parents are not using spanking as their only or primary response to problematic behavior (Wissow, 2001). Similarly, although the proportion of parents who report using corporal punishment remains high, especially among those with young children, public support for corporal punishment has fallen dramatically in past several decades. For example, the percentage of Americans who agreed with the statement, "A good hard spanking is sometimes necessary" dropped 20 percentage points in just 10 years (75% agreed in1988; 55% in 1998) (Straus, 2001). Half as many parents today report using corporal punishment as did in 1975, and fewer parents report using an object to spank (Straus, 2001). In other words, the tide has already turned in some respects. There is also reason to believe that concerns about child abuse are shared by the African American community. For example, Mosby et al.'s (1999) elders voiced the perception that young African American mothers today are using physical discipline too often in anger, and too often accompanied by verbal abuse. The public may be more open than is commonly believed to an antispanking campaign.

IMPLICATIONS FOR FUTURE RESEARCH

Despite several decades of research, there remain numerous outstanding questions regarding the causes and consequences of corporal punishment. As many authors have noted, truly innovative research designs are needed to capture the complexity of dynamics surrounding corporal punishment. Simply assessing the extent and nature of corporal punishment has proven to be a daunting task. Perhaps the biggest problem has been the lack of standard definitions or measures of corporal punishment (Gershoff, 2002a). Until some kind of standardization is achieved, interpreting the research will continue to be a matter of comparing apples to oranges. Similarly, future studies need to move away from methods that rely on retrospective recall over long time periods. Newer methods such as parental diaries, nightly phone calls, and beeper methods may aid in this regard (Parke, 2002).

However, the meaning and impact of corporal punishment cannot be understood simply using a tallying method, no matter how accurate. Laboratory experiments, once a popular way to study corporal punishment, are no longer viewed as ethically acceptable, although they may be helpful in terms of better understanding alternative disciplinary strategies. Moreover, it is difficult to gauge the extent to which laboratory findings can be generalized to real life settings. Parenting practices such as corporal punishment seem to be mediated by complex processes that are challenging to model and test. As Deater-Deckard and Dodge (1997a) suggested, there seem to be a number of curvilinear patterns of association, according to severity of punishment, race, age of child, parent and child temperament, and so forth. The detection of such indirect effects, however, requires large samples and sophisticated statistical techniques. Marshall et al. (2001) suggested that future studies use structural equation modeling to explore the indirect pathways by which fathers, in particular, affect child functioning. Ethnographic methods, often overlooked, also hold some promise for the study of family systems and the interplay of spousal relations with parent-child interactions and overall family culture (Gershoff, 2002a). Holden (2002) emphasized the need to learn about children's experiences and perceptions of corporal punishment, a challenging undertaking considering children's limited ability to self-reflect, and their tendency to rationalize parental behavior (Deater-Deckard et al., 2003).

This study highlights, in particular, the need for more research regarding the role of fathers in child discipline. Unlike much of the research regarding father absence, this study strongly suggests that fathers *are* important when it comes to child discipline, but that the mechanism(s) by which fathers influence corporal punishment are unclear. Under what conditions are fathers likely to be directly involved in child discipline? Are fathers more apt to be "strict" and administer more severe punishment, as suggested by Blankenhorn (1996), or more likely to serve as more recreational, "fun" playmates for their children (Wissow, 2001)? The literature that exists on the subject is sparse and inconsistent, as mothers have been the primary respondents in studies regarding parenting practices and attitudes. Indeed, one study found direct father effects on child outcomes only when fathers themselves were questioned about their own involvement (Black, Dubowitz, & Starr, 1999). This reinforces the need for multiple informants and measures in conducting family research. This is especially true with regard to understanding *children's* experiences, rather than parental behavior. For example, Nobes and Smith (2002) found that low-income children living in two-parent homes were twice as likely as other children were to experience severe or frequent physical punishment when fathers' participation in child discipline was taken into account.

This study also illustrates the need for more information regarding surrogate fathers and the roles they play in families. Again, existing evidence is limited and often contradictory. On the one hand, several studies have reported little difference in child outcomes according to the biological or even residential status of the father (Dubowitz et al., 2000; Furstenburg & Harris, 1993), and it does appear that remarriage and cohabitation often lift mothers and children out of poverty (Lerman, 2002). On the other hand, other studies have documented an increased risk of child abuse in households with surrogate fathers, which is consistent with the findings from this study (Finkelhor et al., 1990; Margolin, 1992; Radhakrishna et al., 2001). The research reviewed likewise suggests a variety of other negative child outcomes associated with remarriage and the presence of stepparents in the home (Hetherington & Stanley-Hagen, 1999). Even in "successful" stepfamilies, it appears that a close bond between stepchildren and stepparents is slow to form and relatively uncommon, although this evidence is drawn primarily from studies of white families (Radhakrishna et al., 2001).

It has been suggested that biological status/residential status of fathers is particularly unimportant in the African American community, where fatherhood may be defined very broadly (Dubowitz et al., 2000). This study, however, found that a mother's coresidence with the biological father of her child(ren) was a protective factor for African American children, but not for white children, a finding which highlights the need for more research regarding the roles played by minority fathers. Several studies have found that father involvement exerts a greater influence on African American children than it does on white children, and that involvement often has relatively little to do with financial contributions to the household (Chase-Lansdale et al., 1999; Coley, 1998; Dubowitz et al., 2000; Marshall et al., 2001). There is also evidence to suggest that remarriage is more likely to benefit African American children than it is white children (Hetherington & Stanley-Hagan, 1999).

By and large, however, relatively little research attention has been paid to this much maligned population of African American fathers (Hamer, 2001). As a number of authors point out, African American fathers are almost universally stereotyped as deadbeat dads who are either weak, criminals, or simply do not care about their children (Gadsen, 1999; Hamer). This study also suggests that multigenerational families are an important yet understudied group, in both low-income African American and low-income white communities. Often portrayed as dysfunctional African

American matriarchies (Gadsen), it appears that multigenerational families may, in some instances, best approximate the two-biological-parent family structure, at least in terms of child discipline.

More generally, it is clear that more research is needed with diverse populations. Attitudes toward child rearing and child discipline practices seem to vary according to culture (whether culture is defined by socioeconomic status, race/ethnicity, religion, geographical area, and so forth), but mainstream parenting advice is typically based on a white, middle-class model of family life. A number of authors have hypothesized that child discipline which is congruent with community norms is likely to be the most effective kind of disciple, and the least harmful to children (Deater-Deckard & Dodge, 1997a; Parke, 2002), but only a handful of studies exist to bolster this claim. Others point to harmful cultural practices such as female circumcision, and argue that cultural rights do not supercede the rights of children (Straus, 2001). Using a less extreme example, Lareau (2002) argued that low-income parents may be doing their children a disservice, at least in terms of social mobility, by socializing them into excessive obedience to authority and a culture of learned helplessness. Although staying out of trouble at school has been represented as one of the beneficial effects of corporal punishment among low-income children, "good" behavior comes at a high cost if it means passivity and a lack of participation in one's education.

What about parents who choose never to spank? As statistics demonstrate, this is a relatively small group of individuals, yet it would be interesting to know more about them, given the general consensus among experts that spanking should be avoided. Davis (1999) identified only three unpublished dissertations regarding nonspanking parents:

> Reasons they gave for not hitting were that they hated being hit when they were children, they realized spanking did not work, they stopped after having more children, they remember feeling embarrassed and degraded when hit as children, and they respected the rights of children because "they are people too." (p. 493)

These rationales are consistent with the kind of human rights orientation to nonspanking reflected by the spanking bans in Europe. However, these samples were extremely small (19 in one study and 15 in another) and drawn from highly educated, arguably privileged populations (e.g., parents from the Northeastern coast and parents involved in the Parent-Teacher Association).

Motivations for not spanking may well vary according to cultural norms. For some parents, nonspanking "may be more a function of lack of involvement with their children than of mastery of less aversive disciplinary strategies" (Wissow, 2001, p. 128). Not much is known about the effects of nonspanking on children. Although one might assume that the negative outcomes of corporal punishment are bypassed, there is evidence to suggest that in some cases, nonspanking may be associated with increased parental frustration, verbal/psychological abuse, and impulsive punishment (Larzelere & Johnson, 1999). The misuse or overuse of alternative strategies, such as time-outs, has also likewise been linked to negative child outcomes. Larzelere (2000) argued that just as there is insufficient evidence to ban corporal punishment, there is insufficient evidence to unequivocally embrace nonspanking, given the known dangers of permissive parenting.

It would be helpful to know more about how parents decide to stop spanking. A significant proportion of parents apparently start out believing in and practicing spanking, but subsequently "convert" to nonspanking (Gershoff, 2002a). Davis (1999) found that parents who stopped spanking or tried to stop spanking were motivated by a variety of factors, including obvious fearfulness on the part of their child(ren); counterproductive responses from their child(en); discomfort with feeling out of control; memory of their own negative experiences with spanking; discovery of new ideas about child development and nonviolence; agency regulations against spanking; and pressure from spouses, family, and friends. Furthermore, the "quitting" process was described as being quite complex, requiring considerable willpower, and often involving so-called relapses along the way. McLoyd et al. (2007) found that African American endorsers and nonendorsers of corporal punishment did not differ significantly in their use of corporal punishment, suggesting that simple attitude change is not enough. Thus, Davis (1999) argued that we should conceptualize a parent's relationship to corporal punishment as a "career," characterized by "starts and stops, lapses and oscillations" (p. 507). A greater understanding of this process is needed in order to design effective parent education efforts: "We do not know whether parents benefit more from instruction in alternative disciplinary techniques or from the fact that some classes and seminars provide a rationale for desistance, offer social support for quitting, and furnish new meanings for spanking" (Davis, 1999, p. 508).

LIMITATIONS OF THE STUDY

This study suffers from a number of methodological limitations. Like most research regarding corporal punishment, it uses cross-sectional data, rather than longitudinal data. A cross-sectional design is appropriate for describing the characteristics and attitudes of a population, allows the simultaneous analysis of multiple variables, and may be useful in hypothesizing explanatory relationships between variables, but it cannot be used to establish causality (Fortune & Reid, 1999). Given the dearth of existing research in this area, a cross-sectional study is a useful and important first step, but the findings must be considered to be, above all else, exploratory. Although family structure and corporal punishment appear to be associated, this study does not "prove" that differences in family structure are responsible for different patterns in corporal punishment.

The possibility that the dependent variable actually caused the independent variable(s), or that a third variable altogether caused both the independent and dependent variables, cannot be ruled out. It seems unlikely that use of corporal punishment would determine family configuration or relationship quality. However, reverse causation or reciprocal/circular causation may well have existed in the case of child externalizing behavior. Shared method variance may have been a problem as well, since both maternal and child behaviors were reported by the mother. This may have resulted in an exaggeration of the apparent relationship between child externalizing behavior and corporal punishment. With regard to third-variable causation, a number of potentially confounding variables were controlled for, including race, education, AFDC status, and maternal age, in order to minimize the possibility of finding a spurious relationship between family configuration and corporal punishment.

The combining of subsamples from multiple study sites represents another significant limitation. Although sample size and diversity were enhanced by combining sites, there is also the very real possibility that study site influenced the findings in ways that were not immediately apparent. Significant differences in race, age, marital status, and AFDC status were found between the sites. Moreover, the sites differed in terms of geographic region, urban/rural composition, and study selection criteria. A number of precautions were taken to try to minimize the untoward influence of these differences, as described in the chapter entitled "Study Methodology." In one case (the race x neighborhood quality interaction), an apparent finding was clearly the result of differences between sites, and that term was subsequently dropped from the model. Particular attention was paid to the possible influence of site on findings regarding family structure. All findings were cross-checked across sites in order to confirm that apparent relationships between family structure and corporal punishment were consistent.

Generalizability of findings is limited by reliance on a convenience sample with very particular characteristics. Because this sample is extremely low income, and has multiple risk factors, the relationships observed between family structure and corporal punishment cannot be said to exist in other populations. In particular, one should be careful not to generalize the findings regarding race to the middle-class, where differences in parenting according to race often seem to be muted or to disappear altogether (Lareau, 2002). Moreover, this sample may not be representative of the population from which it is drawn. With the exception of the South site, potential participants were not selected randomly, and little is known about the characteristics of those who chose to participate compared with those who did not. Conversely, the advantage of using such a sample was that it allowed the detection of more subtle influences on corporal punishment. When more economically heterogeneous samples are used, such influences may be obscured by large differences due to poverty (Kelley et al., 1992).

There are also a number of measurement issues that must be taken into account. In particular, this study suffers from the same flaw observed in so much of the research regarding corporal punishment: the failure to adequately define corporal punishment. For example, the single question that asked about spanking did not describe in any detail what is meant by the term. It is not known whether the spankings were light or hard; delivered on the hand or buttocks; delivered with a hand or an object; resulted in an injury; and so forth. Because interpretations of the word "spank" may be widely divergent, it is difficult to know with certainty what actually transpired. The same is true for many of the questions included in the Minor Assault scale (e.g., "grabbed" or "shook"). Furthermore, no information regarding the contexts of the disciplinary incidents was collected. It is not known what provoked the punishments, whether they were delivered in an impulsive or a controlled fashion; how the children responded; or the level of warmth in the parent-child relationships. In effect, the measures used to assess the use of corporal punishment were rather crude, limiting the extent to which the phenomena under study can be accurately described or understood.

Furthermore, the rates of corporal punishment reported here are almost certainly underestimated. As discussed, LONGSCAN investigators modified the original Conflict Tactic Scale (CTS) so that the highest frequency response category was changed from "more than 20 times in the past year" to "more than 5 times in the past year." Gauging from other studies, typical rates of corporal punishment are much higher, especially with children in the age group represented in this sampie (approximately 4 years old) (Giles-Sims et al., 1995). The cutoffs established between "low" and "high" levels of spanking and minor assault were likewise made somewhat arbitrarily, since no information is available relating to population norms using this modified version of the CTS. As such, the cut offs may not reflect a qualitative difference in behavior, and should not be viewed as establishing a threshold for harmful levels of corporal punishment, as contrasted to harmless ones. In any case, reports of corporal punishment relied on retrospective recall, which was likely to be at least somewhat inaccurate, especially considering the lengthy time frame (1 year). Corporal punishment was also self-reported and may therefore have been subject to social desirability bias, especially considering that some proportion of this sample was likely involved with child welfare services. Finally, it should be reiterated that the children in this study have probably experienced corporal punishment at the hands of other adults in their lives. This study reports only on maternal disciplinary behavior and consequently cannot be said to accurately reflect children's experiences.

The family configuration variables may also have been somewhat flawed, due to the low rates of divorce and remarriage in the sample. In order to construct a large enough group of respondents living with surrogate fathers, remarried and cohabiting respondents were combined in one category. Divorced and remarried respondents were likewise combined, even though it would have been preferable to have separate categories for stepfamilies and cohabiting families. Although imperfect, this categorization has some support in existing literature on the subject. Previous research suggests that rather than ameliorating the effects of divorce, remarriage potentially may be as harmful as divorce, or even more so (Hetherington & Kelly, 2002). In that case, remarried respondents should not be included with always-married respondents, despite the important increase in income that accompanies remarriage. This study, however, was not able to test whether or not the likelihood of corporal punishment by mothers might vary according to the legal status of the surrogate father figure.

Furthermore, it is not clear from this study whether the men defined as surrogate father figures did, in fact, function as such, or were viewed as such by either the mothers or children in question. Surrogate-father status was determined simply by presence in the home, a somewhat crude approximation. It is likely that some proportion of cohabiting boyfriends are not expected to assume a paternal role, and even in stepfamilies, it appears that stepfathers may remain relatively uninvolved in stepparenting (Radhakrishna et al., 2001). Moreover, it is quite possible that other adult males in children's lives, such as uncles, coaches, and so forth, may have functioned as father figures. Therefore, this study only provides an indirect glimpse into the possible influence of surrogate fathers on corporal punishment by mothers.

Measures of relationship quality were also less than precise. For example, perceived relationship quality was derived from scores on the Autonomy and Relatedness Inventory (ARI), yet no established norms or cut point exist for this instrument, so scores were recoded into a dummy variable (low quality/high quality) based on the median split. This may partially explain why relationship quality, contrary to prior research, did not emerge as a significant predictor of corporal punishment by mothers in most of the analyses. Perhaps the cut off used to distinguish a low-quality relationship from a high-quality relationship did not, in fact, capture a substantive difference between the two categories. Moreover, the domestic violence measure used did not distinguish between past and present domestic violence, so it is not clear whether violence in the respondent's relationship at the time of data collection influenced the likelihood of corporal punishment by mothers, whether past violence had an influence, and which of these had a greater influence. Intuitively, it seems reasonable to assume that both would play a role, but this study cannot distinguish between the two.

The race variable must also be treated with some caution. Due to the low occurrence of races/ethnicities other than African American and white in this sample, whites, Hispanics, and other races/ethnicities were combined into one category. Although imperfect, this categorization has some support in the literature. Previous research suggests that Hispanic mothers (by the far the largest proportion of the non-African American/nonwhite race categories) may be more similar to white mothers in terms of corporal punishment than they are to African American mothers (Flynn, 1996; McLeod et al., 1994). The percentage of respondents who fell into the "other" category was so small (2.4%), that the effect of collapsing that category into the white category was probably negligible. Nonetheless, it is possible that including respondents who identified as nonwhite in the "white" category introduced a degree of error into the analysis.

CONCLUSION

Despite its limitations, this study offers a new, more comprehensive model for theorizing the relationship between family structure and corporal punishment than those previously available. The findings suggest that low-income fathers do influence maternal disciplinary behavior, although perhaps not in the generally expected direction. Low-income never-married mothers, often assumed to be at higher risk of using corporal punishment, actually appear less likely to use corporal punishment than their married or partnered counterparts are. Whether this represents an advantage or a disadvantage for children of single mothers is a matter of some interpretation. On the one hand, if corporal punishment represents normative, appropriate discipline in this population, then single mothers may be at risk of overly permissive or neglectful parenting. On the other hand, corporal punishment that is too severe, or is used too frequently, poses a danger to child development. Therefore, child physical abuse may be more likely to occur in married or partnered households, especially those containing a surrogate father figure, than it is in single-mother households.

This complexity illustrates the difficulty of advocating cookie-cutter policy responses to the so-called breakdown of the American family. Although there is general agreement that functional, stable, two-married-parent families represent the optimal environment for child rearing, such families are not so easy to come by, especially for poor women. Coontz (2005) argued that the shift toward a love-based paradigm of marriage has made some marriages much more egalitarian and deeply satisfying than the "typical" duty-based, obligatory marriage of the past. Stable, modern marriage truly is something to celebrate and support. At the same time, however, this new model of marriage can also cause significant psychological distress and family dysfunction when a marriage proves unsatisfying:

> The very things that make marriage so potentially satisfying are for the most part inseparable from the things that make unsatisfying marriage less bearable. The same personal freedoms that allow people to expect more from their married lives also allow them to get more out of staying single and given them more choice than ever before in history about whether or not to remain together. (Coontz, 2005, p. 311)

Thus, marriage today is inherently less stable than it was in the past, and more importantly, perhaps, "bad" marriages may be more likely to negatively affect all members of a family than they used to be. Divorce, although an important option for ending dysfunctional marriages, clearly is painful, and sometimes even traumatic, for both adults and children. In light of such realities, it can be argued that single motherhood represents a rational choice for family formation.

Indeed, several contemporary family researchers have concluded that far from disparaging marriage, low-income mothers hold marriage in high esteem and aspire to marrying one day (Cherlin, 2004; Edin & Kefalas, 2005). As Edin and Kefalas (2005) discovered, low-income women have adopted the same expectations of marriage as more affluent women have: not only do they expect an economic partnership, but they also demand emotional accountability. Too often in disadvantaged neighborhoods, however, neither is commonly forthcoming, and "no marriage education or relationship skills program can permanently immunize couples against the effects of chronic economic and neighborhood stress" (Coontz, 2005, p. 289). In that case, single motherhood actually may benefit children, at least as compared to being raised in a conflict-ridden or even violent family. For these aforementioned reasons, child bearing and rearing are likely to become increasingly detached from marriage, at least among low-income groups.

The question remains of how better to support low-income single mothers in their parenting, or more specifically in this case, with child discipline. Some single mothers might benefit from greater father involvement, although this study offers relatively little insight into the role played by fathers in influencing maternal disciplinary behavior, or into the nature of their own direct involvement in child discipline. More research is needed to better understand the roles fathers play, both positive and negative, in child discipline. Such insight would inform efforts to encourage father involvement in single-mother families, as well as indicating other areas for possible intervention. For example, if it turned out that the primary way in which fathers support maternal disciplinary behavior is by reducing maternal stress (which may be economic and/or emotional), then there might be mechanisms by which public policy could fulfill this role without attempting to orchestrate choices in family formation and structure.

Similarly, more information is needed regarding the circumstances under which father presence may contribute to harsher or more frequent corporal punishment by mothers, as seems to be the case for some reconstituted (both cohabiting and remarried) families. In reality, very little is known about these often marginalized families. Even in the case of stepfamilies, which one might think would be better recognized in the legal arena, the role of stepparents is poorly defined or frankly overlooked by public policy (Mason, 1998). Considering the high rates of cohabitation and remarriage in the United States, this is a significant oversight that potentially endangers the welfare of children. Again, this highlights the need for policies that specifically target and support effective *parenting*, regardless of family configuration.

How corporal punishment fits into society's notion of effective parenting is likely to remain a sticky issue for policy makers. Some argue that the debate around corporal punishment should be driven as much by values as by evidence; the "violent socialization" of children is seen as inherently inhumane and unethical, regardless of its potential efficacy in suppressing unwanted behaviors (Gershoff, 2002b; Straus, 2000). The problem with this position is that it begs the question: Whose values count? Because the evidence does not support a simple condemnation of corporal punishment, the issue—at least for now—seems to boil down to a question of personal choice. Therefore, rather than demonizing corporal punishment (or simply avoiding an open discussion of its use), a better strategy might be to discuss spanking as one possible tool among many other, potentially useful tools for child discipline. For parents who do choose to use corporal punishment, guidelines could be offered to maximize effectiveness and minimize harm. This would seem to be both a more respectful approach to parenting differences in society, and a more pragmatic strategy for protecting children.

In the meantime, opponents of corporal punishment might shift their focus from changing public policy to changing public opinion through respectful, nonsensational educational campaigns regarding the potential risks of and effective alternatives to corporal punishment. Indeed, public support for corporal punishment has waned considerably in just the past few decades, a trend that seems likely to continue in the future. It is important to remember that in Sweden, the first country to ban corporal punishment, support for and use of corporal punishment had already decreased prior to the ban. In effect, social change paved the way for the legislation, rather than the legislation dictating social change. Given the strong emphasis on individual rights, personal freedom, and family privacy in the United States, public education, rather than top-down legislation, would seem a more viable approach to diminishing the practice of corporal punishment.

REFERENCES

Achenbach, T., & Edelbrock, C. (1981). Behavioral problems and competencies reported by parents of normal and disturbed children age four through sixteen. *Monographs of the Society for Research in Child Development, 46*, 1–82.

Achenbach, T. (1991). *Manual for the child behavior checklist/4–18 and 1991 profile*. Burlington, VT: University of Vermont, Department of Psychiatry.

Ackerman, B., D'Eramo, K., Umylny, L., Schultz, D., & Izard, C. (2001). Family structure and the externalizing behavior of children from economically disadvantaged families. *Journal of Family Psychology, 15*(2), 288–300.

Ahn, H. (1990). *Intimacy and discipline in family life: A cross-cultural analysis with implication for theory and practice in child abuse prevention*. Unpublished doctoral dissertation, University of California, Berkeley, CA.

Alvy, K. (1987). *Black parenting: Strategies for training*. New York: Irvington Publishers.

Amato, P. (1999). Children of divorced parents as young adults. In E. Hetherington (Ed.), *Coping with divorce, single parenting and remarriage: A risk and resiliency perspective* (pp. 147–163). Mahwah, NJ: Lawrence Erlbaum Associates.

Amato, P., & Booth, A. (1997). *A Generation at risk: Growing up in an era of family upheaval*. Cambridge, MA: Harvard University Press.

Amato, P., & Keith, B. (1991). Parental divorce and adult well-being: A meta-analysis. *Journal of Marriage and the Family, 53*(1), 43–58.

Amey, C., & Albrecht, S. (1998). Race and ethnic differences in adolescent drug use: The impact of family structure and the quantity and quality of parental interaction. *Journal of Drug Issues, 28*(2), 283–298.

Ammerman, R. (1990). Predisposing child factors. In R. Ammerman & M. Hersen (Eds.), *Children at risk: An evaluation of factors contributing to child abuse and neglect* (pp. 199–224). New York: Plenum Press.

Aquilino, W. (1996). The life course of children born to unmarried mothers: Childhood living arrangements and young adult outcomes. *Journal of Marriage and the Family, 58*(2), 293–310.

Arbuthnot, J., & Gordon, D. (1996). Does mandatory divorce education for parents work? A six-month outcome evaluation. *Family and Conciliation Courts Review, 34*(1), 60–81.

Ards, S., Chung, C., & Myers, S. (1999). The effects of sample selection bias on racial differences in child abuse reporting. *Child Abuse & Neglect, 23*(12), 1211–1215.

Arias, I., & Pape, K. (1999). Psychological abuse: Implications for adjustment and commitment to leave violent partners. *Violence and Victims, 14*, 55–67.

Ashton, V. (2001). The relationship between attitudes toward corporal punishment and the perception and reporting of child maltreatment. *Child Abuse & Neglect, 25*(3), 389–399.

Ateah, C., & Durrant, J. (2005). Maternal use of physical punishment in response to child misbehavior: Implications for child abuse prevention. *Child Abuse & Neglect, 29*(2), 169–185.

Baldwin, A., Baldwin, C., & Cole, R. (1990). Stress-resistant families and stress-resistant children. In J. Rolf, A. Masten, D. Chichetti, K. Neuchterlein, & S. Weintraub (Eds.), *Risk and protective factors in the development of psychopathology* (pp. 257–280). New York: Cambridge University Press.

Bank, L., Forgatch, M., Patterson, G., & Fetrow, R. (1993). Parenting practices of single mothers: Mediators of negative contextual factors. *Journal of Marriage and the Family, 55*(2), 371–384.

Baum, C., & Forehand, R. (1981). Long term follow-up assessment of parent training by use of multiple outcome measures. *Behavior Therapy, 12,* 643–652.

Baumrind, D. (1967). Child care practices anteceding three patterns of preschool behavior. *Genetic Psychology Monographs, 75,* 43–88.

Baumrind, D. (1972). An exploratory study of socialization effects on Black children: Some Black-White comparisons. *Child Development, 43*(1), 261–267.

Baumrind, D. (1997). Necessary distinctions. *Psychological Inquiry, 8*(3), 176–229.

Baumrind, D., Larzelere, R., & Cowan, P. (2002). Ordinary physical punishment: Is it harmful? Comment on Gershoff (2002a). *Psychological Bulletin, 128*(4), 580–589.

Baumrind, D., & Owens, E. (2001). *Does normative physical punishment by parents cause detrimental child outcomes: A prospective longitudinal study.* Manuscript submitted for publication.

Bavolek, S. (1984). *Handbook for the AAPI (Adult-Adolescent Parenting Inventory).* Park City, UT: Family Development Resources, Inc.

Bavolek, S., Kline, D., McLaughlin, J., & Publicover, P. (1979). Primary prevention of child abuse: Identification of high-risk adolescents. *Child Abuse & Neglect, 3,* 1071–1080.

Belsky, J., & Vondra, J. (1989). Lessons from child abuse: The determinants of parenting. In D. Cicchetti & V. Carlson (Eds.), *Child maltreatment: Theory and research on the causes and consequences of maltreatment* (pp. 153–202). New York: Cambridge University Press.

Belsky, J. (1993). Etiology of child maltreatment: A developmental-ecological analysis. *Psychological Bulletin, 114*(3), 413–434.

Bendel, R., & Afiffi, A. (1977). Comparison of stopping rules in forward regression. *Journal of the American Statistical Association, 72*, 46–53.

Berrick, J. (2005). Marriage, motherhood and welfare reform. *Social Policy & Society, 4*(2), 133–145.

Bianchi, S. (1995). The changing demographic and socioeconomic characteristics of single parent families. In M. Hanson, M. Heims, D. Julian, & M. Sussman (Eds.), *Single parent families: Diversity, myths, and realities* (pp. 71–98). New York: Haworth.

Biller, H., & Kimpton, J. (1997). The father and the school-aged child. In M. Lamb (Ed.), *The role of the father in child development* (pp. 143–161). New York: John Wiley & Sons, Inc.

Black, M., Dubowitz, H., & Starr, R. (1999). African American fathers in low income, urban families: Development and behavior of their 3-year-old children. *Child Development, 70*(4), 967–978.

Blankenhorn, D. (1995). *Fatherless America: Confronting our most urgent social problem.* New York: HarperCollins Publications.

Bluestone, C., & Tamis-LeMonda, C. (1999). Correlates of parenting styles in predominantly working- and middle-class African American mothers. *Journal of Marriage and the Family, 61*(4), 881–893.

Bower, M., & Knutson, J. (1996) Attitudes toward physical discipline as a function of disciplinary history and self-labeling as physically abused. *Child Abuse & Neglect, 20*(8), 689–699.

Bradley, K., Boyd-Wickizer, J., Powell, S., & Burman, M. (1998). Alcohol screening questionnaires in women: A critical review. *Journal of the American Medical Association, 280*, 166–171.

Bramlett, M., & Mosher, W. (2002, July). Cohabitation, marriage, divorce and remarriage in the United States: Data from the national survey of family growth (DHHS Publication No. [PHS] 2002-1998). *Vital Health Statistics, 23*(22), 1–93. Hyattsville, MD: National Center for

Health Statistics. Retrieved November 5, 2007, from http://www.cdc. gov/nchs/data/series/sr_23/sr23_022.pdf

Bray, J. (1999). From marriage to remarriage and beyond: Findings from the Developmental Issues in StepFamilies Research Project. In E. Hetherington (Ed.), *Coping with divorce, single parenting and remarriage: A risk and resiliency perspective* (pp. 253–272). Mahwah, NJ: Lawrence Erlbaum Associates.

Broadhead, W., Gehlbach, S., de Gruy, F., & Kaplan, B. (1988). The Duke-UNC functional social support questionnaire. *Medical Care, 26*(7), 709–721.

Bronfenbrenner, U. (1979). *The Ecology of human development: Experiments by nature and design.* Cambridge, MA: Harvard University Press.

Brown, J., Cohen, P., Johnson, J., & Salzinger, S. (1998). A longitudinal analysis of risk factors for child maltreatment: Findings of a 17-year prospective study of officially recorded and self-reported child abuse and neglect. *Child Abuse & Neglect, 22*(11), 1065–1078.

Brown, G., & Moran, P. (1997). Single mothers, poverty and depression. *Psychological Medicine, 27*, 21–33.

Bumpass, L., & Lu, H. (2000). Trends in cohabitation and implications for children's family contexts in the United States. *Population Studies, 54*, 29–41.

Bussman, K. (2004). Evaluating the subtle impact of a ban on corporal punishment of children in Germany. *Child Abuse Review, 13*, 292–311.

Butler, M., & Jones, A. (1979). The health opinion survey reconsidered: Dimensionality, reliability, and validity. *Journal of Clinical Psychology, 35*(3), 554–559.

Caplan, P., Watters, G., White, G., Parry, R., & Bates, R. (1984). Toronto multiagency child abuse research project: The abused and the abuser. *Child Abuse & Neglect, 8*(3), 343–351.

Carlson, M., & Corcoran, M. (2001). Family structure and children's behavioral and cognitive outcomes. *Journal of Marriage and the Family, 63*(3), 779–792.

Cazenave, N., & Straus, M. (1990). Race, class, network embeddedness and family violence: A search for potent support systems. In M. Straus & R. Gelles (Eds.), *Physical violence in American families: Risk factors and adaptations in violence in 8,145 families* (pp. 321–340). New Brunswick, NJ: Transaction Books.

Chaffin, M., Kelleher, K., & Hollenberg, J. (1996). Onset of physical abuse and neglect: Psychiatric, substance abuse, and social risk factors from prospective community data. *Child Abuse & Neglect, 20*(3), 191–203.

Chase-Lansdale, P., Cherlin, A., & Kiernan, K. (1995). The long-term effects of parental divorce on the mental health of young adults: A developmental perspective. *Child Development, 66*(6), 1614–1634.

Chase-Lansdale, P., Gordon, R., Coley, R., Wakschlag, L., & Brooks-Gunn, J. (1999). Young African American multigenerational families in poverty, In E. Hetherington (Ed.), *Coping with divorce, single parenting and remarriage: A risk and resiliency perspective* (pp. 165–191). Mahwah, NJ: Lawrence Erlbaum Associates.

Cherlin, A. (1999). Going to extremes: Family structure, children's well-being, and social science. *Demography, 36*(4), 421–428.

Cherlin, A. (2003). Should the government promote marriage? *Contexts, 2*(4), 22–29. Retrieved October 5, 2005, from http://www.contextsmagazine.org/content_sample_v2-4.php

Cherlin, A. (2004). The deinstitutionalization of American marriage. *Journal of Marriage and the Family, 66*(4), 848–861.

Cherlin, A., & Fomby, P. (2002). *A closer look at changes in children's living arrangements in low-income families* (Policy brief. Welfare, Children and Families: A Three-City Study). Johns Hopkins

University, Baltimore. Retrieved April 16, 2003, from http://www.jhu.edu/~welfare/work_paper_2-20.pdf

Chibnall, S., Dutch, N., Jones-Harden, B., Brown, A., Gourdine, R., Smith, J., et al. (2003). *Children of color in the child welfare system: Perspectives from the child welfare community.* Washington, DC: U.S. Department of Health and Human Services, Children's Bureau, Administration for Children and Families. Retrieved July 11, 2005, from http://nccanch.acf.hhs.gov/pubs/otherpubs/children/children.pdf

Cohen, P., & Casper, L. (2002). In whose home? Multigenerational families in the United States, 1998–2000. *Sociological Perspectives, 45*(1), 1–20.

Coiro, M. (2001). Depressive symptoms among women receiving welfare. *Women & Health, 32*(1/2), 1–25.

Coley, R. (1998). Children's socialization experiences and functioning in single-mother households: The importance of fathers and other men. *Child Development, 69*(1), 219–230.

Collins, K., Schoen, S., Duchon, L., Simantov, E., & Yellowitz, M. (1999). *Health concerns across a woman's lifespan: The Commonwealth Fund 1998 survey of women's health.* New York: The Commonwealth Fund. Retrieved February 15, 2005, from http://www.cmwf.org/usr_doc/Healthconcerns__surveyreport.pdf

Cookston, J. (1999). Parental supervision and family structure: Effects on adolescent problem behaviors. *Journal of Divorce and Remarriage, 32*(1/2), 107–122.

Coolahan, K., McWayne, C., Fantuzzo, J., & Grim, S. (2002). Validation of a multidimensional assessment of parenting styles for low-income African-American families with preschool children. *Early Childhood Research Quarterly, 17*, 356–373.

Coontz, S. (1992). *The way we never were: American families and the nostalgia trap.* New York: Basic Books.

Coontz, S. (2005). *Marriage, a history: From obedience to intimacy or how love conquered marriage*. New York: Viking.

Coontz, S., & Folbre, N. (2002). *Marriage, poverty and public policy: A discussion paper from the Council on Contemporary Families*. Retrieved April 19, 2003, from http://www.prospect.org/webfeatures/2002/03/coontz-s-03-19.html

Coulton, C., Korbin, J., & Su, M. (1999). Neighborhood and child maltreatment: A multi-level study. *Child Abuse & Neglect, 23*(11), 1019–1040.

Cox, C., & Ephross, P. (1997). *Ethnicity and social work practice*. New York: Oxford University Press.

Cox, C., Kotch, J., & Everson, M. (2003). A longitudinal study of modifying influences between domestic violence and child maltreatment [Special issue: LONGSCAN and family violence]. *Journal of Family Violence, 18*(1), 5–17.

Crouch, J., & Behl, L. (2001). Relationships among parental beliefs in corporal punishment, reported stress, and physical child abuse potential. *Child Abuse & Neglect, 25*(3), 413–419.

Curtis, P., & Schneider, M. (1996). *Final report: Consortium for longitudinal studies of child maltreatment: The Capella project* (Report to the National Center on Child Abuse and Neglect, Administration on Children and Families, U.S. Department of Health and Human Services). Chicago: Juvenile Protective Association.

Daly, M., & Wilson, M. (1985). Child abuse and other risks of not living with both parents. *Ethology & Sociobiology, 6*, 197–210.

Darling, N., & Steinberg, L. (1993). Parenting style as context: An integrative model. *Psychological Bulletin, 113*(3), 487–496.

Davis, P. (1999). Corporal punishment cessation: Social contexts and parents' experiences. *Journal of Interpersonal Violence, 14*(5), 492–510.

Day, R. (1998). *Social fatherhood: Conceptualizations, compelling research, and future directions* (Working paper). Philadelphia: National Center on Fathers and Families. Retrieved February 4, 2002, from http://www.ncoff.gse.upenn.edu/briefs/daybrief.pdf

Day, R., Peterson, G., & McCracken, C. (1998). Predicting spanking of younger and older children by mothers and fathers. *Journal of Marriage and the Family, 60*(1), 79–94.

Deater-Deckard, K., & Dodge, K. (1997a). Externalizing behavior problems and discipline revisited: Nonlinear effects and variation by culture, context, and gender. *Psychological Inquiry, 8*(3), 161–175.

Deater-Deckard, K., & Dodge, K. (1997b). Spare the rod, spoil the authors: Emerging themes in research on parenting and child development. *Psychological Inquiry, 8*(3), 230–235.

Deater-Deckard, K., Lansford, J., Dodge, K., Pettit, G., & Bates, J. (2003). The development of attitudes about physical punishment: An 8-year longitudinal study. *Journal of Family Psychology, 17*(3), 351–360.

DeMaris, A., & Greif, G. (1997). Single custodial fathers and their children: When things go well. In A. Hawkins & D. Dollahite (Eds.), *Generative fathering: Beyond deficit perspectives* (pp. 134–146). Thousand Oaks, CA: Sage Publications.

Demo, D., & Acock, A. (1996). Family structure, family process, and adolescent well-being. *Journal of Research on Adolescence, 6*(4), 457–488.

Derezotes, D., Poertner, J., & Testa, M. (Eds.) (2005). *Race matters in child welfare: The overrepresentation of African American children in the system.* Washington, DC: The CWLA Press.

Dinges, N., & Dana, C. (1995). Symptom expression and the use of mental health services among American ethnic minorities. In J. Aponte, R. Young Rivers, & J. Wohl (Eds.), *Psychological interventions and cultural diversity* (pp. 40–56). Needham Heights, MA: Allyn & Bacon.

Dubowitz, H. (May, 1996). *A longitudinal study of child neglect: Final report* (Report to the National Center on Child Abuse and Neglect, Administration on Children and Families, U.S. Department of Health and Human Services). Department of Pediatrics, University of Maryland School of Medicine, Baltimore.

Dubowitz, H., Black, M., Kerr, M., Starr, R., & Harrington, D. (2000). Fathers and child neglect. *Archives of Pediatrics & Adolescent Medicine, 154*, 135–141.

Dubowitz, H., Black, M., Cox, C., Kerr, M., Litrownik, A., Radhakrishna, A., et al. (2001). Father involvement and children's functioning at age 6 years: A multisite study. *Child Maltreatment, 6*(4), 300–309.

Dubowitz, H., Black, M., Kerr, M., Hussey, J., Morrel, T., Everson, M., et al. (2001). Type and timing of mothers' victimization: Effects on mothers and children. *Pediatrics 107*(4), 728–735.

Dunn, J., Deater-Deckard, K., Pickering, K., & O'Connor, T. (1998). Children's adjustment and prosocial behavior in step-, single-parent, and non-stepfamily settings: Findings from a community study. *Journal of Child Psychology and Psychiatry, 39*(8), 1083–1095.

Durrant, J. (1999). Evaluating the success of Sweden's corporal punishment ban. *Child Abuse & Neglect, 23*(5), 435–448.

Durrant, J. (2000). Trends in youth crime and well-being since the abolition of corporal punishment in Sweden. *Youth & Society, 31*(4), 437–455.

Eckenrode, J., Powers, J., Doris, J., Munsch, J., & Bolger, N. (1988). Substantiation of child abuse and neglect reports. *Journal of Consulting and Clinical Psychology, 56*(1), 9–16.

Edin, K., & Lein, L. (1997). *Making ends meet: How single mothers survive welfare and low-wage work.* New York: Russell Sage.

Edin, K., & Kefalas, M. (2005). *Promises I can keep: Why poor women put motherhood before marriage.* Berkeley, CA: University of California Press.

Egan-Sage, E., & Carpenter, J. (1999). Family characteristics of children in cases of alleged abuse and neglect. *Child Abuse Review, 8,* 301–313.

Ellison, C., Musick, M., & Holden, G. (November, 1999). *The effects of corporal punishment on young children: Are they less damaging for conservative Protestants?* Paper presented at the Society for the Scientific Study of Religion, Boston.

Emery, R. (2001). Interparental conflict and social policy. In J. Grych & F. Fincham (Eds.), *Interparental conflict and child development: Theory, research and applications* (pp. 417–439). New York: Cambridge University Press.

Erkman, F. & Rohner, R. (2006). Youths' perceptions of corporal punishment, parental acceptance and psychological adjustment in a Turkish metropolis. *Cross-Cultural Research, 40*(3), 250–267.

Ewing, J. (1984). Detecting alcoholism: The CAGE questionnaire. *Journal of the American Medical Association, 252*(14), 1905–1907.

Executive Office of the President, Council of Economic Advisors (2000)., Chapter 5: The changing American family. In *Executive Office of the President* (pp. 165–197). Washington, DC: United States Government Printing Office. Retrieved February 4, 2002, from http://frwebgate. access.gpo.gov/cgi-bin/multidb.cgi

Fantuzzo, J., Boruch, A., Beriama, R., & Atkins, M. (1997). Domestic violence and children: Prevalence and risk in 5 major U.S. cities. *Journal of the American Academy of Child and Adolescent Psychiatry, 36*(1), 116–122.

Fass, P., & Mason, M. (2000). *Childhood in America.* New York: New York University Press.

Feldman, S., & Wentzel, K. (1990). The relationship between parenting styles, sons' self-restraint, and peer relations in early adolescence. *Journal of Early Adolescence, 10,* 439–454.

Fell, E., Walker, H., Severson, H., & Ball, A. (2000). Proactive screening for emotional/behavioral concerns in Head Start preschools: Promising practices and challenges in applied research. *Behavioral Disorders, 26*, 13–25.

Fields, J. (2003). *Children's living arrangements and characteristics: March 2002. Current population reports, P20–547.*Washington, DC: U.S. Census Bureau. Retrieved November 5, 2007, from http://www. census.gov/prod/2003pubs/p20-547.pdf

Finkelhor, D., Hotaling, G., Lewis, I., & Smith, C. (1990). Sexual abuse in a national survey of adult men and women: Prevalence, characteristics and risk factors. *Child Abuse & Neglect, 14*(1), 19–28.

Flynn, C. (1996). Normative support for corporal punishment: Attitudes, correlates and implications. *Aggression and Violent Behavior, 1*(1), 47–55.

Fortune, A., & Reid, W. (1999). *Research in social work* (3rd ed.). New York: Columbia University Press.

Fox, R., Platz, D., & Bentley, K. (1995). Maternal factors related to parenting practices, developmental expectations, and perceptions of child behavior. *The Journal of Genetic Psychology, 156*(4), 431–441.

Frame, L. (1999). Suitable homes revisited: An historical look at child protection and welfare reform. *Children and Youth Services Review, 21*(9/10), 719–754.

Fergusson, D., Lynskey, M., & Horwood, L. (1996). Child sexual abuse and psychiatric disorder in young adulthood. 1. Prevalence of sexual abuse and factors associated with sexual abuse. *Journal of the American Academy of Child and Adolescent Psychiatry, 35*(10), 1355–1364.

Furstenberg, F., & Cherlin, A. (1991). *Divided families: What happens to children when parents part.* Cambridge, MA: Harvard University Press.

Furstenberg, F., & Harris, K. (1993). When fathers matter/why fathers matter: The impact of paternal involvement on the offspring of adolescent mothers. In D. Rhode & A. Lawson (Eds.), *The politics of pregnancy* (pp. 189–215). New Haven, CT: Yale University Press.

Gadsden, V. (1999). Black families in intergenerational and cultural perspective. In M. Lamb (Ed), *Parenting and child development in "nontraditional" families* (pp. 221–246). Mahwah, NJ: Lawrence Erlbaum Associates.

Gavanas, A. (2001). *Masculinizing fatherhood: Sexuality, marriage and race in the U.S. fatherhood movement.* Unpublished doctoral dissertation, Stockholm University, Stockholm, Sweden.

Gazmararian, J., James, S., & Lepkowski, J. (1995). Depression in Black and White women: The role of marriage and socioeconomic status. *Annals of Epidemiology, 5*(6), 455–463.

Gelles, R. (1989). Child abuse and violence in single-parent families: Parent absence and economic deprivation. *American Journal of Orthopsychiatry, 59*(4), 492–501.

Gelles, R., & Edfeldt, A. (1986). Violence towards children in the United States and Sweden. *Child Abuse & Neglect, 10*(4), 501–510.

Gershoff, E. (2002a). Corporal punishment by parents and associated child behaviors and experiences: A meta-analysis and theoretical review. *Psychological Bulletin, 128*(4), 539–579.

Gershoff, E. (2002b). Corporal punishment, physical abuse, and the burden of proof: Reply to Baumrind, Larzelere, and Cowan (2002), Holden (2002), and Parke (2002). *Psychological Bulletin, 128*(4), 602–611.

Gilbert, N. (1995) *Welfare justice: Restoring social equity.* New Haven, CT: Yale University Press.

Gilbert, N. (2002). *Transformation of the welfare state: The silent surrender of public responsibility.* New York: Oxford University Press.

Giles-Sims, J., Straus, M., & Sugarman, D. (1995). Child, maternal, and family characteristics associated with spanking. *Family Relations, 44*(2), 170–176.

Global Initiative to End All Corporal Punishment of Children. (2007). *Ending legalised violence against children: Global report 2007.* Retrieved from the May 3, 2008, from http://www.endcorporalpunishment.org/pages/pdfs/reports/GlobalReport2007.pdf

Golombok, S. (1999). New family forms: Children raised in solo mother families, lesbian mother families, and in families created by assisted reproduction. In L. Balter & C. Tamis-LeMonda (Eds.), *Child psychology: A handbook of contemporary issues* (pp. 429–446). Philadelphia: Psychology Press, Taylor & Francis Group.

Golombok, S. (2000). *Parenting: What really counts?* London: Routledge.

Golombok, S., Tasker, F., & Murray, C. (1997). Children raised in fatherless families from infancy: Family relationships and the socioemotional development of children of lesbian and single heterosexual mothers. *Journal of Child Psychology and Psychiatry and Allied Disciplines, 38*(7), 783–791.

Gottman, J., Katz, L., & Hooven, C. (1997). *Meta-emotion: How families communicate emotionally.* Mahwah, NJ: Lawrence Erlbaum Associates.

Graziano, A., & Namaste, K. (1990). Parental use of physical force in child discipline: A survey of 679 college students. *Journal of Interpersonal Violence, 5*(4), 449–463.

Grogger, J., Karoly, L., & Klerman, A. (2002). *Consequences of welfare reform: A research synthesis.* Santa Monica, CA: RAND Corporation. Retrieved April 19, 2003, from http://www.acf.dhhs.gov/programs/opre/welfare_reform/rand_report.pdf

Gross, D., Sambrook, A., & Fogg, L. (1999). Behavior problems among young children in low-income urban day care centers. *Research in Nursing Health, 22*(1), 15–25.

Grotevant, H., & Kohler, J. (1999). Adoptive families. In M. Lamb (Ed.), *Parenting and child development in "nontraditional" families* (pp. 161–190). Mahwah, NJ: Lawrence Erlbaum Associates.

Grych, J., & Fincham, F. (1992). Interventions for children of divorce: Toward greater integration of research and action. *Psychological Bulletin, 111*(3), 434–454.

Gunnoe, M., & Mariner, C. (1997). Toward a developmental-contextual model of the effects of parental spanking on children's aggression. *Archives of Pediatrics & Adolescent Medicine, 151,* 768–775.

Hall, L., & Kiernan, B. (1992). Psychometric assessment of a measure of the quality of primary intimate relationships. *Health Values, 16*(4), 30–38.

Hamer, J. (2001). *What it means to be daddy: Fatherhood for Black men living away from their children.* New York: Columbia University Press.

Hamilton, S., & MacQuiddy, S. (1984). Self-administered behavioral parent-training: Enhancement of treatment efficacy using a time-out signal seat. *Journal of Clinical Child Psychology, 13*(1), 61–69.

Hamilton, B., Martin, J., & Ventura, S. J. (2006). Births: Preliminary data for 2005 (DHHS Publication No. [PHS] 2007-1120). *National Vital Statistics Reports, 55*(11), 1–15. Hyattsville, MD: National Center for Health Statistics. Retrieved November 5, 2007, from http://origin.cdc.gov/nchs/data/nvsr/nvsr55/nvsr55_11.pdf

Hampden-Thompson, G., & Pong, S-L. (2005). Does family policy environment moderate the effect of single parenthood on children's academic achievement? A study of 14 European countries. *Journal of Comparative Family Studies, 36*(2), 227–248.

Hashima, P., & Amato, P. (1994). Poverty, social support, and parental behavior. *Child Development, 65*(2), 394–403.

Hawkins, A., & Dollahite, D. (1997). Single custodial fathers and their children: When things go well. In A. Hawkins & D. Dollahite (Eds.), *Generative fathering: Beyond deficit perspectives* (pp. 134–146). Thousand Oaks, CA: Sage Publications.

Heffner, R., & Kelley, M. (1987). Mothers' acceptance of behavioral interventions for children: The influence of parent race and income. *Behavior Therapy, 2*, 153–163.

Hemenway, D., Solnick, S., & Carter, J. (1994). Child-rearing violence. *Child Abuse & Neglect, 18*(12), 1011–1020.

Hetherington, E. (1999). Should we stay together for the sake of the children? In E. Hetherington (Ed.), *Coping with divorce, single parenting and remarriage: A risk and resiliency perspective* (pp. 93–116). Mahwah, NJ: Lawrence Erlbaum Associates.

Hetherington, E., & Kelly, J. (2002). *For better or worse.* New York: W. W. Norton.

Hetherington, E., & Stanley-Hagan, M. (1999). Stepfamilies. In M. Lamb (Ed.), *Parenting and child development in "nontraditional" families* (pp. 137–160). Mahwah, NJ: Lawrence Erlbaum Associates.

Hirshfeld, R. (2001). The comorbidity of major depression and anxiety disorders: Recognition and management in primary care. *Primary Care Companion Journal of Clinical Psychiatry, 3*(6), 244–254.

Holden, G., Coleman, S., & Schmidt, K. (1995). Why 3-year-old children get spanked: Parent and child determinants as reported by college-educated mothers. *Merrill-Palmer Quarterly, 41*, 431–452.

Holden, G., Miller, P., & Harris, S. (1999). The instrumental side of corporal punishment: Parents' reported practices and outcome expectancies. *Journal of Marriage and the Family, 61*, 908–919.

Holden, G. (2002). Perspectives on the effects of corporal punishment: Comment on Gershoff (2002a). *Psychological Bulletin, 128*(4), 590–595.

Houseknecht, S., & Sastry, J. (1996). Family "decline" and child well-being: A comparative assessment. *Journal of Marriage and the Family, 58*(3), 726–739.

Hunter, W. M., Cox, C. E., Teagle, S., Johnson, R. M., Mathew, R., Knight, E. D., et al. (2003). *Measures for assessment of functioning and outcomes in longitudinal research on child abuse. Volume 1: Early childhood.* Retrieved May 12, 2008, from http://www.iprc.unc.edu/longscan/pages/measures/Baseline/index.html

Hunter, W., & Everson, M. (1991). *Mother's History of Loss and Harm* (Unpublished instrument). University of North Carolina, Chapel Hill, NC.

Ispa, J., & Halgunseth, L. (2004). Talking about corporal punishment: Nine low-income African American mothers' perspectives. *Early Childhood Research Quarterly, 19,* 463–484.

Jaccard, J. (2001). *Interaction effects in logistic regression.* Thousand Oaks, CA: Sage Publications.

Jackson, J. (1997). Issues in need of initial visitation: Race and nation specificity in the study of externalizing behavior problems and discipline. *Psychological Inquiry, 8*(3), 176–229.

Jayakody, R. (1998). Race differences in intergenerational financial assistance: The needs of children and the resources of parents. *Journal of Family Issues, 19*(5), 508–533.

Jeynes, W. (2000). The effects of several of the most common family structures on the academic achievement of eighth graders. *Marriage and Family Review, 30*(1/2), 73–97.

Jones, C., Tepperman, L., & Wilson, S. (1995). *Futures of the family.* Englewood Cliffs, NJ: Prentice Hall.

Jones, S. (2000). *Youth exposure to community violence: Neighborhood and familial risk.* Unpublished predissertation paper, Yale University, New Haven, CT.

Kelley, M., Power, T., & Wimbush, D. (1992). Determinants of disciplinary practices in low-income Black mothers. *Child Development, 63*(3), 573–582.

224   CORPORAL PUNISHMENT AND LOW-INCOME MOTHERS

Kelly, J. (2000). Children's adjustment in conflicted marriage and divorce: A decade review of research. *Journal of the American Academy of Child and Adolescent Psychiatry, 39*(8), 963–973.

Kessler, R., McGongle, K., Zhao, S., Nelson, C., Hughes, H., Eshelman, S., et al. (1994). Lifetime and 12-month prevalence of DSM-III-R psychiatric disorders in the U.S. *Archives of General Psychiatry, 51*, 8–19.

Kleist, D. (1999). Single-parent families: A difference that makes a difference? *The Family Journal: Counseling and Therapy for Couples and Families, 7*(4), 373–378.

Kolko, D. (2002). Child physical abuse. In J. Myers, L. Berliner, J. Briere, C. Hendrix, C. Jenny, & T. Reid (Eds.), *APSAC handbook of child maltreatment* (2nd ed.) (pp. 21–54). Thousand Oaks, CA: Sage Publications.

Knight, E., Runyan, D., Dubowtiz, H., Brandford, C., Kotch, J., Litrownik, A., & Hunter, W. (2000). Methodological and ethical challenges associated with child self-report of child maltreatment. *Journal of Interpersonal Violence, 15*(7), 760–775.

Korenmen, S., Kaestner, R., & Joyce, T. (2001). Unintended pregnancy and the consequences on nonmarital childbearing. In L. Wu & B. Wolfe (Eds.), *Out of wedlock: Causes and consequences of nonmarital fertility* (pp. 259–286). New York: Russell Sage Foundation.

Kotch, J., Browne, D., Dufort, V., & Winsor, J. (1999). Predicting child maltreatment in the first 4 years of life from characteristics assessed in the neonatal period. *Child Abuse & Neglect, 23*(4), 305–319.

Kreider, R., & Fields, J. (2002). *Number, timing and duration of marriages and divorces: 1996. Current Population Reports, P70–80.* Washington, DC: U.S. Census Bureau. Retrieved November 5, 2007, from http://www.census.gov/prod/2002pubs/p70-80.pdf

Lake, C., Snell, A., & Kolling, S. (2002). *Poll results on welfare reform.* Washington, DC: Lake, Snell, Perry & Associates, Inc. Retrieved

February 11, 2002, from http://www.raisethefloor.org/lsp_welfare_ memo.pdf

Lamb, M. (1997). Fathers and child development: An introductory overview and guide. In M. Lamb (Ed.), *The role of the father in child development* (pp. 1–8). New York: John Wiley & Sons, Inc.

Lamb, M., Sternberg, K., & Thompson, R. (1997). The effects of divorce and custody arrangements on children's behavior, development and adjustment. *Family and Conciliation Courts Review, 35*(4), 393–404.

Lamb, M. (Ed.) (1999). *Parenting and child development in "nontraditional" families*. Mahwah, NJ: Lawrence Erlbaum Associates.

Lansford, J., Dodge, K., Malone, P., Bacchini, D., Zelli, A., Chaudhary, N., et al. (2005). Physical discipline and children's adjustment: Cultural normativeness as a moderator. *Child Development, 76*(6), 1234–1246.

Lareau, A. (2002). Invisible inequality: Social class and childrearing in Black families and White families. *American Sociological Review, 67*(5), 747–776.

Larzelere, R. (2000). Child outcomes of nonabusive and customary physical punishment by parents: An updated literature review. *Clinical Child and Family Psychology Review, 3*(4), 199–221.

Larzelere, R. (2004). *Sweden's smacking ban: More harm than good.* Essex, England: Families First. Retrieved November 12, 2005, from http://www.families-first.org.uk/art/sweden.pdf

Larzelere, R., & Johnson, B. (1999). Evaluations of the effects of Sweden's spanking ban on physical child abuse rates: A literature review. *Psychological Reports, 83*, 381–392.

Larzelere, R., Sather, P., Schneider, W., Larson, D., & Pike, P. (1998). Punishment enhances reasoning's effectiveness as a disciplinary response to toddlers. *Journal of Marriage and the Family, 60*(2), 388–403.

Larzelere, R., & Smith, G. (2000, August). *Controlled longitudinal effects of five disciplinary tactics on antisocial behavior.* Paper presented at the annual convention of the American Psychological Association, Washington, DC.

Lerman, R. (2002). *Married and unmarried parenthood and economic well-being: A dynamic analysis of a recent cohort.* Washington, DC: The Urban Institute. Retrieved April 19, 2003, from http://www.urban.org/url.cfm?ID=410540

Levin-Epstein, J. (2005). *To have and to hold: Congressional vows on marriage and sex.* Washington, DC: Center for Law and Social Policy. Retrieved June 2, 2005, from http://www.clasp.org/publications/have_and_hold.pdf

Levine, M., Doueck, H., Freeman, J., & Compaan, C. (1996). African-American families and child protection. *Children & Youth Services Review, 18*(8), 693–711.

Litrownik, A., Newton, R., Hunter, W., English, D., & Everson, M. (2003). Exposure to family violence in young at-risk children: A longitudinal look at the effects of victimization and witnessed physical and psychological aggression. *Journal of Family Violence, 18*(1), 59–73.

Loeber, R., Drinkwater, M., Yin, Y., Anderson, S., Schmidt, L., & Crawford, A. (2000). Stability of family interaction from ages 6 to 18. *Journal of Abnormal Child Psychology, 28*, 353–369.

Ludtke, M. (1997). *On our own: Unmarried motherhood in America.* New York: Random House.

Lutenbacher, M. (2001). Psychometric assessment of the adult-adolescent parenting inventory in a sample of low-income single mothers. *Journal of Nursing Measurement, 9*(3), 291–308.

Maccoby, E., & Martin, J. (1983). Socialization in the context of the family: Parent-child interaction. In P. Mussen (Ed.), *Handbook of child psychology* (Volume IV) (pp. 1–101). New York: John Wiley & Sons.

MacMillan, A. (1957). The health opinion survey: Technique for estimating the prevalence of psychoneurotic and related types of disorder in communities. *Psychological Reports, 3*, 325–339.

Mahoney, A., Donnelly, W., & Lewis, T. (2000). Mother and father self-reports of corporal punishment and severe physical aggression toward clinic-referred youth. *Journal of Clinical Child Psychology, 29*(2), 266–281.

Margolin, L. (1992). Child abuse by mother's boyfriends: Why the over-representation? *Child Abuse & Neglect, 16*(4), 541–551.

Marshall, D., English, D., & Stewart, A. (2001). The effect of fathers or father figures on child behavioral problems in families referred to child protective services. *Child Maltreatment, 6*(4), 290–299.

Marsiglio, W., Amato, P., Day, R., & Lamb, M. (2000). Scholarship on fatherhood in the 1990s and beyond. *Journal of Marriage and the Family, 62*(4), 1173–1191.

Martin, J. (1981). A longitudinal study of the consequences of early mother-infant interaction: A microanalytic approach. *Monographs of the Society for Research in Child Development, 46* (3, Serial No. 190).

Martin, J., Hamilton, B., Sutton, P., Ventura, S., Menacker, F. & Kirmeyer, S. (2006). Births: Final data for 2004 (DHHS Publication No. [PHS] 2006-1120). *National Vital Statistics Reports, 55*(1), 1–88. Hyattsville, MD: National Center for Health Statistics. Retrieved November 5, 2007, from http://www.cdc.gov/nchs/data/nvsr/nvsr55/nvsr55_01.pdf

Mason, M. (1998). The modern American stepfamily. In M. Mason, A. Skolnick, & S. Sugarman (Eds.), *All our families: New policies for a new century* (pp. 95–116). New York: Oxford University Press.

Mason, M. (1999). *The custody wars: Why children are losing the legal battle and what we can do about it.* New York: Basic Books.

Mathurin, M., Gielen, U., & Lancaster, J. (2006). Corporal punishment and personality traits in the children of St. Croix, U.S. Virgin Islands. *Cross-Cultural Research, 40*(3), 287–305.

Mauldon, J. (1998). Families started by teenagers. In M. Mason, A. Skolnick, & S. Sugarman (Eds.), *All our families: New policies for a new century* (pp. 29–65). New York: Oxford University Press.

Mayfield, D., McLeod, G., & Hall, P. (1974). The CAGE questionnaire: Validation of a new alcoholism screening instrument. *American Journal of Psychiatry, 131,* 1121–1123.

McCabe, K., Clark, R., & Barnett, D. (1999). Family protective factors among urban African American youth. *Journal of Clinical Child Psychology, 28*(2), 137–150.

McCord, J. (1997). On discipline. *Psychological Inquiry, 8,* 215–217.

McGuigan, W., & Pratt, C. (2001). The predictive impact of domestic violence on three types of child maltreatment. *Child Abuse & Neglect, 25*(7), 869–883.

McLanahan, S., & Sandefur, G. (1994). *Growing up with a single parent: What hurts, what helps.* Cambridge, MA: Harvard University Press.

McLanahan, S. (1999). Father absence and children's welfare. In E. Hetherington (Ed.), *Coping with divorce, single parenting and remarriage: A risk and resiliency perspective* (pp. 117–145). Mahwah, NJ: Lawrence Erlbaum Associates.

McLanahan, S., & Teitler, J. (1999). The consequences of father absence. In M. Lamb (Ed), *Parenting and child development in "nontraditional" families* (pp. 83–102). Mahwah, NJ: Lawrence Erlbaum Associates.

McLaughlin, A. (2001, June 4). Bush's controversial bid to promote marriage. *The Christian Science Monitor.* Retrieved January 28, 2002, from http://www.csmonitor.com/2001/0604/p1s3.html

McLeod, J., Kruttschnitt, C., & Dornfeld, M. (1994). Does parenting explain the effects of structural conditions on children's antisocial behavior? A comparison of Blacks and Whites. *Social Forces, 73,* 575–604.

McLoyd, V. (1990). The impact of economic hardship on Black families and children: Psychological distress, parenting and socioemotional development. *Child Development, 61*(2), 311–346.

McLoyd, V., Kaplan, R., Hardaway, C., & Wood, D. (2007). Does endorsement of physical discipline matter? Assessing moderating influences on the maternal and child psychological correlates of physical discipline in African American families. *Journal of Family Psychology, 21*(2), 165–175.

McLoyd, V., & Smith, J. (2002). Physical discipline and behavior problems in African American, European American and Hispanic children: Emotional support as a moderator. *Journal of Marriage and the Family, 64*(1), 40–53.

McNeil, C., Eyberg, S., Eisenstadt, T., Newcomb, K., & Funderburk, B. (1991). Parent–child interaction therapy with behavior problem children: Generalization of treatment effects to the school setting. *Journal of Clinical Child Psychology, 20*(2), 140–151.

Menard, S. (2002). *Applied logistic regression analysis* (2nd ed.). Thousand Oaks, CA: Sage Publications.

Midanik, L., Zahnd, E., & Klein, D. (1998). Alcohol and drug CAGE screeners for pregnant, low-income women: the California perinatal needs assessment. *Alcoholism: Clinical and Experimental Research, 22*(1), 121–125.

Mintz, S., & Kellogg, S. (1988). *Domestic revolutions: A social history of American family life.* New York: The Free Press.

Moffit, R. (1998). *Welfare, the family, and reproductive behavior.* Washington, DC: National Academy Press.

Morris, P., Huston, A., Duncan, G., Crosby, D., & Bos, J. (2001). *How welfare and work policies affect children: A synthesis of research.* New York: Manpower Demonstration Research Corporation. Retrieved April 19, 2003, from http://www.mdrc.org/Reports2001/NGChildSynth/NG-ChildSynth.pdf

Mosby, L., Rawls, A., Meehan, A., Mays, E., & Pettinari, C. (1999). Troubles in interracial talk about discipline: An examination of African American child rearing narratives. *Journal of Comparative Family Studies, 30*(3), 489–523.

Moynihan, D. (1965). *The negro family: The case for national action.* Washington, DC: U.S. Department of Labor.

National Data Archive on Child Abuse and Neglect (NDACAN) (2001). *Longitudinal studies of child abuse and neglect (LONGSCAN), assessments 0–4.* (NDACAN dataset number 87, user's guide). Family Life Development Center, Cornell University, Ithaca, NY.

National Institute of Mental Health (2001). *The numbers count: Mental disorders in America.* Bethesda, MD: National Institute of Mental Health. Retrieved October 5, 2005, from http://www.nimh.nih.gov/publicat/numbers.cfm

Nobes, G., & Smith, M. (2002). Family structure and the physical punishment of children. *Journal of Family Issues, 23*(3), 349–373.

Nord, C., Brimhall, D., & West, J. (1997). *Fathers' involvement in their children's schools.* Washington, DC: National Center for Education Statistics. Retrieved May 5, 2003, from http://nces.ed.gov/pubsearch/pubsinfo.asp?pubid=98091

Nordlinger, P. (1998, March 2). The anti-divorce revolution: The debate on marriage takes a surprising turn. *The Weekly Standard.* Retrieved November 12, 2005, from http://www.smartmarriages.com/weeklystandard.html

Olson, R., & Roberts, M. (1987). Alternative treatments for sibling aggression. *Behavior Therapy, 18,* 243–250.

Olson, M., & Haynes, J. (1993). Successful single parents. *Families in Society, 74,* 259–267.

Parke, R. (2002). Punishment revisited–Science, values and the right question: Comment on Gershoff (2002a). *Psychological Bulletin, 128*(4), 596–601.

Paquette D., Bolté, C., Turcotte, G., Dubeau, D., & Bouchard, C. (2000). A new typology of fathering: Defining and associated variables. *Infant and Child Development, 9*, 213–230.

Patterson, G. (1982). *Coercive family process.* Eugene, OR: Castalia.

Patterson, C., & Chan, R. (1997). Gay Fathers. In M. Lamb (Ed.), *The role of the father in child development* (pp. 245–260). New York: John Wiley & Sons, Inc.

Patterson, C., & Chan, R. (1999). Families headed by lesbian and gay parents. In M. Lamb (Ed.), *Parenting and child development in "nontraditional" families* (pp. 191–219). Mahwah, NJ: Lawrence Erlbaum Associates.

Pelton, L. (1991). Beyond permanency planning: Restructuring the public child welfare system. *Social Work, 36*(4), 337–343.

Pinderhuges, E., Dodge, K., Bates, J., Pettit, G., & Zelli, A. (2000). Discipline responses: Influences of parents' socioeconomic status, ethnicity, beliefs about parenting, and cognitive-emotional processes. *Journal of Family Psychology, 14*(3), 380–400.

Pleck, J. (1997). Paternal involvement levels, sources, and consequences. In M. Lamb (Ed.), *The role of the father in child development* (pp. 66–103). New York: John Wiley & Sons, Inc.

Polhamus, B., Dalenius, K., Thompson, D., Scanlon, K., Borland, E., Smith, B., et al. (2004). *Pediatric nutrition surveillance 2002 report.* Atlanta, GA: U.S. Department of Health and Human Services, Centers for Disease Control and Prevention. Retrieved November 12, 2005, from http://www.cdc.gov/pednss/pdfs/PedNSS_2002_Summary.pdf

Pong, S., & Ju, D. (2000). The effects of change in family structure and income on dropping out of middle and high school. *Journal of Family Issues, 21*(2), 147–169.

Popenoe, D. (1996). *Life without father: Compelling new evidence that fatherhood and marriage are indispensable for the good of children and society.* Cambridge, MA: Harvard University Press.

Pruett, K. (2000). *Fatherneed: Why father care is as essential as mother care for your child*. New York: The Free Press.

Pulkkinen, L. (1982). Self-control and continuity from childhood to adolescence. In P. Baltes & O. Brim (Eds.), *Life-span development and behavior* (Volume 4) (pp. 63–105). Orlando, FL: Academic Press.

Radhakrishna, A., Bou-Saada, I., Hunter, W., Catellier, D., & Kotch, J. (2001). Are father surrogates a risk factor for child maltreatment? *Child Maltreatment, 6*(4), 281–289.

Radloff, L. (1977). *Center for epidemiological studies-depression scale (CES-D)*. Retrieved May 4, 2008, from http://www.assessments. com/catalog/CES_D.htm

Reiss, D. (1995). Genetic influence on family systems: Implications for development. *Journal of Marriage and the Family, 57*(3), 543–560.

Ripoll-Nunez, K., & Rohner, R. (2006). Corporal punishment in cross-cultural perspective: Directions for a research agenda. *Cross-Cultural Research, 40*(3), 220–249.

Roberts, D. (1998). The absent black father. In C. Daniels (Ed.), *Lost fathers: The politics of fatherlessness in America* (pp. 145–162). New York: St. Martin's Press.

Rohner, R., Bourque, S., & Elordi, C. (1996). Children's perceptions of corporal punishment, caretaker acceptance, and psychological adjustment in a poor, biracial Southern community. *Journal of Marriage and the Family, 58*(4), 842–852.

Rohner, R. (2006). Preface to special issue. *Cross-Cultural Research, 40*(3), 215–219.

Rolock, N., & Testa, M. F. (2005). Indicated child abuse and neglect reports: Is the investigation process racially biased? In D. Derezotes, J. Poertner, & M. Testa (Eds.), *Race matters in child welfare: The overrepresentation of African American children in the system* (pp. 119–130). Washington, DC: The CWLA Press.

Rubin, G. (1992). Multicultural considerations in the application of child protection laws [Special issue: Social distress and families in crisis: A multicultural perspective]. *Journal of Social Distress and the Homeless, 1*(3/4), 249–271.

Runyan, D., Curtis, P., Hunter, W., Black, M., Kotch, J., Bangdiwala, S., et al. (1998). LONGSCAN: A consortium for longitudinal studies of maltreatment and the life course of children. *Aggression and Violent Behavior, 3*(3), 275–285.

Sack, W., Mason, R., & Higgins, J. E. (1985). The single-parent family and abusive child punishment. *American Journal of Orthopsychiatry, 55*(2), 252–259.

Salem, D., Zimmerman, M., & Notaro, P. (1998). Effects of family structure, family process, and father involvement on psychosocial outcomes among African American adolescents. *Family Relations, 47*(4), 331–341.

Sarason, I., Johnson, J., & Siegel, J. (1987). Assessing the impact of life changes: Development of the life experiences survey. *Journal of Consulting and Clinical Psychology, 46*(5), 932–946.

Sariola, H., & Uutela, A. (1992). The prevalence and context of family violence against children in Finland. *Child Abuse & Neglect, 16*(6), 823–832.

Schaefer, E., & Edgarton, M. (1982*). Autonomy and relatedness inventory*. Unpublished paper for the School of Public Health, University of North Carolina, Chapel Hill, NC.

Scott, E., Edin, K., London, A., & Mazelis, J. (2001). My children come first: Welfare-reliant women's post-TANF views of work-family trade-offs and marriage. In Chase-Lansdale & Duncan (Eds.), *For better and for worse: Welfare reform and the well-being of children and families* (pp. 132–153). New York: Russell Sage.

Sears, R. (1961). Relation of early socialization experiences to aggression in middle childhood. *Journal of Abnormal and Social Psychology, 63*, 466–492.

Shaw, D. (1999). A prospective study of the effects of marital status and family relations on young children's adjustment among African American and European American families. *Child Development, 70*(3), 742–755.

Siegel, L. (1994). Cultural differences and their impact on child welfare. *Journal of Multicultural Social Work, 3*(3), 87–96.

Simons, L., Chen, Y-F., Simons, R., Brody, G., & Cutrona, C. (2006). Parenting practices and child adjustment in different types of households: A study of African American families. *Journal of Family Issues, 27*(6), 803–825.

Simons, R., & Chao, W. (1996). Conduct problems. In R. Simons (Ed.), *Understanding differences between divorced and intact families: Stress, interaction, and child outcome* (pp. 125–143). Thousand Oaks, CA: Sage Publications.

Simons, R., Johnson, C., & Conger, R. (1994). Harsh corporal punishment versus quality of parental involvement as an explanation of adolescent maladjustment. *Journal of Marriage and the Family, 56*(3), 591–607.

Simons, R., Lorenz, F., Wu, C-I., & Conger, R. (1993). Social network and marital support as mediators and moderators of the impact of stress and depression on parental behavior. *Developmental Psychology, 29*(2), 368–381.

Smith, C. (1996). The use of research in local policy making: A case study of corporal punishment in public education. *Educational Policy, 10*(4), 502–517.

Smith, J., & Brooks-Gunn, J. (1997). Correlates and consequences of harsh discipline for young children. *Archives of Pediatrics & Adolescent Medicine, 151*, 777–786.

Smith, M., Lindsey, C., & Hansen, C. (2006). Corporal punishment and the mediating effects of parental acceptance-rejection and gender on empathy in a Southern rural population. *Cross-Cultural Research, 40*(3), 287–305.

Snyder, H., & Sickmund, M. (1999). *Juvenile offenders and victims: 1999 national report.* Washington, DC: Office of Juvenile Justice and Delinquency Prevention. Retrieved February 12, 2002, from http://www.ncjrs.org/html/ojjdp/nationalreport99/frontmatter.pdf

Socolar, R., & Stein, R. (1995). Spanking infants and toddlers: Maternal belief and practice. *Pediatrics, 95*(1), 105–111.

Sorensen, E. (2003). *Child support gains some ground. Snapshots of America's Families III.* Washington, DC: The Urban Institute. Retrieved on May 4, 2008 from http://www.urban.org/UploadedPDF/310860_snapshots3_no11.pdf

Sorensen, E., & Halpern, A. (1999). *Series A, No. A-31, Child support enforcement is working better than we think.* Washington, DC: The Urban Institute. Retrieved February 4, 2002, from http://newfederalism.urban.org/pdf/Anf31.pdf

SPSS for Windows, Rel.11.5. 2002. Chicago: SPSS Inc.

Stacey, J. (1998). Dada-ism in the 1990s: Getting past the baby talk about fatherlessness. In C. Daniels (Ed.), *Lost fathers: The politics of fatherlessness in America* (pp. 51–84). New York: St. Martin's Press.

Steely, A. & Rohner, R. (2006). Relations among corporal punishment, perceived parental acceptance and psychological adjustment in Jamaica. *Cross-Cultural Research, 40*(3), 268–286.

Steinberg, L., Lamborn, S., Dornbusch, S., & Darling, N. (1992). Impact of parenting practices on adolescent achievement: Authoritative parenting, school involvement, and encouragement to succeed. *Child Development, 63*(5), 1266–1281.

Stiffman, M., Schnitzer, P., Adam, P., Kruse, R., & Ewigman, B. (2002). Household composition and risk of fatal child maltreatment. *Pediatrics, 109*(4), 615–702.

Stolley, K., & Szinovacz, M. (1997). Caregiving responsibilities and child spanking. *Journal of Family Violence, 12*(1), 99–112.

Straus, M. (1979). Measuring intrafamily conflict and violence: The conflict tactics scales. *Journal of Marriage and the Family, 41*(1), 75–88.

Straus, M. (2000). Corporal punishment and primary prevention of physical abuse. *Child Abuse & Neglect, 24*(9), 1109–1114.

Straus, M. (2001). *Beating the devil out of them: Corporal punishment in American families and its effects on children* (2nd ed.). New Brunswick, NJ: Transaction Publishers.

Straus, M., & Donnelly, D. (1993). Corporal punishment of adolescents by American parents. *Youth and Society, 24*(4), 419–442.

Straus, M., & Gelles, R. (Eds.). (1990). *Physical violence in American families: Risk factors and adaptations to violence in 8,145 families.* New Brunswick, NJ: Transaction Books.

Straus, M., Hamby, S., Finkelhor, D., Moore, D., & Runyan, D. (1998). Identification of child maltreatment with the parent-child conflict tactics scales: Development and psychometric data for a national sample of American parents. *Child Abuse & Neglect, 22*(4), 249–270.

Straus, M., & Mathur, A. (1996). Social change and change in approval of corporal punishment by parents from 1968 to 1994. In D. Frehsee, W. Horn, & K-D. Bussman (Eds.), *Family violence against children: A challenge for society* (pp. 91–105). New York: Walter deGruyter.

Straus, M., & Mouradian, V. (1998). Impulsive corporal punishment by mothers and antisocial behavior and impulsiveness of children. *Behavioral Sciences and the Law, 16*, 353–374.

Straus, M., & Smith, C. (1990). Violence in Hispanic families in the United States: Incidence rates and structural interpretations. In M. Straus & R. Gelles (Eds.), *Physical violence in American families: Risk factors and adaptations in violence in 8,145 families* (pp. 341–363). New Brunswick, NJ: Transactions Books.

Straus, M., & Stewart, J. (1999). Corporal punishment by American parents: National data on prevalence, chronicity, severity and duration, in relations to child and family characteristics. *Clinical Child and Family Psychology Review, 2*(2), 55–70.

Straus, M., Sugarman, D., & Giles-Sims, J. (1997). Spanking by parents and subsequent antisocial behavior of children. *Archives of Pediatrics & Adolescent Medicine, 151*, 761–767.

Studenmund, A. (1997). *Using econometrics: A practical guide* (3rd ed.). Boston: Addison Wesley.

Sugarman, S. (1998). Single-parent families. In M. Mason, A. Skolnick, & S. Sugarman (Eds.), *All our families: New policies for a new century* (pp. 13–38). New York: Oxford University Press.

Thomas, G., Farrell, M., & Barnes, G. (1996). The effects of single-mother families and nonresident fathers on delinquency and substance abuse in Black and White adolescents. *Journal of Marriage and the Family, 58*(4), 884–894.

Thompson, R., Christiansen, E., Jackson, S., Wyatt, J., Colman, R., Peterson, R., et al. (1999). Parent attitudes and discipline practices: Profiles and correlates in a nationally representative sample. *Child Maltreatment, 4*(4), 316–330.

Tousignant, M., Denis, G., & Lachapelle, R. (1974). Some considerations concerning the validity and use of the health opinion survey. *Journal of Health and Social Behavior, 15*(3), 241–252.

Tucker, M., & James, A. (2005). New families, new functions: Postmodern African American families in context. In V. McLoyd, N. Hill, & K. Dodge (Eds.), *African American family life: Ecological and cultural diversity* (pp. 86–110). New York: The Guildford Press.

U.S. Census Bureau (2001a). *Poverty: 2000 highlights*. Washington, DC: U.S. Census Bureau. Retrieved January 20, 2002, from http://www.census.gov/hhes/poverty/poverty00/pov00hi.html

U.S. Census Bureau (2001b). *Labor force participation for women with infants declines for first time*. Washington, DC: U.S. Census Bureau. Retrieved July 21, 2005, from http://www.census.gov/Pressrelease/www/releases/archives/fertility/000329.html

U.S. Census Bureau (2006). *Current population survey reports: America's families and living arrangements 2006*. Washington, DC: U.S. Census Bureau. Retrieved November 5, 2007, from http://www.census.gov/population/www/socdemo/hh-fam/cps2006.html

U.S. Department of Education (1993). *Youth indicators 1993: Trends in the well-being of American youth, Indicator 17: Mother's employment*. Washington, DC: National Center for Education Statistics. Retrieved January 20, 2002, from http://www.ed.gov/pubs/YouthIndicators/indfig17.gif

U.S. Department of Health and Human Services, Administration for Children and Families (2002). *Child maltreatment 2000: Reports for the states to the national child abuse and neglect data system.* Washington, DC: United States Government Printing Office. Retrieved May 4, 2008, from http://www.acf.hhs.gov/programs/cb/pubs/cm00/index.htm

U.S. Department of Labor. (2007) *Employment characteristics of families in 2006.* Washington, DC: U.S. Bureau of Labor Statistics. Retrieved November 5, 2007, from http://www.bls.gov/news.release/pdf/famee.pdf

Vandewater, E., & Lansford, J. (1998). Influences of family structure and parental conflict on children's well-being. *Family Relations, 47*(4), 323–330.

Vostanis, P., Graves, A., Meltzer, H., Goodman, R., Jenkins, R., & Brugha, T. (2006). Relationship between parental psychology, parenting strategies and child mental health: Findings from the GB national study. *Social Psychiatry and Psychiatric Epidemiology, 41*, 509–514.

Wallerstein, J. (1998). Children of divorce: A society in search of policy. In M. Mason, A. Skolnick, & S. Sugarman (Eds.), *All our families: New policies for a new century* (pp. 66–94). New York: Oxford University Press.

Wallerstein, J., Lewis, J., & Blakeslee, S. (2000). *The unexpected legacy of divorce: A 25 year landmark study*. New York: Hyperion.

Walsh, W. (2002) Spankers and nonspankers: Where they get information on spanking. *Family Relations, 51*(1), 81–88.

Wang, J. (2004). The difference between single and married mothers in the 12 month prevalence of major depressive syndrome, associated factors and mental health service utilization. *Social Psychiatry and Psychiatric Epidemiology, 39*(1), 26–32.

Warner, J. (2005). *Perfect madness: Motherhood in an age of anxiety.* New York: Riverhead Books.

Webster, P., Orbuch, T., & House, J. (1995). Effects of childhood family structure on adult marital quality and perceived stability. *American Journal of Sociology, 101*, 404–432.

Wells, L., & Rankin, J. (1991). Families and delinquency: A meta-analysis of the impact of broken homes. *Social Problems, 38*(1), 71–93.

Whaley, A. (2000). Sociocultural differences in the developmental consequences of the use of physical discipline during childhood for African Americans. *Cultural Diversity and Ethnic Minority Psychology, 6*(1), 5–12.

Whipple, E., & Richey, C. (1997). Crossing the line from physical discipline to child abuse: How much is too much? *Child Abuse & Neglect, 21*(5), 431–444.

Whitehead, B. (1997). *The divorce culture*. New York: Knopf.

Widom, C., & Shepard, R. (1996). Accuracy of adult recollections of childhood victimization: Part 1. Childhood physical abuse. *Psychological Assessment, 8*, 412–421.

Wilcox, W. (1998). Conservative Protestant childrearing: Authoritarian or authoritative? *American Sociological Review, 63*(6), 796–809.

Wilson, W. (1996). *When work disappears: The world of the new urban poor*. New York: Knopf.

Wissow, L. (2001). Ethnicity, income, and parenting contexts of physical punishment in a national sample of families with young children. *Child Maltreatment, 6*(2), 118–129.

Wu, L., & Wolfe, B. (Eds.) (2001). *Out of wedlock: Causes and consequences of nonmarital fertility*. New York: Russell Sage Foundation.

Xu, X., Tung, Y., & Dunaway, R. (2000). Cultural, human, and social capital as determinants of corporal punishment: Toward an integrated theoretical model. *Journal of Interpersonal Violence, 15*(6), 603–630.

Yarrow, M., Campbell, J., & Burton, R. (1968). *Child rearing: An inquiry into research and methods*. San Francisco: Jossey-Bass.

Youssef, R., Attia, M., & Kamel, M. (1998). Children experiencing violence: I. Parental use of corporal punishment. *Child Abuse & Neglect, 22*(10), 959–973.

Zeiler, C., Nemes, S., Holtz, K., Landis, R., & Hoffman, J. (2002). Responses to a drug and alcohol problem assessment for primary care by ethnicity. *American Journal of Drug and Alcohol Abuse, 28*(3), 513–524.

Zimmerman, M., Salem, D., & Maton, K. (1995). Family structure and psychosocial correlates among urban African American males. *Child Development, 66*(6), 1598–1613.

INDEX

abstinence, 184. *See also* sexuality
  education
*Adolescent and Adult Parenting
  Inventory*, 98
Aid to Families with Dependent
  Children (AFDC), 63
alcohol use. *See* maternal mental
  health
anxiety. *See* maternal mental health
*Autonomy and Relatedness
  Inventory*, 92, 202

breakdown of the family, 15

CAGE, 98
*Center for Epidemiologic Studies-
  Depression Scale (CES-D)*, 96
Child Behavior Checklist, 82, 96
child maltreatment, 6, 70–72, 88,
  103, 169, 180, 183, 189
  association with corporal
    punishment, 6, 56, 59
  presence of surrogate father, 10
  single motherhood as risk
    factor, 70–71
child welfare system, 3, 188–189
  discrimination against African
    American families, 3, 188–190
  regulating women's relationships
    with men, 183
cohabitation, 6, 17–20, 28, 32, 37,
  166, 180, 183, 195, 205
  differences by income and race,
    18–20
  effects on children, 43, 65

cohabitation (*continued*)
  effects on family income,
    91, 180, 195
  increase in, 15–16, 26–27, 51–52,
    67, 71, 91, 140, 145, 151, 155,
    187, 201
  international comparison, 18
  policy to discourage, 10, 180
conduct problems. *See* externalizing
  behavior in children
*Conflict Tactics Scales – Caregiver
  to Child*, 87
continuum of violence, 4
corporal punishment, 2–13, 25,
  39–50, 52–65, 67–70, 72–73,
  75–78, 87–89, 94–95,
  98–99, 119–120, 129–131,
  135, 140, 145, 151, 155,
  161–165, 167–171, 173–176,
  178–180, 185–194, 196–203,
  205–206
  attitudes toward, 39, 56, 60, 196
  and child age, 46, 58
  and child temperament, 193
  definition, 40–42
  differences by income and race/
    ethnicity, 7–9, 53–57, 60–64
  effects of, 2–5, 7, 9–10, 15, 20,
    24–26, 29, 32, 34, 36, 42–46,
    49, 53, 55, 59–60, 67, 74, 76,
    91, 163, 168, 178, 183, 185,
    188, 196–197, 201, 205
  and family stability, 76
  impulsive, 3, 67–68, 174, 180,
    187, 197, 200

corporal punishment (*continued*)
international comparisons,
186–187, 192, 206
limitations of the research, 42–45
and maternal characteristics, 28,
73, 93
movement to ban, 2
as normative parenting practice,
9, 39, 55, 76, 163, 177,
185, 188
rates of, 16–17, 23, 29,
32, 34–35, 58, 62–63,
67–69, 76, 88, 119, 122,
184, 187, 200–201, 205
relationship quality, 6, 74, 77,
89–90, 92–93, 106, 117, 126,
129, 131, 139, 142, 146, 151,
161–162, 167, 198, 202
role of religion, 132
severity of, 6, 44, 46, 75, 165,
178, 185, 193
sign of parenting dysfunction,
185, 188
cultural differences, 3
in effects of corporal punishment,
3–5, 7, 9–10, 42, 44, 46, 49,
53, 55, 57, 178, 185, 196
in endorsement of corporal
punishment, 7, 48, 61–62,
99, 130–131
in parenting, 3, 56, 76, 104,
132, 199
in use of corporal punishment,
3–5, 7–9, 11–12, 43–44, 48,
57, 60, 62, 67–69, 73, 75–77,
161–163, 167, 169, 173, 176,
178, 186–187, 190–191, 198,
200, 206

depression. *See* maternal mental
health
discipline methods
child-centered vs.
parent-centered, 47
time-out, 12, 41, 51–53, 55,
89, 121, 191, 197
verbal reprimand, 12, 191
withdrawal of privileges
(response cost), 45
divorce, 1–2, 15, 17–20, 22–28,
30–32, 35, 37, 67–68, 91–92, 166,
183–184, 201, 204
effects of, 2–5, 7, 9–10, 15,
20, 24–26, 29, 32, 34, 36,
42–46, 49, 53, 55, 59, 60,
67, 74, 76, 91, 163, 168,
178, 183, 185, 188, 196–197,
201, 205
rates of, 16–17, 23, 29, 32,
34–35, 58, 62–63, 67–69,
76, 88, 119, 122, 184, 187,
200–201, 205
remarriage, 20–21, 26, 28,
30, 32–33, 91, 194–195,
201, 205
domestic violence, 30, 69, 71, 90,
92–93, 115, 117, 126, 129, 131,
139, 144, 150, 154, 161, 167,
169, 182, 202. *See also* maternal
mental health

ecological model, 5, 36, 73, 95
economic stress model, 67
education, 12, 16, 22, 28, 59, 61, 63,
71, 92–93, 96, 174, 179, 183–185,
196, 198–199, 205–206
ethnographic methods, 193

eurocentric notions of the family, 1
externalizing behavior in children
    association with corporal
        punishment, 49–50, 173, 199
    association with family conflict,
        27, 31
    association with family structure,
        27–28, 30, 35
    differences by income and
        race/ethnicity, 35, 173
    role of genetics, 50
extrafamilial influence. *See* neighbor-
    hood quality, social support

families, single-earner (two parent)
    families, 29–30, 32–33, 70,
    76, 169
    and child maltreatment, 71
    and corporal punishment,
        5–6, 9, 25, 40–41, 58–59,
        63–64, 69, 76, 94, 135, 165,
        198–199, 203
    differences by income and
        race, 19
    postmodern, 2
family conflict, 30
    effects on child behavior, 72
family structure, 2–7, 9, 16–17, 21,
    24–29, 31–32, 34–36, 64–68,
    72–73, 77, 89–91, 105–106,
    111–112, 122, 126, 131–132,
    135–137, 139, 142–146, 148,
    151–152, 154–156, 158, 161,
    163–167, 170–172, 178–180,
    196, 198–199, 203. *See also*
    single mothers, stepfamilies,
    multigenerational families,
    same-sex

fathers, 1–2, 6–7, 10, 20, 23–25,
    30, 32–34, 36, 54, 58–59, 66,
    70–73, 76–77, 90, 164–165,
    168–169, 172, 179–182, 193–195,
    201–203, 205
    absence of, 1, 24, 31, 34, 73, 171
    criminal activity by, 32, 182
    deadbeat dads, 23, 195
    definition of, 25
    differences by income and race,
        34, 195
    drug abuse by, 1
    infidelity by, 30
    influence of, 167
    noncustodial, 19, 32
    support for mother, 33–34
    surrogate, 6, 10, 32–33, 66–67,
        71–72, 76–77, 89–90, 115,
        123, 126, 129, 135, 137, 142,
        148, 151–152, 161, 163–166,
        168–169, 172, 180, 194–195,
        201–203
    unemployment of, 29, 34
feminism, 2
fertility, 15–16, 184. *See also*
    nonmarital birth
    decline in, 15
    differences by income
        and race, 16–17
Functional Social Support Scale, 100

grandparents. *See* multigenerational
    families

harsh parenting. *See* corporal
    punishment
Head Start, 8, 185
Health Opinion Survey, 97

Healthy Marriage Initiative,
    179, 182. *See also* marriage
    promotion
History of Loss and Harm, 92, 98
human rights perspective, xiv, 188, 197

income inequality, 15
    association with family structure,
        23–24
    effects on children, 43, 65
    growth of, 15
    influence on family formation,
        23–24
intentional families, 25. *See also*
    same-sex families

Life Experiences Survey, 91
LONGSCAN, 79, 81–82, 87–88,
    90–91, 93, 95–104, 111,
    120–121, 200

main effects models, 34
marriage 2, 7, 10–11, 16–21, 23, 27,
    29, 66, 165, 179–184, 204–205
    changing notions of, 2
    differences by income
        and race, 7, 17, 19, 21, 60,
        165, 182, 204
    rates of, 17, 23
maternal mental health 74, 94, 96,
    139, 144, 150, 155, 167
    abuse as a child, 98, 119, 126,
        131–132, 150, 155, 162,
        169, 175
    alcohol use, 94, 139, 155, 167, 174
    anxiety (psychosomatic
        symptoms), 162
    depression, 94, 96–97, 118, 140,
        145, 150

maternal mental health (*continued*)
    history of domestic violence,
        69, 71
minor assault, 6, 10, 40–41, 75, 77,
    87–89, 106, 120–122, 126, 129,
    131–132, 135–136, 148–156,
    162–165, 167, 170, 173–176,
    181, 200
multigenerational families, 9, 36,
    67, 137, 163–166, 178, 183,
    195–196

neglect, 11, 70–72, 79–80, 98–99,
    102–103, 179, 183
neighborhood quality, 75, 95, 100,
    155, 176–177, 199
nonmarital childbirth, 15
    and cohabitation, 18, 195
    by age, 18
    differences by income and
        race/ethnicity, 10, 16
    increase in, 15–16
nonspanking, 196–197

parental warmth, 4, 44, 47, 49, 52,
    56, 161, 177
parenting attitudes, 74, 93, 95, 98,
    126, 130, 175–176
    age-appropriate expectations, 119,
        140, 145, 151, 170
    empathy, 98, 119, 126, 140, 145,
        151, 170, 176
    importance of religion, 75, 140,
        151, 176
    support for corporal punishment,
        13, 39, 186, 189–190, 192, 206
parenting style, 5, 47–48, 54, 56–57,
    68, 76, 176, 189
    authoritarian, 47–48, 54, 68

parenting style (*continued*)
  authoritative, 47–48
  permissive, 47, 68, 76
parenting toolbox, 12
Parson's structural-functional
  theory, 31
poverty, 1, 15, 22–24, 28–30, 35, 63,
  71, 82, 164, 184, 195, 200. *See
  also* income inequality
psychosomatic symptoms. *See*
  maternal mental health
punishment as a packaged variable, 7

relationship quality, 6, 74, 77, 89–90
  92–93, 106, 117, 126, 129, 131,
  139, 142, 146, 151, 161–162, 167,
  198, 202
  differences by income and race,
    6–7, 10, 30, 181–182
  effects on parenting, 43, 65
relationship stability, 89, 91, 135, 167
reliance on white, middle-class
  samples, 53
remarriage. *See* stepfamilies
role overload model, 66–67

same-sex families, 31
spanking. *See* corporal punishment
stepfamilies, 9, 19, 21, 26, 28, 37,
  67, 69, 180, 195, 201, 205
  effects on children, 43, 65
  family functioning, 31
  lack of research, 194–195, 205
  rates of remarriage, 19
  risk for divorce, 19

shotgun marriage, 10, 181
single motherhood, 1–4, 6, 11,
  19–20, 24–25, 36–37, 68,
  70–71, 166, 171, 181, 183,
  204–205
  child discipline, 68
  child maltreatment, 70–71, 88,
    103, 169, 180, 183, 189
  child supervision, 72
  differences by income and
    race/ethnicity, 19–21
  divorced, 37
  international comparison, 11–12
  never-married, 29–30
  supports for, 11
social support, 11, 30, 60,
  75, 95, 100–101, 106,
  119, 126, 140–142, 145,
  151, 155
socialization theory, 66
stress. *See* maternal mental health
structural equation modeling, 193
Sweden
  effects of ban on corporal
    punishment, 186–187

talk therapy, 182
teen motherhood, 16–17
Temporary Assistance For Needy
  Families (TANF), 10

violent socialization, 13, 206

welfare reform, 2, 35, 179, 184
women's labor force participation, 21